THE BRAVE BLUE LINE

DICK KIRBY
has also written

Rough Justice – Memoirs of a Flying Squad Detective

'Real Boys' Own stuff, this. Tinged with a wry sense of humour which makes this an excellent read.' METROPOLITAN POLICE HISTORY SOCIETY

The Real Sweeney

'These are the real-life accounts of a tough London cop.' DAILY EXPRESS

You're Nicked!

'It's full of dark humour, tense busts and stand-offs. As crime rates rocket, this book will go down well.' DAILY SPORT

Villains

'All of the stories are told with Dick Kirby's acerbic, black humour in a compelling style, by a detective who was there.' AMERICAN POLICE BEAT

The Guv'nors – Ten of Scotland Yard's Greatest Detectives

'Scotland Yard legends are vividly brought to life by a man who has walked the walk, the Flying Squad's own Dick Kirby. What a brilliant TV series this would make!' JOSEPH WAMBAUGH, AUTHOR OF *THE CHOIRBOYS*

The Sweeney – The First Sixty Years of Scotland Yard's Crimebusting Flying Squad

'This thoroughly researched and enjoyable history, crammed with vivid descriptions ... races along like an Invicta Tourer at full throttle.' DAILY EXPRESS

Scotland Yard's Ghost Squad

'A superb description of crime-busting at the front end.' BERTRAMS – THE HEART OF THE BOOK TRADE

THE BRAVE BLUE LINE

100 YEARS OF METROPOLITAN POLICE GALLANTRY

DICK KIRBY

True Crime

First published in Great Britain in 2011 by
Wharncliffe Local History
an imprint of
Pen & Sword Books Ltd
47 Church Street
Barnsley
South Yorkshire
S70 2AS

Copyright © Dick Kirby 2011

ISBN 978 1 84884 652 4

P   of
P   ry,
Pen &   . & Sword
Discover   History, Wharncliffe True Crime,
Wharncliffe Transport, Pen & Sword Select, Pen & Sword
Military Classics, Leo Cooper, The Praetorian Press,
Remember When, Seaforth Publishing and
Frontline Publishing

For a complete list of Pen & Sword titles please contact
PEN & SWORD BOOKS LIMITED
47 Church Street, Barnsley, South Yorkshire, S70 2AS, England
E-mail: enquiries@pen-and-sword.co.uk
Website: www.pen-and-sword.co.uk

Contents

This book is dedicated to my parents,
Win and Charlie Kirby – God bless your memory.
And to all the Metropolitan Police officers
who aspire to be heroes –
this is your manual.

Acknowledgements

I would like to express my appreciation to the staff at Pen & Sword Books for their hard work, especially my publishing manager, Brigadier Henry Wilson for his encouragement and wisdom. In addition, my thanks go to my editor, George Chamier, for his eagle-eyed expertise.

My thanks go to Lord Stevens of Kirkwhelpington for his splendid foreword. The following cast a wide net to find contributors for the book: Sioban Clark, Maureen Whitford and Linda Bailey of the Metropolitan Women Police Association, Bob Fenton QGM, Secretary of the ex-CID Officers' Association of the Metropolitan Police and Susi Rogol, editor of the London Police Pensioner magazine; my thanks to them all.

I received the most enormous assistance from the Friends of the Metropolitan Police Historical Collection, including Alan Moss of History by the Yard and Keith Skinner of Causeway Resources. In addition, Phillip Barnes-Warden, Neil Paterson and Paul Dew from the Met Collection, Pamela Pappé and Katie Hamilton from the Peel Centre Library and especially my son, Mark Kirby; all provided diligent and painstaking research on my behalf.

Others who kindly gave of their time and assistance were: Keith Foster, Research Advisor, London Metropolitan Police, Andrew Brown, Assistant Departmental Record Officer, Metropolitan Police Directorate of Information, Leanne Fagan, Croydon Local Studies Library and Archives Service, my son Robert Kirby and Catherine Powell of Police Review. My grateful thanks go to my granddaughter, Jessica Cowper, for her translating skills.

I would like to thank the following for the use of their photographs: the Metropolitan Police, John Barrett BEM, Steve Bocking, Sioban Clark, Harry Clement BEM, Alan Fairfax, Arthur Garner GM, Anthony Gledhill GC, William Griffiths CBE, BEM, QPM, Derek Hall QGM, Julian Hurst, Media & Information Manager, Metropolitan Police, Margaret Jackson GM, Diane Lowrie, Maurice Marshall, Terence McFall GM, Kathleen Parrott GM, Ernie Pawley GM, Rod Phillips BEM, Jan Scott and Phillip Williams GM. Every effort has been made to contact copyright holders; the publishers and I apologise for any inadvertent omissions.

The following – and others who, for a variety of reasons wished to remain anonymous – provided unstintingly of their time to provide the content of this book and I am grateful to all of them: Raymond Charles Adams BEM, QPM; John Anthony Allport MBE, QGM, BEM; Peter Ansell; Jacqueline Ashley-Collins; Peter Atkins; John Henry Barrett BEM; Barry Baulch; James Wallace Beaton GC, CVO; Steve Bocking; Dave Bowen; Derek Bradley; Ethel Violet Bush GM; Mick Carter; Harry Charles Clement BEM; Peter Connor JP; Dave Dixon; Russ Dunlop; Brian Ford; Jeanette French; Stuart French; Arthur Howard Garner GM; Anthony John Gledhill GC; Alan Goodman; Mick Gray; William Ian Griffiths CBE, BEM, QPM; Derek Arnsby Hall QGM; Michael Hills GM; Steve Holloway; William Hucklesby QPM, FRGS; Margaret Shaw Jackson GM; Reginald Alfred Walter George Jenkins BEM; Marion Jones; Dave Little; Diane Lowrie; Maurice Marshall; Terence Frederick McFall GM; Roy Medcalf; Graham Melvin; Jim O'Connell; Kathleen Flora Parrott GM; Brian Ernest Walter Pawley GM; Rodney Andrew Phillips BEM; Mick Purchase; Susan Raif; Gordon Reynolds; Bob Robinson; Jan Scott; the late Lou van Dyke and Phillip John Dixon Williams GM.

I have already mentioned several members of my family, but it would be quite wrong not to include my daughter Suzanne Cowper and her husband Steve, who came to my rescue on a number of occasions when my lack of computer skills became so blatantly obvious that help was required and assistance was made immediately available. So to them and my youngest daughter, Barbara Jerreat and her husband, Rich, plus my lovely, assorted grandchildren – Emma, Harry, Samuel and Annie Grace – my thanks for your help, love and encouragement. Most of all, my love and my thanks to my dear wife Ann, who despite being privy to all my faults and foibles has stuck with me for almost fifty years.

Any faults or imperfections in this book are mine alone.

Dick Kirby

Foreword

I was in the Police Service for forty-two years, serving from Police Constable to Commissioner of the Metropolitan Police and was very proud to be known on retirement as the 'Copper's Copper'. The Police Service is in my blood. Part of that is the incredible pride I have in all those officers and staff who are serving or have served this country within the Police Service.

I served with the Metropolitan Police at the start of my police career and I finished my police career there. Since Sir Robert Peel instigated the first thousand or so officers in 1829, there have been rightly justified awards for gallantry, and surely many more that should have been so recognised, but for whatever reason or circumstance at the time were not.

This book rightly highlights the brave exploits of a few, but reflects the courage and devotion to duty of all those who served or serve today. Dick Kirby has meticulously researched this subject, speaking to recipients of these awards, or (in cases of their death or incapacity) their surviving relatives and colleagues, in order to get the most factual record possible, in addition to perusing official records of the various incidents. Indeed, during my career I not only witnessed acts of courage by those who I served alongside, but was able to both recognise and reward those individuals through commendation or recommendation for further awards.

These accounts of outstanding courage and devotion to duty start with a story from 1909, recounting the award of the first King's Police Medal by King Edward VII. The book concludes with the courage of an individual awarded the Queen's Gallantry Medal, first struck in 1974. Between these accounts the book is littered with individual stories of courage resulting in the award of the George Cross, George Medal, King's (and Queen's) Police Medal for Gallantry, Queen's Gallantry Medal and the British Empire Medal for Gallantry.

This book of courageous accounts of outstanding bravery should serve as an inspiration to all young officers today. Additionally though, it is a fitting tribute which should be read by a far wider audience to understand how every day officers step out on to the streets, not knowing what they may face, yet always doing their duty and protecting the public, come what may.

Lord Stevens of Kirkwhelpington
Commissioner of the Metropolitan Police 2000–2005

Chapter 1

Gunmen in Hampstead

What became known as 'The Tottenham Outrage' occurred on 23 January 1909; two Eastern Europeans, Jacob Lepidus and Paul Hefeld, carried out an armed robbery at a factory in North London. They were chased by police for six and a half miles, and during the course of the pursuit they fired over 400 rounds of ammunition, shot and killed both Police Constable William Tyler (who had heroically attempted to stop them) and a ten-year-old boy, and shot and wounded twenty-one other people, before turning their weapons on themselves. Three police officers – Police Constables John William Cater and Charles Eagles and Detective Constable Charles Dixon – acted with outstanding bravery, so much so that King Edward VII signed a Royal Warrant on 7 July 1909 which instituted the award of the King's Police Medal. The medal, with the face of the sovereign on the obverse and a figure of justice with the words on his shield 'To guard my people' on the reverse, had a dark blue ribbon, one and three-eighths of an inch wide, with a narrow silver stripe down each side. The Royal Warrant stipulated that only 120 such medals were to be presented annually to recipients within the British Empire, including awards 'For Distinguished Service' as well as 'Gallantry'. The three officers – Cater, Eagles and Dixon – were all awarded the medal and each was promoted to sergeant, as well as receiving £10 from the Bow Street Reward Fund and being presented with medals from the Carnegie Hero Trust. Unfortunately, there was no recognition for PC Tyler's gallantry; his widow was granted a pension of £15 per year, and although £1,055 was raised for her through a public appeal, the money was invested and she was only permitted to receive the interest from it.

What follows are incidents which, one way or another, were linked – the bravery and friendship of two police officers and the death of one of them, the theft of crown jewels, four sleazy crooks and the independent awards of two very well-deserved King's Police Medals.

* * *

After the Irish Crown Jewels were paraded through the streets of Dublin following the opening of the Irish International Exhibition on 4 May 1907, they were placed in the twin-lock Ratner safe in the library of Dublin Castle. On 6 July it was discovered that they had been stolen. Chief Inspector John Kane of Scotland Yard (whose experience, stated the *Daily Mail* on 10 May 1906, 'has been very wide') was called in to investigate the theft. Suspicion fell upon two men, the first of whom was Frank Shackleton, the Dublin Herald of the Castle and the brother of the celebrated explorer, Sir Ernest Shackleton. He was a deeply unsavoury character whose notorious sexual conquests included Queen Victoria's son-in-law, the Duke of Argyll. Although there may have been complicity on his part in the plot to steal the jewels it is fairly certain that he was not the main culprit. The second (and prime) suspect was Richard William Howard Gorges, whose character was even more loathsome than Shackleton's. Born in 1876, his early life was tainted with allegations of 'precocious sexual malpractice'. His career with the British South African Police came to an abrupt halt after nine months when he was discharged 'By Order'. He enrolled as a private soldier with Thorneycroft's Mounted Infantry, but when he was discovered mounting a drummer boy instead of a steed, he was quite literally kicked out of the regiment, inasmuch as the Colonel lined up the unit, 'and every man had a kick at him'. But Gorges was a survivor; he later obtained a commission in the 3rd Royal Irish Regiment in 1903, although following the report of the commissioners in respect of the missing crown jewels – they were never recovered and nobody was ever prosecuted for the theft – he was forced to resign his commission. There we can leave the odious Gorges; it will not be too long before he, like so many other unpleasant objects, rises to the surface again.

★   ★   ★

Alfred Young joined the Metropolitan Police on 17 February 1902 and was posted to 'S' Division. A keen and conscientious officer, he was commended time and again for good and courageous police work and by 15 December 1908 had achieved the rank of 'permanent patrol' (or detective constable). At 8.30 that night, Young was patrolling the area of Swiss Cottage on his bicycle when he saw two men loitering in the vicinity. They were Dennis White, aged thirty, a ship's steward and Lucas Garcia, aged thirty-three, a fireman who had been paid off from his ship, the SS *Pydla*, at Southend, three weeks previously. Since then,

Garcia had been in White's company. They had already committed a housebreaking, in which they had stolen two overcoats and other items, including a revolver.

Young kept observation on the two men but then lost sight of them. Getting back on his bicycle, he continued his patrol. Meanwhile, White and Garcia had entered Belsize Lane where they encountered Thomas Wood, a nineteen-year-old coachman. Suddenly Garcia pointed a revolver at Wood and said, "Get them up – get them up!" Both Garcia and White were wearing masks covering the lower parts of their faces, and Garcia then shouted, "I mean it – I mean it!" As Wood later stated in court, "I was terrified and instantly ran," but his departure was witnessed by Young, who saw him run off in the direction of Fitzjames Avenue. Young pretended to examine his bicycle, passed the two men and met up with a fellow officer, Police Constable 297 'S' Frederick Street, telling him to stop the two men, which he did. Young then strolled over to the group.

"I'm a police officer," said Young. "What are you doing loitering about here?"

"Nothing," was the reply. "We're not loitering about – we're strangers here."

"What did you stop that gentleman in Belsize Lane for?" asked Young and was told, "We haven't stopped anyone." At this stage, Young said, "I'm not satisfied with your answers; I shall take you into custody," whereupon, as PC Street would later say in court, "a fearful struggle broke out." As Street took hold of Garcia, White drew a revolver from his coat pocket and Young called out, "Come here, Street – he's got a firearm!" and fought with White for possession of the revolver. There was a flash – Young later admitted that it could have been light reflecting on the nickel plate of the revolver – but he very definitely heard the sound of a 'click' before seizing the gun. Street released his hold on Garcia, who started to escape, until White shouted to him, "Come here, you heifer!" As Garcia approached him, Young kicked him in the stomach. Street blew his whistle and the four men crashed to the ground, where they struggled violently. Police Constable 667 'S' Hills then arrived, took possession of the revolver and other officers turned up and secured the prisoners.

Searched at the police station, both men were found to be in possession of black masks ("made out of kid gloves, I should say," remarked Young), and Garcia had ten rounds of ammunition in his pocket, similar to the bullets in the five chambers of the revolver. It was unloaded by Inspector George Wallace, who later said, "I noticed on the cap of the cartridge under the hammer there was a scratch and a slight indentation. I have experimented by pulling the trigger. It sticks or hitches on the fifth or sixth pull." Edwin John Churchill, who had started his gunmaking business at 8 Agar Street, The Strand, in 1891, agreed. "I have had a life experience of firearms," he told the jury at the Old Bailey on 12 January 1909. "I have examined this revolver. It is in very bad working order. It would be possible to fire it. It hangs up every now and then on pulling the trigger and does not come down with sufficient force to explode, but would leave a mark on the cartridge. That occurs about every fifth pull, otherwise there is nothing to prevent it exploding. There are some scratches on three. There is a slight scratch on this as if the chamber had been tried to be pushed round to bring under another cap, or to admit of the hammer being pulled."

It was clear that the 'click' which Young had heard was White pulling the trigger of the revolver and the hammer descending on the cap with insufficient force to discharge the round – he was an exceptionally lucky man, as well as a very brave one.

White gave evidence from the dock – he was not on oath, and therefore not cross-examined by the prosecution – saying, "There was no intention on my part to injure the detective but only to get away from him." Telling the jury, "I leave it to yourselves to give me the benefit of the doubt," he was largely unsuccessful, and at the end of the two-day trial the Recorder of London sentenced White, who unsurprisingly had a previous conviction, to five years' penal servitude and Garcia to three.

Highly commended by the commissioner, Young was awarded £15 from the Bow Street Reward Fund and in the New Year's Honours List of 1910 was decorated with the King's Police Medal.

★   ★   ★

In May 1911 our old friend Gorges appeared at West London Police Court, charged with obtaining sums of money by means of dishonoured cheques from the female licensee of Barons Court Hotel, West Kensington. He was charged under his rank of Captain, and the magistrates were highly impressed when his solicitor produced testimonials from senior officers who stated that Gorges had been wounded three times in battle and had been awarded four medals. In fact, he possessed just one campaign medal, the British South Africa Company's Medal 1890–97, not four for valour, as had been tacitly suggested. Whichever officers sent the testimonials, it may be assumed that

Colonel Thorneycroft was not among them; and whatever wounds Gorges may or may not have received, it was highly unlikely that they had been sustained in combat with the enemy. They might have been sustained in the course of a murder and two highway robberies of which he was strongly suspected, but if Gorges' solicitor was aware of this suggestion he prudently kept that information to himself.

According to one source, Gorges was 'a man known to the English police, a man of absolutely depraved character'; but if this was indeed the case, that information was not filtered through to the bench at West London Police Court, who bound Gorges over in the sum of £2 to be of good behaviour.

Gorges fared far better than his former associate. The previous year, Frank Shackleton had persuaded several prominent (and gullible) people to invest their money in the Montevideo Public Works Corporation. The shares were utterly valueless, and after acquiring £17,000 in cash the company was wound up with a deficit of £943,000. Shackleton was declared bankrupt and fled the country, leaving debts of £84,441 behind him. Two years later, he was extradited from Portuguese West Africa, and in January 1913 at the Old Bailey he was convicted of fraudulent conversion and sentenced to fifteen months' imprisonment.

Following the outbreak of the Great War, Gorges was commissioned as a temporary captain with the 9th Border Regiment but lasted only four months before he was dismissed. Thereafter, he portrayed himself as a hero, discharged after being gassed on the Western Front. Inevitably, the truth was somewhat different: Gorges had been caught in what the Sunday tabloids used to refer to as 'a compromising position' with a certain Lance Sergeant Bullock and forced, once more, to resign his commission. On 2 June 1915 he had moved into two rooms, together with a professional boxer named Charles Thoroughgood, at 1 Mount Vernon, Hampstead, the property of Mr and Mrs Caraber. By now, Gorges was a chronic alcoholic, leaving in his wake a trail of unpaid bills and dishonoured cheques. The police had acquired a warrant for his arrest, not for his swindling practices but for his sexual predation on boys – and the officers who were going to execute the warrant were Detective Constable Alfred Young KPM and Detective Sergeant Askew.

★   ★   ★

Arthur Walter Askew had joined the Metropolitan Police four years after Young; but unlike the latter, Askew had gone for promotion and by 1913 had achieved the rank of detective sergeant (third class), a rank which would become defunct by 1921. He and Young were friends and had often worked together on 'S' Division. Like Young, Askew was a conscientious worker and was acquiring an impressive number of commendations; his cousin, Police Constable Ambrose Askew (later a detective inspector) had been highly commended by the commissioner in 1911 when he had tackled a burglar who had shot him in the arm; the gunman, Harry de Vere, was sentenced to fourteen years' penal servitude.

But now, Arthur Askew and Alfred Young arrived at Gorges' lodgings at 11.30 on the morning of 14 July 1915. The matter was a serious one, because a magistrate had been roused from his bed to sign the warrant at two o'clock that morning. It is possible that Young felt a sense of *déjà vu*; the premises were less than a mile away from the scene where he had carried out the arrest which earned him his King's Police Medal, almost seven years previously. Or perhaps he experienced a premonition. Gorges was known to be dangerous and unstable – the boxer Thoroughgood would later say that two weeks prior to the detectives' visit, Gorges had told him that unless he cleared out of the house he would blow his brains out – and Young had brought with him a thick, ash walking stick. However, their suspect was absent from his room, having left the house a quarter of an hour earlier; nevertheless, the detectives carried out a search and in a chest of drawers by Gorges' bed they discovered a service revolver and 197 cartridges, 127 of which fitted the weapon. The remainder of the ammunition fitted a smaller calibre revolver, which was not found. The service revolver and all the ammunition they took with them back to the police station. Gorges returned to his lodgings at eight o'clock that evening; he had spent the day with a young boy named Alfred Muncer, visiting a number of public houses. "When he found his revolver and cartridges were missing," said Muncer, "he got into an awful rage. He paced up and down, clutched at his throat and foamed at the mouth." This was confirmed by Gorges' landlord, Mr Caraber, himself a former police officer, who said, "He behaved like a madman. I had never seen him so bad before."

At 9.50 that evening the detectives returned. Muncer had already packed a bag for Gorges and urged him to escape, but, drunk and truculent, Gorges waited in the corner of the basement. The landlady, Mrs Caraber, led the way down the poorly lit, narrow steps to the basement, with Young and Askew following. As Young reached the sixth step he stopped, and Askew saw Gorges standing in the corner, his hands behind his back. "Are you Captain Gorges?" asked Young, and Gorges replied, "Yes. Who are you? What do you want?" He then added, "I have heard a lot of …," but Askew was unable to hear the rest of the sentence. "We are police officers," said Young, and as he did so Gorges began to fumble behind his back. Askew told him that they wished to speak to him privately, and Gorges told his landlady to bring a light to his living room.

Gorges then told the officers, "You go first," but Young replied, "No, you go up."

"Am I under arrest?" asked Gorges, and when Young replied, "Yes," it was the last word he would utter. Askew saw Gorges bring his right arm out from behind his back. Immediately, Askew leapt at Gorges and flung his arms around him in a bear-hug but failed to secure his right arm. He saw that in his right hand Gorges was holding a revolver. Within a split second he fired, and Young, hit in the chest, fell headlong down the stairs; he was dead by the time he reached the bottom. With Gorges struggling violently, Askew smashed him head-first through the wooden balusters supporting the banister rail and then overpowered him, snatching the revolver from his grasp.

On his way to the police station, Gorges said, "I hope I have not killed him. I don't give a fuck about myself. I am sorry if I have. I did not intend to kill him."

At the police station, the revolver was examined. It was five-chambered, contained four live cartridges and one spent cartridge and was a hammerless model, in so far as the hammer was concealed inside the revolver. It could, as the expert gunsmith, Robert Churchill (whose father had given evidence at the previous trial in which Young had also given evidence) would later tell the jury at the Old Bailey, "Only be fired deliberately."

Gorges' mood changed at the police station. "If I had had a free hand," he stated, "I would have shot fifty of them. I don't care a fuck for the whole Police Force and if I had two guns I would have fired the lot of them."

He later made a written statement:

I had been drinking to some extent and I heard when I came home that two detectives had been calling for me. I asked my landlady what for and she did not know. I found on going upstairs that my large service revolver was gone and about two hundred bullets and also one hundred bullets of a small revolver. I loaded a small revolver and put it in my pocket and about fifty cartridges. The officers said they wanted to talk to

me, as man to man. I asked them to come upstairs when Young
said, "What have you got in your pocket?" I said, "That is my
business." He tried to take the revolver from me and he is
dead. That is all I have got to say. I had no intention of
shooting him.

After being charged, Gorges replied, "I wish to say it was
accidental. It was his [Askew's] fault for having tried to take the
revolver from me. I had no more intention of shooting him than
shooting you. I was in liquor."

However, early the following morning, his mood changed once
more. "Good evening, officer," he said to a police officer who
visited him in his cell. "I have shot one of your fellows tonight.
How many policemen are there at this station – fifty? Well, I had
enough rounds for them."

It is only slightly surprising that Gorges entered the Police
Court later that morning with his teeth still intact.

Two months later, Gorges appeared before Mr Justice Low at
the Old Bailey. At the judge's request, Askew took the revolver
and imitated Gorges' actions on that fateful night. Slowly
bringing his arm around from behind his back, Askew pointed
the weapon in the direction of the Clerk of Arraigns and Cecil
Whitely, counsel for the prosecution, and pulled the trigger. Both
of those legal gentlemen undoubtedly expelled a sigh of relief
when all they heard was a sharp click.

"Was it not your prime purpose to get the prisoner's revolver
when you got into that house?" asked Mr Gordon Hewart KC,
one of the three barristers for the defence.

"We expected some difficulty but my intention was to read and
execute the warrant," replied Askew.

"You knew, or shrewdly expected," pursued Hewart, "that the
prisoner had a revolver?"

"I certainly expected it," answered Askew.

When Gorges entered the witness box, he stated that he had
been drinking all day and that he had been in possession of the
smaller of the two revolvers. He realized that he should have left
it at one of the public houses he had visited, because he had fired
it several times out of the pub window and had thought that this
was the reason for the detectives' visit.

This, of course, was nonsense. He was fully aware that the two
officers had first arrived at the house prior to his and Master
Muncer's pub crawl. Gorges went on to say that during the
confrontation on the stairway, when he produced the revolver
from behind his back, it was lying on his open palm, so that the

detectives might see it. It was, admitted Gorges, quite possible that one finger was inside the trigger guard.

"The production of the revolver," dramatically stated Gorges, "was a signal for a general assault on me. Sergeant Askew commenced by giving me a violent kick on the right knee. Detective Young caught me by the right wrist and tried to take the revolver from me. In the struggle, the weapon went off."

The main thrust of Gorges' defence was two-pronged; firstly, that he was an alcoholic, he was drunk at the time of the shooting and was not responsible for his actions; and secondly, that it was an accident. The Hampstead Police Surgeon, Dr Payne, was called; he gave evidence that on the night of the shooting he had examined Gorges and he was not drunk. Gorges' pugilistic friend, Charles Thoroughgood, stated that he was never drunk.

For the defence, Dr Seymour of Hampstead stated that he had been treating Gorges since May for chronic alcoholism, and Major Ritchie DSO, told the court that when he knew Gorges as a volunteer in the Matabele War in 1896 he was 'normal' but when he saw him again during the Boer War he was not. It must be assumed that Ritchie was referring to Gorges' sobriety rather than his sexual predilections. Brigadier General Charles Ridley was called to say that during Gorges' very brief service during the Great War with the Border Regiment he had an opportunity to observe Gorges when he was 'in drink'. He did not mention whether or not he had had an opportunity to observe Gorges when he was inside Lance Sergeant Bullock.

Summing up, the judge told the jury that the law was this: if through the overwhelming consequences of drink, a man at that moment was in such a state as not to be capable of forming an intention, then although he had taken in these circumstances the life of another, that should be regarded as manslaughter and not murder.

After a two-day trial Gorges was acquitted of murder but convicted of manslaughter. Telling him, "Manslaughter is a crime of infinite variety, and the variety which you committed was near akin to murder," Mr Justice Low sentenced Gorges to twelve years' penal servitude. He was discharged from Parkhurst Prison in 1925 and died in London in 1944.

Awarded the King's Police Medal in 1917, Askew, who was also rewarded from the Bow Street Reward Fund, remained on 'S' Division for twenty-two years, gradually rising through the ranks until in 1928, with the rank of detective chief inspector, he was posted to C1 Department at the Yard. He became head of what was inaccurately referred to as 'The Murder Squad' and was deeply admired by his men, both as a gallant officer and a shrewd investigator. When Detective Inspector (later Detective Superintendent) Fred Narborough gave evidence at the police court in respect of a woman he had arrested for murder, he had not had the time to put notes in his pocket-book; Askew was in court, taking notes which he presented to Narborough at the conclusion of the proceedings. He also kept a fatherly eye on the Flying Squad, and when he retired with the rank of detective superintendent in 1938 he had served the Metropolitan Police for over thirty-two years and had been awarded no fewer than sixty-nine commissioner's commendations.

Aged fifty-seven, Askew's services were still much in demand, and he worked as senior security officer for the Foreign Office. In 1951, just after his seventieth birthday, his service to the Government was recognised with the award of the British Empire Medal (Civil Division). He retired to his Finchley home and died at the grand age of ninety-four.

Young and Askew had been awarded the same medal, although there were slight differences; on Young's medal was shown the face of King Edward VII, while Askew's bore the profile of King George V. And Askew's medal ribbon had changed from that of his contemporary's – a third silver stripe had been added down the middle in 1916. It made little difference; whatever the changes, the medals reflected the gallantry of two very brave officers from 'S' Division.

CHAPTER 2

Heroes All

It cannot be said that Field Marshal Sir Henry Hughes Wilson, 1st Baronet, GCB, DSO, MP was the most popular man in the world. Born in 1864 in Co. Longford, Ireland, he was commissioned into the Rifle Brigade, served in a number of campaigns, was severely wounded, mentioned in dispatches and won the Distinguished Service Order in the Boer War. In 1914, as a major general and a staunch Ulsterman, he surreptitiously supported the British officers who refused (in the so-called Curragh Mutiny) to lead their troops against the Ulster Unionist opponents of the Third Irish Home Rule Bill. After a successful career in the First World War he was appointed Chief of the Imperial General Staff (CIGS) in 1918 and adviser to Prime Minister Lloyd George. He had been regarded as a fine Corps Commander, and following the end of the war he was awarded £10,000 by a grateful British Government plus a baronetcy by Lloyd George (a fellow officer drily remarked, "Whenever Wilson came within a mile of a prominent politician he suffered from a sexual disturbance") and was showered with awards, world-wide. But when a treaty was signed between the provisional Irish government (headed by Michael Collins) and the British to form the Irish Free State, in Knightsbridge in December 1921, Wilson could not agree with government policy. He fell out of favour with Lloyd George, resigned from his post as CIGS in 1922, became Member of Parliament for North Down and was invited to become Northern Ireland's adviser on security. In addition, Wilson (who was hurtfully known as 'The Ugliest Man in the British Army') was said to be a scandalmonger and a lover of intrigue. But if he was no longer popular with Lloyd George, this was nothing compared to how the Irish Republican Army felt about him. In fact, Wilson had been on their death list since 1921, but apparently his execution had not been sanctioned by Collins who, it was said, 'wanted to give the treaty a chance'.

★   ★   ★

The Field Marshal had spent the morning of 22 June 1922 unveiling a plaque for a war memorial at Liverpool Street station

and afterwards returned to his house at 36 Eaton Place, SW1. He
was in full uniform, and as he paid off the taxi he was taking out
his front door key when two men approached him from behind.
The first was Reginald Dunne (also known as John O'Brien),
who was aged twenty-four and had served as a private with the
Irish Guards in the First World War; currently, he was employed
as a teacher at Strawberry Hill College, London. The second man
was Joseph O'Sullivan (also known as James Connelly), aged
twenty-five; he was currently employed as a clerk at the Ministry
of Labour in Whitehall. O'Sullivan had also served in the First
World War as a lance corporal with the London Regiment; he had
lost a leg at Ypres in 1917. Disabled or not, O'Sullivan, like
Dunne, was a fervent, paid-up member of the IRA; their mission
was to murder Field Marshal Wilson. Although Dunne and
Michael Collins had been close friends, it is possible that what
was to follow had not been instigated by Collins.

The two men drew their revolvers and fired a total of nine
shots. Two bullets hit Wilson in his right arm as he endeavoured
to draw his sword to defend himself, another lodged in his left
forearm, two in his right shoulder, two more in his right leg and
one in each of his armpits; these last two were the fatal ones,
puncturing his lungs. Their work complete, the heroic duo
scuttled away, but Police Constable Walter March had been
patrolling at nearby Eaton Square; hearing the shots, he ran into
Eaton Place West where he confronted the two gunmen. March
immediately tackled Dunne but as he did so O'Sullivan shot him,
at close range, in the stomach.

Detective Constable Cecil Charles Sayer had joined the
Metropolitan Police in 1913 and had served as a constable on 'F',
'H', and 'D' Divisions before being appointed detective constable
on 'B' Division in August 1920. He had been twice commended
by the commissioner, once for the arrest of four men for
conspiracy and larceny and, just three weeks previously, for the
arrest of two men for cheque frauds. The commendations were
made even more acceptable by the award of six shillings for the
first and fifteen shillings for the second. Now he was on patrol in
Elizabeth Street when he too heard the shots; the initial fusillade
came from almost straight ahead of him, then after he had started
running across the busy King's Road there was another shot, off
to his left. March, although seriously wounded, was able to
provide a good description of the two assassins to Sayer, and he
set off in pursuit, re-crossing the King's Road and chasing them
into South Eaton Place. As he did so, both men turned and fired
at him (and also hit and wounded Alexander Clarke, a chauffeur

who had joined in the chase), but Sayer, a married man aged twenty-nine, gamely continued his pursuit, pausing only long enough to draw his truncheon and fling it, hitting O'Sullivan on the back of the head. Dunne stopped, turned and fired, hitting Sayer in the leg and bringing him crashing to the ground. The blow to O'Sullivan's head had slowed him considerably, as had his wooden leg, but as he and Dunne ran on and into Ebury Street, the alarm had been well and truly raised, and two constables ran out of Gerald Road police station into Eaton Place to take up the pursuit.

Police Constable James Alexander Duff had joined the Metropolitan Police just three months previously, and was not even on duty when he rushed from the station; not that that mattered. The former gamekeeper from Castle Douglas, aged twenty-one and single, now joined his colleague and they turned right, chasing the suspects into Ebury Street.

The other officer was Police Constable Walter Bush, who after spending twelve years in the British Army had joined the police in 1919. A married man, twenty-nine-year-old PC Bush, at almost six feet two, was a powerful adversary, as Reginald Dunne was about to discover. As the police officers dashed towards their quarry a number of shots were fired at them, but they were more fortunate than their colleagues. All of the shots missed, but PC Bush did not miss his mark. With one carefully aimed punch from his ham-like fist, he caught Dunne flush on the jaw, flattening him. At the same moment, Duff flung his truncheon at O'Sullivan, striking him in the face, and then tackled him to the ground.

As news of the murder emerged, the House of Commons adjourned as a mark of respect; a dinner to celebrate the birthday of the Prince of Wales at Buckingham Palace was cancelled. The following day, *The Times*, with more than a hint of jingoism, noted: "The murderers were Irishmen. Their deed must rank amongst the foulest in the foul category of Irish political crimes." It appears that Field Marshal Wilson was rather better regarded in death than he had been in life.

Dunne and O'Sullivan stood trial at the Old Bailey on 18 July 1922 before Mr Justice Shearman and pleaded not guilty to Wilson's murder. The noted pathologist Sir Bernard Spilsbury had carried out his initial examination of Wilson's body on the couch at Wilson's home in Eaton Place and he was able to tell the jury not only where the murderers had been standing as they fired their fatal shots but also the probable order in which the shots had been fired. That testimony, together with the evidence of the four police officers, was sufficient for the jury to return a verdict of guilty, and although Dunne attempted to read some heroic rhetoric from a prepared script in the dock, he was prevented from doing so. Instead, he and O'Sullivan were obliged to listen to some rhetoric from the judge, who sentenced both of them to death.

Following the sentence, the foreman of the grand jury handed a note to the Recorder, who read it aloud:

> I have been asked by the foreman of the grand jury to express their appreciation of the conduct of the police at the arrest of the two prisoners charged with the murder of Sir Henry Wilson. They feel that their conduct in unflinchingly facing almost certain death by the performance of their duties is worthy of the highest praise and commendation. They also wish to express their appreciation of the conduct of the civilians concerned in the case.

The Recorder expressed his concurrence with those sentiments which he directed be communicated to the proper authorities. Three days after the conclusion of the court case there was a presentation at the London home of the Duke and Duchess of Atholl, 84 Eaton Place. Lord Arthur Hill informed the assembly that following Field Marshal Wilson's murder he had gone from house to house in Eaton Place, and without exception all of the residents had given generously to a fund to recognise the gallantry of Police Constable March, Detective Constable Sayer and Alexander Clarke, all of whom had been wounded during their endeavours to stop the two gunmen. The three men were each presented with a gold watch and chain by the Duchess.

The double execution was carried out at Wandsworth Prison on 10 August 1922 and Dunne and O'Sullivan were buried in the grounds of the prison. Sir Henry's own funeral was a more grandiose affair; he was buried in a crypt at St Paul's Cathedral. Twelve days after the hangings Michael Collins was shot dead in an ambush just outside Cork, and shortly afterwards the Irish Civil War commenced.

In addition to being commended by the grand jury and the trial judge, the four officers were congratulated by the coroner at Westminster Court and highly commended by the commissioner. On 18 September the officers appeared before the Chief Metropolitan Magistrate, Sir Chartres Biron. March and Sayer were presented with cheques for £20 each and Duff and Bush with cheques for £15. In a wonderfully flowery speech, Sir Chartres declared:

In few countries has that wild savagery of spirit which inevitably followed a Great War been less in evidence than in our own; this is due largely not only to the firm administration of the law, but to the kind and generous spirit which is always behind that administration. That the two murderers of Sir Henry Wilson were brought to justice was largely due to those considerations and to the fact that the police can always be relied upon to do their duty, as in this instance with a bravery which might, if there were not so many other examples of it, be called exceptional. The police who secured the men and the members of the public who assisted them did so at the imminent risk of their lives, and one of the constables (March) is still maimed and lame as a consequence of his injuries. The constables deserve the thanks and the gratitude of the community and I feel certain that they will prize more than any pecuniary reward the consciousness of having rendered valuable service to the public and of having upheld to the fullest degree the best traditions of the Force to which they belong and to which the country and London in particular owe so much.

On 15 February 1923, at Buckingham Palace, the four officers were personally decorated with the King's Police Medal by His Majesty King George V.

★   ★   ★

PC March was so badly injured that eventually he had to be invalided out of the Force. The heroic former soldier, PC Bush, was later transferred to 'S' Division and after three years' service there transferred to 'X' Division. There, aged forty-four, he received another commissioner's commendation, this time for stopping a runaway horse; but his wartime service had taken its toll of him and after twenty-five years he developed angina and was pensioned off. He died twenty years later, just before his seventy-third birthday.

PC Duff, the keen newcomer, had acquired a taste for adventure early in his career and in 1929 he joined the CID. By now he was married and had two children. As he rose through the ranks, he received commendation number thirteen from the commissioner for the arrest of 'three violent, alien female pickpockets', followed by another, six months later, for an arrest in a case of housebreaking. And then, six months after that came promotion to detective sergeant (first class) and a posting to C1 Department at the Yard. This lasted, however, less than two years and was followed by a posting to 'R' Division where he remained for the rest of his service; it appears that much of the fire had gone out of him. He had passed his examination for detective inspector (second class) in 1936 but for some unknown reason he was never promoted. His next commendation was sixteen years after his previous one, followed by another two years later, both for the arrest of housebreakers; three years after that he resigned, still with the rank of detective sergeant, the rank he had held for twenty years, after thirty-three years' and one day's service. He died six years later, aged fifty-nine.

DC Sayer recovered from his leg wound and within a year he was active again, being commended in a case of false pretences. In the next few years, until he was promoted to detective sergeant (first class) in 1934, he notched up a total of sixteen commissioner's commendations for a multiplicity of offences: for a variety of breakings – office-, shop-, warehouse- and church- (although this was better known as sacrilege) – and for his last, in a case of robbery with violence. In addition, he received monetary rewards from the commissioner on an astonishing eleven occasions, bringing in a total of over £25.

And yet, like Duff, Sayer had passed the examination for detective inspector (second class), in his case in 1930, and again, like Duff, was never promoted. He was a man who had travelled within the Metropolitan Police; commencing his service on 'F' Division, he was posted to 'H', 'D', 'B', 'M' and 'K' Divisions, before finally returning to 'H' Division. He had served in West, South and East London.

With his posting to East Ham in 1928, he and his wife settled into Police Married Quarters at 61 Haldane Road, just a short walk across Central Park to the police station. However, in 1941 he was pensioned off as being unfit for further duty due to clinical depression. He had served almost twenty-eight years, was awarded a pension of exactly £4 per week and lived on for another twenty-two years, dying at the age of seventy.

That was the fate of those gallant Metropolitan Police officers: to suffer ill health, to be denied promotion or longevity.

On the other hand, Dunne and O'Sullivan, those heroes of the IRA, fared far better; their remains were permitted to be disinterred from the unmarked graves in Wandsworth Prison and in 1968 they were reburied in the Republican plot at Dean's Grange cemetery in Dublin, where Dunne's dramatic words were finally read to an enraptured audience, forty-six years later than originally intended. The following year, the IRA offensive commenced in Northern Ireland, then in mainland Britain, and it continued for the next twenty-eight years. It seemed a curious way of saying thank you.

CHAPTER 3

Gang Warfare

For a variety of reasons, 1919 could not be said to be the finest year for London's police; nor, indeed, for the rest of the country. The previous year, one third of the 18,000-strong personnel of the Metropolitan Police had gone on strike for the third time in the history of the Force; their pay was atrocious, police officers were in debt, their families were suffering from malnutrition. In fact, as a result of the strike, a constable's pay was more than doubled, from £1 12s 6d per week to £3 10s 0d. And yet, in 1919, because the Prime Minister Lloyd George had said one thing but meant another, the police struck again; this time it was nationwide. There was fighting in the streets between striking and non-striking police officers, mobs smashed their way into department stores at night and actually switched the lights on to see what they were stealing, and in Liverpool the rioting was so bad that a signal was sent to the destroyers *Venomous* and *Whitley*, detaching them from their flagship and ordering them to make for Liverpool at maximum speed. This time the government did not accede to the strikers' demands; the 1,056 Metropolitan Police officers who went on strike were immediately dismissed. Nor were police the only strikers; London's Underground came to a standstill over a dispute about shorter working hours. Even more worrying was a massive meeting held in Glasgow on 31 January 1919 which sparked fears of a Russian-style revolution.

Nor was that all. A pandemic known as 'Spanish Flu' was sweeping the globe; it had commenced in 1918 and it did not abate until 1920. It is estimated that it claimed the lives of 100,000,000 people; five times that number were infected and 1,500 Metropolitan Police officers went sick, all on the same day.

And on top of all that, the First World War had ended the previous year; a war in which one man in ten under the age of forty-five had perished. World trade had all but collapsed, inflation would more than double between 1919 and 1920 and unemployment (which would soon double, from one to two million) awaited the hundreds of thousands of returning servicemen. This, coupled with the existence of young men who had not known paternal guidance through the war years plus the hordes of immigrants who had been flooding unchecked into London, meant that violent and organised crime went through the roof.

A new and revolutionary concept of crime-fighting was needed, whereby groups of detectives could go from one hotspot of crime in the capital to another – fast. It heralded the birth of the Flying Squad, the brainchild of Detective Chief Inspector (later Chief Constable of the CID) Frederick Porter Wensley. Fortunately, Wensley was a career detective through-and-through, and during his career which by then had lasted thirty-one years, he got to know the East End underworld inside-out – and he knew detectives. He was given authority to pick twelve detectives from all over London to form the Flying Squad, and he knew exactly who he wanted. From 'G' Division, one of the toughest areas in London's East End, he selected Detective Constable John Alec Rutherford. It was a wise choice.

Rutherford was born on 24 October 1892 in Eastbourne, Sussex and joined the Metropolitan Police on 4 August 1913, aged twenty; following a period as a 'winter patrol' (the forerunner of the aid to CID system), he was appointed as 'permanent patrol' (later, detective constable) on New Year's Eve, 1917 – this was considered to be very quick work, indeed. One month later he married Elizabeth, two years his junior, at the Parish Church, St Pancras. By the time Wensley summoned him to the Yard in October 1919, Rutherford had been rewarded and commended on seven occasions; but more importantly, he had acquired an acute knowledge of the gangs in and around the area of 'G' Division.

It was early days for the Flying Squad; their initial patrols were made in the back of a horse-drawn wagon leased from the Great Western Railway and fitted with interchangeable boards displaying names of businesses to suit the area which they were patrolling; and the criminals simply did not know what had hit them. The trial period of the Squad was a success, and within a year the horse-drawn wagons were withdrawn and Crossley Tenders were brought into service. They were badly needed, to combat the growing menace of the 'motor car bandit'.

On 15 September 1920 Rutherford was one of a number of detectives in a tender who set off on a patrol to catch a gang of south London villains, who with the use of motor vehicles had been carrying out a series of smash and grab raids. On the third night's patrol the Squad ambushed the gang, who were about to break into a clothier's shop, and there was a tremendous fight, the villains using a variety of weapons and the Squad their truncheons. There were severe injuries on both sides but the Squad – particularly Rutherford, who at five feet nine-and-a-half inches possessed a sturdy build – acquitted themselves well. They were commended by the Magistrate at Westminster police court and by Sir Henry Dickins, the trial judge at the Old Bailey, who sentenced the seven-man gang to varying periods of penal servitude and hard labour. Rutherford was one of twelve Squad officers commended by the commissioner and given monetary – in Rutherford's case, £1 5s 0d – awards. In 1920 alone, Rutherford received nine more commendations.

However, there was a menace to society far more prevalent than the 'motor car bandit'; what were known as 'the Racetracks Gangs' were perpetuating violence not only at the racetracks but also on the streets on Britain. And what was more, the violence was escalating at a frightening rate.

★ ★ ★

Following the end of the First World War, there were a large number of gangs running protection rackets among the bookmakers at racecourses nationwide. Two gangs stood out head and shoulders above the rest: the Italian Mob and the Birmingham Boys, also known as the Brummagem Hammers.

In charge of the Italian Mob was Charles 'Darby' Sabini. He and his brothers – George, Fred, Harryboy and Joseph – hailed from Saffron Hill, Clerkenwell. Darby was a sly, illiterate, charismatic tough, who had boxed professionally as a middleweight, and he had formed a coalition with Jewish bookmakers from the East End. The Italian Mob ran the protection rackets at the racecourses in the south of England.

On the opposing side, Billy Kimber from Bordesley, Birmingham, was the head of the Birmingham Boys. He was an intelligent strategist, had formed some useful alliances with other gangs and was running the racecourses in the Midlands and the north of England. Kimber had set up headquarters in Islington and formed a further fruitful (if uneasy) partnership with the Hoxton Gang, the Finsbury Boys and the Camden Town Gang; the common denominator was that these gangs shared a hatred for Sabini and his associates. Kimber's principal lieutenants were Fred Gilbert, who had boxed as a welterweight under the ring name of George Langham (principally because he was an army deserter) and George 'Brummy' Sage. But in addition, Kimber reinforced the Birmingham Boys with some of the local colour who originated from south of the River Thames, and the waters were further muddied when a number of the combatants changed sides.

In 1921 there was a pitched battle between the two factions at Alexandra Park; shots were fired and severe injuries were inflicted on both sides. On 23 February that year Darby Sabini was attacked by the Birmingham Boys, led by 'Brummy' Sage, at Greenford Trotting Track; Sabini fired a shot at his attackers and although he was arrested for possessing a firearm with intent to endanger life, he was acquitted after he pleaded self-defence, and for unlawfully possessing a pistol he was bound over. Fred Gilbert, who was also present, had the charges against him dismissed. When Billy Kimber endeavoured to broker a deal with Darby Sabini, he was found shot outside Sabini's address; Kimber survived, and Alfie Soloman, a Jewish bookmaker, was acquitted of the shooting a month later. But while he was awaiting trial, two Birmingham bookmakers' touts were beaten up, and in retaliation two Jewish taxi-drivers working for the Sabinis were attacked and one of them was shot. No one was convicted of these offences and it was not until Derby Day, after the Leeds Mob were attacked by their allies the Birmingham Boys (who had mistaken them for the Italian Mob), that there were successful prosecutions, in which much of the evidence was given by the police. In February 1922 two of the Birmingham Boys were slashed with razors in London's Coventry Street by Sabini's gang, led by Alfie Soloman, and in April Fred Gilbert was slashed in the legs, again by Alfie Soloman, but he refused to press charges. However, this did not herald the end of the violence – not by any means.

★   ★   ★

Although Rutherford would later say that on the night of 28 July 1922 he was 'off-duty' in the Red Bull Public House, Gray's Inn Road, it is more likely that he was meeting an informant and the 'off-duty' remark was made to distance himself from that suggestion. But whatever the circumstances, at 10.30 that evening Rutherford saw William Edwards, a forty-year-old labourer from Hoxton, enter the premises, together with Arthur Phillips, a fruiterer aged twenty-four from Clerkenwell and a man named Tobin. Suddenly they ran into the street followed by some other men and Rutherford heard a shot fired.

So too did a gang member who was in Gray's Inn Road and who made his way towards the sound of the shot until he was stopped by Fred Gilbert, who told him, "Go the other way or I shall blow your fucking brains out." Running into the street, Rutherford saw that the three men were in possession of revolvers, as was Joseph Jackson, a thirty-four-year-old dealer from Bermondsey and a number of other men. Tobin fired a shot at a group of men, Rutherford advanced towards him and Tobin shouted, "There's Rutherford – let him have one!" With that, he took a few steps backwards and from a distance of fifteen yards fired at Rutherford. The men then backed away down the adjacent Portpool Lane for twenty yards before Jackson took aim at the detective and fired. Jackson ran off towards Leather Lane chased by Rutherford and a colleague, and when the men had reached a spot about forty yards away from the junction with Gray's Inn Road, Edwards and Phillips stopped and turned in the middle of the road. There was a shout of "Go back, Rutherford!" and both men opened fire. Rutherford avoided injury, as he had all the way through the chase by dodging into doorways. Meanwhile, Jackson had turned into Hatton Garden and then faced Rutherford and, pointing his revolver at him, shouted, "Go away or I'll do you in!" But before he had a chance to do so, Rutherford dashed up, punched him in the face and, as Jackson fell to the ground, relieved him of his revolver. Upon examination, it was found to contain four used cartridge cases. Also arrested was George Fagioli, a twenty-one-year-old labourer from Wakefield Street who was charged with possessing a firearm with intent to injure. Jackson was charged with shooting at Rutherford with intent to murder him, and within a week more of the gang were rounded up and charged, including George Baker, a labourer. It was madness that they had shot at Rutherford, whom they obviously knew, and they were highly fortunate that no one was hit; one of the shots struck a tramcar in Gray's Inn Road, the bullet entering one side of the car and burying itself in a panel at the rear of the tram – it had missed one of the passengers by about twelve inches.

Fred Gilbert was not arrested on that occasion; however he was, three weeks later. The day started early for violence and intimidation on 22 August. A fleet of taxis drew up in Mornington Crescent and men got out and opened fire on George 'Brummy' Sage and Fred Gilbert who was walking with his wife. This time, Gilbert did prosecute. Members of the Italian Mob – George West, Paul Boffa, Simon Nyberg, Tommy Mack, Alf White and Joseph Sabini – were all arrested. But this inspired piece of grassing by Gilbert could not pass unnoticed or unpunished.

The Italian Mob retaliated; on the same day, a Jewish bookmaker told the police that three days previously, on 19 August, whilst he was waiting for a train at Waterloo station to convey him to Brighton for the racing, he was confronted by George 'Brummy' Sage who told him, "You Jew bastard. You're one of the cunts we're going to do. You're a fucking bastard Jew and we're going to do you and the Italians and stop you going racing." And the same day, again at Waterloo in a pub, another Jewish bookmaker stated that he was approached by Fred Gilbert, Jim Brett and Sage; grabbing hold of the bookmaker, Sage said, "This is one of the bastards; do him Fred, through the guts." Pressing a revolver into the bookmaker's side, Gilbert allegedly said, "Give us a tenner and you can go." Pulling out a butcher's knife on a second bookmaker, Brett asked, "Shall I do him?" This meant that as well as the Gilbert family's attackers being locked up, so too were Gilbert, Brett and Sage.

There was a series of trials at the Old Bailey; on 1 November the three men were acquitted of demanding money with menaces from the Jewish bookmakers. Nor were they alone in their good fortune; a number of other men in both the shootings in Mornington Crescent and Gray's Inn Road were similarly found not guilty. But others were not so fortunate, and on 3 November 1922 all the men were brought up for judgement before Mr Justice Roche, who before passing sentence told the court:

> I am going to teach people to act through the police and rely on them for protection, and as far as I can, to stop people taking the law into their own hands.

For shooting at Rutherford and being in possession of firearms, Joseph Jackson was sentenced to seven years' penal servitude and George Baker to five years' penal servitude. George Fagioli, for being in possession of a firearm, was sentenced to nine months' hard labour.

When Alf White was sentenced to five years' penal servitude for the Mornington Crescent shooting, women screamed at the back of the court, White put his hand to his forehead and groaned, "My God!" and one of the women advanced towards the judge in the well of the court, appealing for clemency. His Lordship directed that she be 'gently removed'. In fact, White was later cleared on appeal; not so Joseph Sabini, who was sentenced to three years' penal servitude, or Simon Nyberg (who during the past ten years had been convicted on sixteen occasions), who was sentenced to twenty-one months' hard labour for riot. Thomas Mack was sentenced to eighteen months' hard labour for riot, with six months concurrent for wounding a woman in a tramcar. Not that it can be said that Mack learnt a salutary lesson; following his release, he was sentenced to a month's hard labour for an incident at Wye races, and twelve years after that, for his part in 'The Battle of Lewes Racetrack', he was sentenced to three years' penal servitude.

Chief Inspector Brown, the officer in charge of the case, castigated Jackson, convicted of shooting at Rutherford, as 'having the character in the neighbourhood of Bermondsey of a man who blackmailed tradesmen and bookmakers'; and when Mr J. D. Cassells for the defence pointed out that Rutherford had stated that Jackson was not connected with any of the racing parties, Brown stated emphatically that Cassells' client was 'a confirmed and dangerous thief'. But it was clear whose side the police were on. White, Chief Inspector Brown stated, had given information to the police previously in connection with racing matters and dangerous criminals who frequented race courses; he also said that Joseph Sabini 'had never been in conflict with the police before'. Former Detective Chief Inspector Tom Divall (now an official of the Jockey Club) echoed Brown's commendation of White; he also later applauded Billy Kimber as being 'one of the best' and praised him and George Sage for being 'generous and brave fellows ... who would rather die than send those men to prison'.

Divall had previously been Fred Wensley's divisional detective inspector and Wensley hated him. It is easy to understand why. With men like Divall – to all intents and purposes, an upright and well-respected former senior police officer – championing the cause of both the Italian Mob and the Birmingham Boys, it is only slightly amazing that the Racetrack wars did not last longer than they did.

In *Police Orders* dated 1 January 1923 Rutherford, together with Detective Constable Cory and Police Constables 204 'E' Rauscher, 594 'E' Underwood and 378 'E' Ackerman were all highly commended by the commissioner, and each (with the exception of Rutherford) was awarded £2; in addition, all were commended by the magistrate at Clerkenwell Police Court and the judge and the grand jury at the Old Bailey. Rutherford was also awarded £10 from the Bow Street Reward Fund for his courageous conduct.

In the *London Gazette* dated 1 January 1924 it was announced that Rutherford's courage was to be recognised with a very well merited King's Police Medal, and the medal was awarded to Rutherford personally by His Majesty King George V at Buckingham Palace on 28 February 1924.

On the very evening of the day of his investiture, Rutherford was part of a Flying Squad team assisting 'D' Division officers under the command of Detective Chief Inspector George Cornish ('The murder wizard of Scotland Yard', as the press liked to call him) who were keeping observation on the offices of Messrs Ewart & Son, Euston Road. They had received information that a four-man gang was going to break into the safe using explosives. The four men entered the premises and bolted the door behind them. Two hours later, one of the men, Edward Wood, left the building and, standing in the street opposite, ostentatiously wiped his face with his handkerchief, obviously a signal to the others waiting in the offices. Then he walked off, only to be grabbed by Rutherford, who relieved him of his raincoat and bowler hat. As Wood was taken to Albany Street police station, so Rutherford, now suitably disguised in Wood's coat and hat, took his place in the street. A second man, Harris, was similarly arrested as he left the premises, and two more, James and Russell, were found hiding in the office. The safe had been drilled, the lock was packed with explosives and a fuse was held in place with a piece of soap; this had been thought the most viable way of cracking the safe, although a number of other items of the safe cracker's armoury were laid out in front of the safe. Wood and Harris both pleaded not guilty, rather improbably claiming a case of mistaken identity, but it did them little good; at the Old Bailey two of the gang each received three years' penal servitude, another fifteen months' hard labour and the fourth six months' – and Rutherford had his twenty-third commendation.

★   ★   ★

But still the Racetrack warfare continued, not only in London, but nationwide. In 1924 a bookmaker in Cardiff was attacked in his office, a man was murdered in Sheffield, in London a man was severely wounded in Tottenham Court Road and on a Doncaster to London train there was a pitched battle between the gangs. There was also a gang fight on the streets of Brixton and bystanders were caught up in the violence. In 1925 the violence on the streets actually escalated, with ten riots in London and other major cities. It was high time that decisive action was taken, and it prompted the often controversial Home Secretary, Sir William Joynson-Hicks Bt PC, DL – he was known as 'Jix' and had been appointed the previous year – to inform Parliament:

I intend to break up the race gangs. These fights show the existence of a state of affairs which cannot be tolerated in a civilised community. It may be difficult to break these gangs all at once, but give me time. The responsibility is mine; I mean to discharge it. It is monstrous that in a civilised country, this kind of rowdyism should take place. I shall take the necessary steps to put an end to this particular kind of atrocity.

He was supported by Edward Shortt KC who, as Secretary of State for the Home Department, had helped bring the police strike to an end and had earned the respect of the police. He had brought in a bill for the licensing of firearms and believed that the Racetrack gangster was as dangerous as a mental patient and should be treated as such. He stated:

In his case, I would remove the prison limit of ten years' jail and substitute an indeterminate sentence confining him to an institution as a criminal lunatic during the King's pleasure.

But despite this impressive rhetoric, it would be a decade before the gangs were brought under control. The Racetrack gangs were largely defeated following 'The Battle of Lewes Racetrack' on 8 June 1936. Opponents of the Italian Mob carried out an attack on Alfie Soloman (who had been acquitted of the attempted murder of Billy Kimber in 1921 and had been sentenced to three years' penal servitude for manslaughter after stabbing one Barnett Blitz in the back of his head with a stiletto at the Eden Social Club in 1924), sixteen gang members appeared at Lewes Assizes and were sentenced to a total of forty-three-and-a-half years' penal servitude, hard labour and imprisonment. Not that Rutherford was around to witness or take part in the proceedings.

Five years previously, on 17 April 1931, after less than eighteen years' service and aged thirty-eight, Rutherford voluntarily retired. His conduct was described as 'very good' and he received a pension of £79 16s 9d – annually; his weekly pension amounted to just £1 10s 1d. It seems strange that a married man aged eight with a weekly wage which (including rent allowance) amounted to £5 5s 6d, who to all intents and purposes was very much on top of his job and who had been honoured by a succession of commissioners, judges and magistrates – and his Sovereign – should walk away from a well-paid job. That, however, was what he did, and little else is known about him; his pension was sent to him at 30 Howard House, Cleveland Street, London W1 until his death, aged seventy-two, on 26 February 1965.

But whatever the circumstances of the retirement of John Rutherford there is no denying that he was an intrepid detective – and a very brave one.

CHAPTER 4

Cowards and Heroes

This chapter deals with a series of events which in one way or another are inextricably linked.

The story commences on 8 December 1944, when a stolen black Vauxhall saloon pulled up outside Frank Wordley Ltd, a jeweller's shop in Birchin Lane in the City of London. Three young men got out, and one smashed the window of the premises with a long-handled axe and scooped out valuables worth £3,800 (by today's standards, over £87,000); then the men scrambled back into the car, which roared away. As the Vauxhall accelerated towards the junction with Lombard Street a man stepped into its path, his arms raised in an effort to stop the raiders. He was Captain Ralph Binney, a fifty-six-year-old Royal Naval officer, close to retirement. The car smashed into him, knocking him on to his back, and the front wheels ran over him. The driver, twenty-six-year-old Thomas Hedley, stopped, reversed, then ran over Binney again, and as he did so Binney's clothing became trapped in the car's suspension. Hedley then drove off, scattering pedestrians and pulling Binney along underneath the car as he went. A motorist who gave chase heard Binney shouting, "Help! Help!" as he was dragged for over a mile through Lombard Street and across Tower Bridge, before he was flung from the vehicle in Tooley Street outside London Bridge Station. By coincidence, the noted pathologist Professor Keith Simpson was passing, and although he rushed Binney to the conveniently nearby Guy's Hospital, it was too late to save him. His lungs had been crushed and punctured by his broken ribs when the car ran over him, and the battering and bruising that his whole body had suffered was sufficient to end his life within three hours of his admission to hospital.

The car was found abandoned near Tower Bridge and the hunt was on for the murderers. Hedley was soon arrested, as were two brothers named Jenkins. At the Old Bailey in March 1945 Hedley was convicted of murder and sentenced to death. His appeal failed, but surprisingly his sentence was commuted to penal servitude for life. One of the brothers, Thomas James Jenkins, was convicted of manslaughter and sentenced to eight years' penal servitude; his younger brother, twenty-year-old Charles Henry

'Harry-Boy' Jenkins, was not even charged. When he was brought to the police station to stand on an identity parade, he punched a police sergeant in the face, breaking his jaw. This might have been thought to be the height of folly, but young Harry-Boy had a hidden agenda. Having received a retaliatory beating from the police, which he knew was as inevitable as it would be painful, Jenkins insisted that his injuries be dressed with sticking plaster. He then demanded that the faces of every member of the identity parade were similarly adorned with sticking plaster, and to nobody's surprise none of the witnesses from Birchin Lane picked him out. It was a ploy which might have suggested the acumen of a much older criminal, but Jenkins was nothing if not streetwise. He had first been convicted at the age of twelve and since that time had notched up seven convictions. He was, of course, sent to Borstal for his attack on the sergeant, but he undoubtedly thought that this was a better result than the alternative.

⋆   ⋆   ⋆

Binney's friends and colleagues set up a subscription fund to commemorate his bravery, and the Binney Medal was struck, to be awarded annually to a member of the public – not a police officer – who demonstrated outstanding bravery in the prevention of crime, in assisting the police, or contributing to the maintenance of law and order. The medal shows an effigy of the gallant captain and it comes without a ribbon; it is not intended that it should be worn. At the suggestion of Sir Hugh Turnbull, the (then) Commissioner of the City of London Police, the naval officers who had collected the fund invited the Goldsmiths' Company to act as trustees. As well as the medal, a number of Certificates of Merit are awarded annually – up to twenty – for similar acts of courage for which the medal cannot be awarded but which deserve special recognition. This decision is made by the Selection Committee, comprised of the Chairman, the Chief Metropolitan Magistrate, the Commissioners of both the Metropolitan Police and the City of London Police, the Chief of Fleet Support and the secretary of the trust, the Clerk of the Goldsmiths' company.

Hedley was released after nine years and expressed contrition for causing the death of Captain Binney – which made everybody feel so much better. We have, however, not yet finished with the brothers Jenkins.

⋆   ⋆   ⋆

On Christmas Day 1946 Divisional Detective Inspector Robert Mold Higgins was forty-three years of age and had been a police officer for twenty-one years. A very tough character, Higgins served several tours with the Flying Squad (which would include being the Squad's deputy chief), and by the end of his career spanning thirty-two years had been commended by the commissioner on fifty-eight occasions. Commander Hugh Young CBE, KPM described him as being, "the best informed detective on my staff'. So when Higgins' home telephone rang at 12.30 on that Christmas morning, a call which would lead to an encounter with a man whom Higgins would later describe as "probably the greatest individual menace I encountered", one of his sources of information would be put to the test and would not be found wanting.

Frederick Rowland Westbrook was born in 1919 and his life of crime had commenced at Crewe when he was just fifteen. Sent to an approved school for stealing, he escaped and later, for garagebreaking and theft at the Old Bailey in March 1939, was sentenced to two years' Borstal Training. Released early, he was arrested for housebreaking in Surrey, wriggled free from his captors and was chased across country by police for five miles before swimming a river in order to escape. Stopped in possession of a bicycle, he threw it at the police officers' legs and ran off. When he was finally cornered, he produced an automatic pistol and threatened the officers, but it was kicked from his hand and he was arrested. At the Old Bailey in January 1940 he was convicted of officebreaking, larceny of a gun and ammunition and making use of it to resist arrest, and was sentenced to three years' Borstal Detention. Confronted by the police on Putney Bridge in 1942, he leapt twenty feet from the parapet and got clean away. Prison sentences of nine, six and twelve months followed. Arrested again, this time at Kingston, Surrey in April 1945, Westbrook made the following, astonishing statement:

> I shall continue thieving until I am thirty. Then I shall have sufficient capital to keep me free from worrying for a few years and if there is a next time, when a copper comes for me, it won't be so easy and I will have something ready for him.

These turned out to be prophetic words. Conscripted into the Army, Westbrook deserted from the South Wales Borderers in October 1946, and carried out at least forty-four housebreakings in the Thames Valley area. He was now twenty-seven years of age and the possessor of fourteen previous convictions. He was variously described as 'short and skinny' or 'a smallish, lithe man with a rather reedy voice', but it was clear that when cornered by police he would use any ruse to escape. What was less clear was that he could be provoked into violence with little or no pretext, and what was not known at all was that he was in possession of a fully loaded 9mm Browning automatic.

On Christmas Eve 1946 Westbrook arrived in Soho and met up with a blonde woman and her male companion. They went from pub to pub until they arrived at Esther's, an all-night café in New Cavendish Street, just off Tottenham Court Road. Already in the premises were a group of Jamaicans, one of whom was twenty-seven-year-old Aloysius Abbott, an aircraftsman serving with the RAF and spending a few days' leave in London. Westbrook demanded priority in being served before the black customers, and when the waitress refused he punched her on the chin; she, in turn smashed a plate over his head and demanded that he leave. Two of the Jamaican group, Emmanuel Williams, a medical student, and an RAF sergeant ejected Westbrook from the café before the violence escalated any further; Westbrook scampered away, but then stopped, produced the Browning and fired into the group of Jamaicans. Abbott was hit three times, once in the shoulder and twice in the lungs, and fell to the pavement, fatally wounded; he died an hour later. Westbrook fired more shots at the group before escaping with his blonde companion; they later booked into a hotel in Woburn Square, under the names of 'Mr & Mrs French'.

With the descriptions of Westbrook and his companions, Higgins now put his expertise to good use; a prostitute who was a regular informant provided him with the name of the blonde's original companion and a probable address. The man was spoken to, he identified Westbrook as the killer, and as a result, the cafés, boarding houses and hotels in the Bloomsbury area which Westbrook was known to have previously frequented were checked.

It paid off; on the morning of 27 December two aids to CID, Police Constables Bertie Joseph Charles Rowswell and Norman Harold Strange were on patrol in Woburn Place when they saw Westbrook and his blonde companion and realized that they fitted the descriptions of the wanted couple. The officers confronted Westbrook, told him they were police officers and asked to see his identity card. Westbrook immediately pulled out his automatic and rammed it into PC Strange's stomach, saying, "If you come another inch, I'll blow your guts in." He then turned and ran, with the officers in hot pursuit.

Westbrook was pitted against two determined adversaries. Rowswell was thirty-six years of age and at one-eighth of an inch under six feet three and weighing sixteen stone, he was a powerful opponent. With fifteen years' service in the Metropolitan Police, he had proved his abilities time and again. Within two years of joining he had received a commissioner's commendation for effecting the arrest of two men for larceny and in 1939 another for 'courage and promptitude in rescuing a woman from drowning whilst on annual leave at Skegness'; he was also awarded a testimonial on vellum from the Royal Humane Society. Two years later, he was awarded the British Empire Medal for 'meritorious service in connection with war activities', and now it was quite clear that he was determined to stop Westbrook. He jumped on to a passing taxi, but Westbrook, standing in its path, fired a shot at his pursuer which hit the taxi's roof.

Norman Strange first jumped on to a passing lorry, but due to its slowness opted instead for a lift in a car to pursue Westbrook. Strange had joined the Metropolitan Police in 1925 and today was his forty-fourth birthday; he too was making it clear that the finest birthday present he could receive was the capture of Westbrook. Strange had been commended twice by the commissioner, first in 1929 for his action in a case of housebreaking, then two years later for effecting the arrest of a thief, on each occasion receiving monetary awards of 7s 6d. However, it seemed at one time that his career was about to come to an untimely end. Three months after his second commendation he appeared before a disciplinary board, in respect of two charges. The first was that he had omitted to proceed to a police station for duty, and for this offence he was fined one day's pay. This amounted to 11s 6d, so at least that left 3s 6d from his two awards. However, the second charge was considered far more serious: he had failed to work his patrol and, to further aggravate the matter, he had been found in a police section house with his helmet off and his jacket removed. He was fined four days' pay (£2 6s 0d), severely rebuked and cautioned. Perhaps his commendations acted as mitigation; other officers faced dismissal for similar offences.

But now, fifteen years later, his youthful impetuosity behind him, Norman Strange chased Westbrook as he ran in and out of premises, down back-alleys and over walls, firing at the two officers as he went. Householders were spilling out of their homes, passers-by stood and stared, as Westbrook dashed into a hotel in Cartwright Gardens, ran up the stairs and got out on to the flat roof. Following him up to the roof, Strange paused only to grab hold of a crowbar before emerging out of the skylight. By now, the police had been called and a hundred officers ringed the scene; but although, for all his Houdini-style escapes, Westbrook must have realized that a getaway was now impossible, he turned and fired at Strange, who was almost within striking distance on the slippery roof. Strange saw a flash and dropped the crowbar as he felt a tug at his arm; the bullet had passed right through the sleeve of his raincoat. A moment later, Westbrook fired again. The bullet just missed Rowswell but struck some brickwork which splintered and flew into his right eye, causing him to stagger, and he cried out, "I've been hit!" Nevertheless, he picked himself up and held a handkerchief to his bleeding eye while he and Strange followed Westbrook who, still firing at them, disappeared through the skylight.

Meanwhile, Higgins had been alerted and was racing to the hotel, armed with a service revolver. Meeting up with Police Sergeant Lacey, who was also armed, they searched the premises and found Westbrook in one of the rooms. "I give in," he said simply – his gun, secreted behind a cushion, was empty. Even as he left the hotel he tried to make a final break for it; he was dissuaded from doing so.

On 13 February 1947 at the Old Bailey Westbrook was found not guilty of the murder of Aloysius Abbott, claiming that he had only fired his pistol to frighten the Jamaicans who, he feared, were going to attack him, and he was convicted of manslaughter. He had already pleaded guilty to possessing a firearm with intent to resist arrest and asked for the forty-four cases of housebreaking to be taken into consideration; the trial judge, Mr Justice Atkinson, listened with incredulity as Higgins outlined Westbrook's criminal career. Told of his two Borstal Training sentences, the judge snapped, "That illustrates the futility of letting them out before training could have done any good at all," but when Higgins informed the judge that following his conviction for twenty-four offences at the Old Bailey in November 1942, Westbrook had been bound over to keep the peace for three years, it was too much.

"And he was *bound over*!" gasped the judge.

Sentencing him to eleven years' penal servitude, Mr Justice Atkinson told Westbrook:

If ever a criminal had a chance given to him when he did not deserve it, you were he. Not only Borstal but probation was turned into a farce by the way you have been treated. The jury have given you the benefit of a very slender doubt. It is plain you fired the pistol in a most reckless way and I imagine the jury thought there was an element of bad luck in that two shots killed Abbott. That crime was followed by two crimes where luck was all your way, where you might very well have killed two police officers, as well.

He then highly commended Rowswell and Strange, as did the jury, a commendation that was echoed by the commissioner three months later. Both officers were awarded £15 from the Bow Street Reward Fund, and on 5 September 1947 both men were awarded the King's Police and Fire Services Medal for Gallantry.

Strange never did realize his ambition to become a permanent member of the CID; he failed his second-class Civil Service examination (a necessity, then, to join the CID) on three occasions. He retired after twenty-five years service and died aged seventy-four.

Rowswell's damaged eye had to be removed but he was assured that he would keep his job, and he did. On 15 December 1947 he was appointed detective constable and was given duties in the office of the divisional detective inspector on 'J' Division. Not that this proved to be a purely sedentary duty – seven years later he was commended by both the North London Magistrates' Court and the commissioner for ability and initiative in arresting two persistent housebreakers.

He soldiered bravely on until 30 September 1963 when, still serving but off-duty, he collapsed and died from coronary thrombosis and a gastric ulcer. Married, with two sons, he was fifty-three years of age and had served with the Metropolitan Police for almost thirty-two and a half years. The Force turned out in droves to salute the memory of their highly decorated, resourceful comrade. Rowswell was the only Metropolitan Police officer to be awarded both the King's Police and Fire Services Medal and the British Empire Medal, both for gallantry.

Bob Higgins, on the other hand, rose to the rank of detective superintendent and enjoyed forty-five years of retirement, keeping extremely active until his death, three weeks prior to what would have been his ninety-ninth birthday. He was a good friend to me and an amusing correspondent – and never forgot that he was a hard-line copper. "Clearing out the riff-raff," was one of his favourite descriptions of his way of dispersing disagreeable members of society. I was one of those fortunate to be considered 'a good scout'; his contempt was reserved for those officers who obtained their promotion by 'driving a desk'. And I know he was furious at the jury's decision after just one hour's deliberations to acquit Westbrook of Abbott's murder, especially after two of the women jurors were heard to say as they left the Old Bailey that at least it would not be on their consciences that they had sent a man to be hanged.

"I wonder how they'd have felt if Abbott had been one of their loved ones?" he bitterly commented to me.

There we shall leave Bob Higgins, but only momentarily; two months after Westbrook's conviction he would re-emerge in another story of murder and firearms.

★ ★ ★

On 23 April 1947 Charles Henry 'Harry-Boy' Jenkins was released from Borstal, having served just twenty-one months of his sentence. Known as 'The King of Borstal' during his incarceration, he had become friends with another South London tearaway, twenty-year-old Christopher James Geraghty, who had carried out two armed raids at jewellers in 1945. Geraghty had escaped twice during his stay at Sherwood Borstal; he was released in November 1946. Now he and Jenkins were reunited and they teamed up with seventeen-year-old Terence Peter Rolt. Within two days, the three young men, together with two other criminals, Michael Joseph Gillam (who had met Geraghty and Jenkins whilst similarly serving a Borstal term) and thirty-seven-year-old William Henry Walsh, carried out an armed robbery at A.B. Davis Ltd, a jeweller in Queensway, which netted them £4,500; and two days after that, Rolt, Geraghty and Jenkins had broken into F. Dyke & Co, a gunsmith's in Union Street and made off with a number of revolvers and a quantity of ammunition.

On 29 April, just six days after his release, Jenkins, together with his two trusted lieutenants, Geraghty and Rolt, stole a Vauxhall 14 saloon, intending that it should be the getaway car for a robbery at Jay's, a jeweller's shop in Charlotte Street, W.1. Rushing into the shop, the three masked tearaways brandished the stolen guns, threatened the staff and coshed the director with a gun barrel; but when the seventy-year-old manager threw a stool at them, a shot was fired and the three robbers fled, only to discover that their getaway car had been obstructed by a lorry. As they ran off on foot, a motor mechanic named Alec d'Antiquis, married with six children, was riding past the scene on his motorcycle. Seeing what was going on, he slewed his machine in front of the fleeing gunmen and Geraghty paused, only to shoot him in the head. As he lay dying, face down on the pavement, d'Antiquis murmured to a passer-by, "They have shot me ... stop them ... I did my best."

DDI Bob Higgins immediately contacted his senior officer. Robert Honey Fabian was the acting detective superintendent of No. 1 Area and he was already a legendary character in the Metropolitan Police. Just two years away from retirement, forty-six-year-old Fabian had been commended by the commissioner on forty occasions and had been awarded the King's Police Medal for Gallantry in 1940, after dismantling an IRA bomb by the simple expedient of pulling the detonators out of the unstable, sweating sticks of Polar Ammon gelignite and then, to ensure that no more detonators were secreted, cutting up the gelignite with his pocket knife.

Fabian, a brilliant murder investigator and a former head of the Flying Squad, got to work with his deputy Higgins, and in a twenty-day period all of the criminals in all of the cases were arrested and later convicted. Rolt, too young to hang, was ordered to be detained at His Majesty's Pleasure, but Geraghty and Jenkins were sentenced to death.

Whilst Geraghty and Jenkins were achieving heroic status amongst their equally gormless chums, Mrs d'Antiquis was experiencing problems of her own, quite apart from the murder of her husband. Due to her husband's neglect of his motorcycle business, she had accumulated debts of £650; these were alleviated by donations, gathered by the *Daily Mail*, of £1,521 – that and the award, on behalf of her brave husband, of the Binney Medal. It was curious that the Binney Medal was originally struck partly because of Thomas Jenkins' conviction for Binney's manslaughter, since his brother, Harry, who was not convicted for that offence, was convicted of the murder of d'Antiquis. As the hangman, Albert Pierrepoint, slipped the noose over Jenkins' head at Pentonville Prison on the morning of 19 September 1947, thus providing him with a one-way ticket to eternity, it is possible that Thomas Jenkins, then in the second year of his sentence at Dartmoor, paused to wonder if the existence that he and his brother had been leading – a life of guns and death – was entirely worthwhile. But if this was indeed the case, it was just a momentary thought and one which he quickly dismissed.

★   ★   ★

If the Jenkins brothers were bad through and through and Westbrook was a gun-toting borderline psychotic, then Robert Harrington Sanders was a criminal who was totally out of control. Deserting from his regiment, the Black Watch, in wartime Germany, twenty-year-old Sanders undertook an orgy of violence, including two cases of robbery with aggravation, four cases of rape and an indecent assault. At his court martial in June 1945 he was sentenced to fifteen years' penal servitude, and although the sentence was later reduced to one of seven years, he escaped and managed to return to England. During an attempted armed robbery of a garage owner, the police were called and overpowered Sanders; he broke away, leapt over the parapet of a viaduct and, landing thirty feet below, made his getaway. Jumping played an important part in his escapes; a few months later he was traced to a house at Clacton-on-Sea and leapt from a first floor window, sixteen feet off the ground. Unfortunately, a police officer was waiting for him, and at Essex Quarter Sessions on 14 March 1946 he was convicted of possessing a loaded pistol with intent to endanger life and sentenced to fourteen years' penal servitude. At the same time, for attempting to steal a car, a wireless set and other offences, he was sentenced to concurrent terms of one, three and seven years' imprisonment.

Incarcerated in Wakefield Prison, Sanders waited for six years before making his next move; then, just before Christmas 1952, he climbed over the prison wall and escaped. Within a month, Sanders had led a six-man gang into a robbery at an East London pub, the Prospect of Whitby; all disguised themselves with red scarves and not unnaturally were christened 'The Red Scarf Gang'. Sanders was their leader; it was known that he had obtained a gun and detectives all over London were pressed into service to discover his whereabouts. It paid off. The police received a tip-off that a robbery was planned when wages were delivered to Messrs Cedra Mantles Ltd, a clothing company situated in Chatham Place, a thoroughfare just south of the junction with Morning Lane, Hackney. On Friday 6 February 1953 police were keeping observation when they saw two men, later joined by a third, acting suspiciously in the area; from their actions it was clear that they were the men who intended to rob the employees of the clothing company. The three men were Robert Sanders, John Joseph Cracknell, a thirty-two-year-old market porter and – recently released from prison – thirty-three-year-old Thomas James Jenkins. The detectives telephoned for reinforcements, but in the meantime the taxi containing the wages clerk, Leslie Moutrie, was arriving at the premises. He had returned from another branch, having collected between £700 and £800 in wages. Suddenly, Sanders and Jenkins walked up the stairs to the office, where the factory manager, Benjamin Izen, picked up an iron bar to confront them. As Sanders reached inside his jacket pocket the manager lunged at him, and he and some of the company's workmen chased them into the street, with Jenkins exclaiming, "We've been tumbled!" However, by this time police assistance arrived, Cracknell had disappeared in the confusion.

The crew of the 'J' Division 'Q' Car who tore into Chatham Place saw Sanders and Jenkins being pursued by the company's employees. The driver followed the men as they ran into Meeting Fields Path, through Rivaz Place and across a bombsite. At the junction of Mead Road and Cresset Road the two men split up. Jenkins turned into Cresset Road and Sanders continued along Mead Road towards the junction with Elsdale Street; with that, the 'Q' Car pulled up. Police Constable George Kenneth Frank Baldwin was first out of the car and he took up the pursuit of Jenkins, eventually catching and overpowering him in the gardens of Lennox Buildings; his actions were later recognised with the award of a Queen's Commendation for Brave Conduct.

Meanwhile, Sanders was chased by the other two officers; the driver was Police Constable George Edward Dorsett. At thirty-one years of age, Dorsett had spent six years with the RAF as a despatch rider and had been mentioned in dispatches in 1941; he had joined the Metropolitan Police as soon as he was demobilised. At the Hendon driving school he had been authorised to ride all types of motorcycles, and just six months previously he had been appointed a Class I driver, authorised to drive any type of fast police vehicle, up to and including Flying Squad cars.

But leading Sanders' pursuit was Detective Constable Edward Norman Snitch, who during the 1930s had served as a military policeman. Joining the Metropolitan Police one year prior to the Second World War, Snitch had been recalled to the Army in 1942 and served for the next four years with the rank of sergeant. Demobilised in 1946, he rejoined the police, was posted back to 'J' Division and, after a short period as an aid to CID, was appointed detective constable in 1947. Married, with a son aged four, the thirty-four-year-old officer had been commended by the commissioner just six months previously for his ability in a case of robbery; now, once more, his abilities would be put to the test.

Closing in on Sanders at Collent House, Snitch called out, "Stop – I'm a police officer." Sanders turned and shouted, "Keep away from me you bastard, or I'll put a bullet through you!" and reaching under his raincoat he produced a Smith & Wesson .38 revolver. Snitch had no illusions about the danger posed by this jail-breaker, who had used firearms on other occasions; at a distance of ten feet from the man pointing a gun right at him, Snitch simply went straight for him. Sanders fired, the bullet grazed the side of Snitch's face and he stumbled. Dorsett saw his colleague fall and, believing that he had been shot, dashed at Sanders. Snitch got to his feet as Dorsett drew level with him and together the two officers closed with Sanders who fired two more shots at them, one providentially lodging in the belt of Snitch's raincoat. Dorsett seized hold of Sanders by the head whilst Snitch wrestled the revolver from his grasp. The gun was found to contain three used cartridges plus three live ones.

After being searched at Hackney police station, Sanders was found to be in possession of another twelve rounds of .38 ammunition, as well as a leather holster. A flat in Sydenham, Kent, where Sanders had been staying, was searched and a second gun, a loaded automatic pistol with 100 rounds of ammunition, was discovered. Yet another revolver was discovered in a telephone kiosk, not far from the factory in Chatham Place. When he was charged, Sanders replied, "Fuck you, you've caught me. I'll take the lot," and in fairness, there was little else he could do. Cracknell was later picked up, and Sanders manfully absolved Jenkins of any knowledge of the weapons.

The trial commenced at the Old Bailey on 26 March 1953. Sanders was charged with shooting at Snitch with intent to murder him, plus wounding with intent to murder; in addition, he was charged with Jenkins and Cracknell for conspiring to rob Leslie Moutrie. All pleaded not guilty.

In the witness box Sanders admitted being a convict 'on the run' and stated that he had agreed to meet Jenkins at four o'clock on 6 February to discuss with him the possibility of finding new accommodation, plus the chance of going abroad. Through his barrister, Mr H.M. Croome, Sanders said there was never any agreement to rob anybody. He and Jenkins were walking by the factory when he saw a police car. "I soon discovered I was being chased," he told the jury. "Detective Snitch didn't call out and I didn't say anything to him. I looked over my shoulder and saw Snitch closing in on me. I couldn't run any farther as I had been ill, and I turned round, drew my gun from my holster and waited until he was a yard or so away and then fired three shots into the ground. Snitch made a dive at me and we had a struggle. He grasped my hand and I placed my feet behind his legs and threw him to the ground. In doing so, the gun fell from my hand. I was standing over Snitch when Police Constable Dorsett came up, and in the struggle I was overpowered."

"Did you fire those shots with the intention of killing Snitch?" asked his barrister.

"No," replied Sanders. "If I wanted to kill him, I would have had no trouble in doing so."

Jenkins went into the witness box to tell the jury that since he had been released from Dartmoor in June 1950 he had been 'working straight'. He also stated that he had no idea that Sanders had a gun or a cosh and that it was just coincidence that they were near the factory at the time Leslie Moutrie was delivering the wages. They had never discussed robbing anyone, he added.

In his defence, Cracknell denied ever being anywhere near Chatham Place on the day of the wages delivery.

On 30 March the jury found all of the defendants guilty of the offences with which they had been charged. Mr Justice Streatfeild sentenced Cracknell, who had a number of minor convictions, to three years' imprisonment and Jenkins, who had been working as a labourer (and had given his employer 'every satisfaction'), to five years' imprisonment.

Sentencing Sanders to life imprisonment, the judge told him:

You have committed this offence with a firearm just once too often. Once before you were sentenced to fourteen years' penal servitude for being in possession of a firearm with intent to endanger life. Quite clearly, you are a thoroughly dangerous man. In my view you are a danger to society every moment you are at liberty and you force a judge, for the first time in his life, and I hope it will be the last, to take a very extreme view of an offence of this gravity. The public must be protected as far as it possibly can be against the activities of a man, such as yourself.

With a rather feeble attempt at braggadocio, the twenty-eight-year-old, short, stocky gunman with a tell-tale scar above his eye gave a sardonic bow and replied, "My Lord is most gracious."

As the larcenous trio were led away, the judge called the officers before him, saying:

Before parting from this case, I would just like to express the appreciation and admiration of the court for the great gallantry and devotion to duty shown by Detective Constable Snitch and PC Dorsett and I very much welcome the rider which the jury have added to their verdict expressing a similar appreciation. I trust that the conduct of these two police officers which in my view deserves the highest commendation will be drawn to the attention of the commissioner of police.

On 20 June, the three officers were each awarded £15 from the Bow Street Reward Fund, and three days later all were highly commended by the commissioner; it took another four months before Snitch and Dorsett were each awarded very well deserved George Medals.

Two years later, Snitch was promoted to detective sergeant (second class) and posted to 'G' Division, where he served the rest of his service at City Road police station. He retired after twenty-five years service and later moved, with his wife Eileen to East Sussex. In 1985 he began to lose his balance, and the shot from Sanders' gun causing the wound which originally had been thought to be 'superficial' was diagnosed by the specialists as being the start of a progressive illness. For the last four years of his life he was unable to move or speak. His wife wrote to the Metropolitan Police Welfare Department on three occasions without receiving a reply; therefore Mrs Snitch wrote directly to the commissioner. Sir Kenneth Newman GBE, QPM had received criticism both from inside and outside the Force during his tenure, but in Mrs Snitch's eyes he could do no wrong. He replied, almost by return of post, and Mrs Snitch received considerable assistance in converting their garage into a bedroom, where she nursed her husband until his death, aged seventy-four, in 1992.

But his colleague George Dorsett carried on; his gallantry had not yet been expended.

* * *

On a Saturday afternoon in December 1958 Dorsett was asleep at home in Chingford, having finished a tour of night duty, when he was awoken by the sounds of an explosion, of breaking glass and someone screaming. Looking out of his bedroom window, he saw a youth standing in the roadway and pointing a shotgun at a neighbour. It was clear that the explosion he had heard was the noise of the shotgun being discharged at the neighbour's windows. Quickly putting on a dressing gown, he ran downstairs and out into the street, where the youth – he was just sixteen – was screaming threats. It later transpired that the father of the youth's girl-friend had had opposed their friendship, and this had caused the boy, carrying his brother's shotgun, to arrive at his paramour's house, blow out the windows and threaten to kill her father.

It appeared that the fears of the girl's father were justified; Dorsett called out to the boy, who swung round, the gun pointing at Dorsett and his finger on the trigger. "I'm a police officer," said Dorsett, quietly. "Now, don't be silly."

"Keep away," replied the boy. "I'm not afraid to use this." Dorsett continued to advance towards the obviously troubled youth, speaking quietly and soothingly to him. And then, when he was a yard away from the twin muzzles of the shotgun, Dorsett pounced. He knocked the gun aside and, with the assistance of a neighbour, overpowered the youth.

The gun contained one live twelve-bore cartridge, the other having been expended during the window-blowing episode; but Dorsett then noticed that the gun was not cocked and mentioned this to the youth. "I know it wasn't cocked," said the boy, "because I pulled the trigger and nothing happened."

"So you did intend to shoot me?" asked Dorsett and received the chilling reply, "Of course I did."

After his appearance at Chingford and Waltham Abbey Magistrates' Court, where the boy hopefully received the type of treatment he so obviously needed, the Bench congratulated Dorsett for his courage, as did the commissioner on 10 February 1959 for 'outstanding courage and determination'. Six weeks later he was awarded a second cheque for £15 from the Bow Street Reward Fund, and three months after that a bar to his George Medal.

Dorsett had exhibited absolutely cold-blooded courage. At the time of advancing upon the obviously agitated youth, whose finger was on the trigger, he was unaware that the shotgun was not cocked but he knew that although one barrel had been discharged it was reasonable to assume that the second barrel contained a live cartridge, as indeed it did. And as an experienced police officer with a knowledge of firearms, he was also aware that if the shotgun had been fired at him from a distance of three feet it would have quite literally blown him in half.

Dorsett was quite properly regarded as a legend. "He was smart – immaculately smart," recalled former Police Constable Brian Ford, a newcomer to Walthamstow police station, adding, "Everybody looked up to him."

An accident a few years later when his right elbow and left wrist were fractured meant the end of Dorsett's active police career; his injuries were so severe that he taught himself to write with his other hand. He spent the rest of his twenty-six years service as a court officer and he died on 1 February 2006, aged eighty-four.

At his death, Dorsett had the unique distinction of being the only Metropolitan Police officer to be awarded the George Medal, a bar to it, and a wartime mention in dispatches. Together with his Police Long Service and Good Conduct Medal, plus his war medals, the decorations are held in the Met Collection at the Empress State Building and are a fitting tribute to a very brave man.

CHAPTER 5

Alone on a Footpath

hen a series of especially brutal handbag snatches was
carried out on women crossing Tooting Bec Common
early in 1947, a decoy was needed – a woman police
officer of extraordinary pluck and resolution. The
investigating officers did not have far to look; newly promoted
Woman Detective Sergeant Alberta 'Bertie' Mary Law had
arrived at 'W' Division fifteen months previously and, as it turned
out, would fit the bill admirably.

★   ★   ★

Born in Hawarden, Flintshire, just west of Chester, in 1914,
Bertie Law received an elementary education before working as a
shop assistant, but the attractive, dark haired young woman
decided that she wanted more excitement out of life than serving
behind a shop counter and in July 1939 she enrolled as a woman
police constable with the Metropolitan Police. Posted as WPC 28,
first at Cannon Row's 'A' Division, then three months later, still
bearing the same divisional numerals, to 'V' Division, within four
years' service she was appointed detective constable. It was not
surprising; in 1941 she had been commended for her actions in a
case of a woman posing as a fortune teller and in 1943 she had
been commended again, this time for detecting offences in
contravention of the Betting and Licensing Acts. Just two months
later another commendation followed, this time for good work in
clearing up offences contrary to the Licensing Act. In June 1943,
one month after her last commendation, she was posted to West
End Central police station, now completely rebuilt since being
destroyed by a parachute mine three years previously. Within six
months of her transfer to 'W' Division in 1945 Bertie was
promoted to woman detective sergeant; and a few months later
the attacks on Tooting Bec Common commenced.

The Tooting Commons consist of two separate areas of
common land stretching between Balham, Streatham and
Tooting: Tooting Bec Common and Tooting Graveney Common,
a huge area covering a total of over 200 acres. The woodland

areas are a natural habitat for the wildlife of the area – also for thugs who prey on women with handbags.

★   ★   ★

Bertie immediately volunteered for this highly dangerous decoy work; her undercover work combating offences against the betting and licensing acts had instilled great confidence in her, but on 24 January 1947, the very first night of her lone patrol, her handbag slung over her arm, she was attacked. It was already dark and bitterly cold, and as she commenced her lonely walk at six o'clock she noticed a man standing on the corner of the common. Arthur Burland followed her, caught up with her and then passed her; it was clear that he was surveying the area to see if there was any chance of interruption by a third party. Bertie stopped, turned on her heel and casually walked off in the direction from which she had come. It was now quite clear to her that an attack was imminent. Suddenly she heard the sound of running footsteps, and Burland grabbed her from behind, threw her to the ground struck her on the head with a bottle and kicked and punched her. Bertie struggled fiercely but, wrenching her arm as he seized her handbag, Burland ran off. Dazed, she got to her feet and, despite sustaining these crippling injuries, dashed after her attacker. Fit, and above average height at five feet six-and-a-quarter, Bertie shouted for assistance and, catching up with Burland, she grappled with him and hung on until other officers arrived and arrested him.

She was placed sick for two weeks, suffering from the effects of shock and the bruising, but she was commended by the Bench when Burland was committed for trial from South-western Magistrates' Court; it was the first of several commendations for her. At the Old Bailey Burland admitted the attack on Bertie, plus two other cases of robbery with violence and, sentencing him to five years' penal servitude, Sir Gerald Dodson, the Recorder of London, congratulated Bertie, stating, "His arrest was only possible by the extreme bravery and heroism of this officer. No one can speak too highly of her or commend her too strongly."

An award of £15 from the Bow Street Reward Fund marked the first time since the fund was first established in 1869 that a woman had been a recipient. On 13 May 1947 Bertie was highly commended by the commissioner for 'courage and resource' and four months later, she was the first – and only – woman officer with the Metropolitan Police to be awarded what normally would have been the King's Police Medal for Gallantry. However, since the medal had first been struck, amendments had been made to the Royal Warrant.

It had originally been stipulated that the medal would be forfeited in the event that the recipient was convicted of a criminal offence (although nobody in the Metropolitan Police ever was), but this rule was varied on 1 October 1930 to permit the sovereign to restore the medal should that eventuality arise. And three years later, a central red stripe was added to the medal ribbon to denote that the medal had been awarded for gallantry, plus a further silver strip in the middle of the ribbon. The words, 'For Gallantry' or 'For Distinguished Service' were added, as appropriate.

Then on 6 September 1940 the name of the medal was changed to the King's Police and Fire Services Medal, to incorporate the eligibility of the Fire Service. In addition, there was to be no limit on the number of medals issued annually. From 1950 the King's Police and Fire Services Medal was only awarded posthumously for gallantry, and this remained the case when the medal was superseded by the Queen's Police Medal which was struck on 19 May 1954. It was only in 1969 that recipients of the medals were permitted to use the letters, KPM, KPFSM and QPM after their name.

★   ★   ★

Both the high commendation and the investiture raised some confusion; Bertie had changed her name, since she had married on 29 March, and both awards were made in her married name of Watts. The waters were further muddied when, at the same investiture, the same medal was awarded to Bertie Rowswell. And two weeks before the announcement of the commendation, Bertie Watts had been transferred to 'P' Division – but it would be a short-lived posting. Exactly five months later, on 28 September 1947, she voluntarily resigned, having served eight years and sixty days. Her character was described as 'exemplary' but aged thirty-three she received no pension; she took with her a gratuity of £82 2s 9d – approximately £2,240 at today's values.

She retired to Cornwall and was a member of the Metropolitan Women Police Association; she attended several of their functions in Falmouth, where she was regarded as 'great company'. After Bertie's husband died, she lived with her daughter, a health visitor, and it was in Cornwall that she died on 22 December 2002, aged eighty-eight. Just one-eleventh of her life had been spent in the Metropolitan Police, but it had been put to hugely productive – and heroic – use.

CHAPTER 6

Left in the Snow

It is hard to imagine more conspicuous bravery than that exhibited by Detective Sergeant Bill Deans.

He knew he was going to be brutally assaulted on a lonely footpath by any number of vicious criminals out of a gang of six. After he had been attacked, he knew he would be kidnapped; not only that, but he was aware that all this would be witnessed by colleagues who could do nothing to help him. He was told it would happen on a specific Friday, but it did not. Then he was told it would occur on the following Friday, but again it did not. It was only on the third Friday that he was savagely attacked and badly hurt, just as he knew he would be; he had volunteered to be a decoy. The plan – to liberate Deans after his ordeal, thwart a well thought out robbery and bring about the arrest of six professional criminals – had been meticulously set out. Nothing could go wrong.

Until it did.

★   ★   ★

Early in 1947, word had filtered to the Flying Squad from a highly placed informant that a six-man gang were observing the movements of a Mr Snell, the manager of the Kentish Town branch of the Midland Bank. They had carefully monitored his route home from the bank; they knew that he caught the Northern Line train at Kentish Town, then travelled to Woodside Park Station, Finchley. He would leave the station, walk down a footpath to Holden Road, cut through to Avondale Avenue, turn right into Argyle Road and then arrive home, in Westbury Road. It was a route Mr Snell always took, without exception.

The plan, the informant told the Flying Squad, was to kidnap the manager on a Friday evening; the gang were working on the fairly certain assumption that by then the bank vaults and strongroom would be full. Having subdued and abducted Mr Snell, the keys to the bank – the exterior doors and the vaults

– would be taken from him, leaving the way open for the depositories to be plundered. But not all of the gang would be required to kidnap one man; four would carry out the snatch and two more would wait in the vicinity of the bank. Therefore it was essential to arrest all of them simultaneously. If the kidnappers alone were arrested at the scene, the other two would get clean away. Not only that; the informant knew that the organiser of the robbery would not be involved in the actual kidnap. Therefore, if he were not arrested, through lack of evidence, he would be at liberty to recruit new gang members and carry out a further robbery, details of which the informant might not know.

It was inconceivable that the Squad could let the plan go ahead, because of the danger to the unsuspecting Mr Snell; he had been seen by several members of the Squad and his frail physical appearance suggested that if the gang did indeed attack him, it could result in a fatality. What was required was a daring plan. Detective Superintendent George Hatherill of C1 Department at the Yard – which at that time included the Flying Squad – was informed of the circumstances, but the planning of this complex operation was wisely left to Detective Inspector (later Detective Chief Superintendent) Len Crawford.

Leonard William Crawford had joined the Metropolitan Police in 1927 and at the time of this investigation was on his third tour with the Flying Squad. The former Royal Navy telegraphist was now forty-five years of age and what he lacked in height – he was just under five feet ten – he made up for in toughness and guile. Amongst his commendations (which numbered twenty-nine at the time of this case) were arrests for grievous bodily harm, the capture of a violent criminal for prisonbreaking and, after he had arrested a fiercely struggling IRA man on a roof top fifty feet above ground level, the calm defusing of a row of ticking bombs.

Crawford knew that absolute secrecy was paramount. Had the plan been formed because of an inside agent in the bank informing the gang? It was impossible to say. What was needed was a decoy, someone to impersonate the bank manager; but he would have to be convincing – the gang had already seen Mr Snell on several occasions. Crawford idly looked around the Flying Squad office – it was known as 'The Bungalow' at the Yard – until his eye settled on one particular officer. Bill Deans bore an almost uncanny resemblance to Mr Snell.

★   ★   ★

Formerly a plumber, William Hosie Deans had joined the Metropolitan Police in 1932. Married with two children, a girl then aged eight and a boy then aged three, Deans had learnt his trade as a detective on 'L' and 'P' Divisions, collecting ten commendations along the way. One of them, awarded almost exactly three years prior to this operation, was for 'devotion to duty, whilst off-duty, in a case of larceny dwelling'. Born in Glasgow, Deans was now aged thirty-six, five feet ten tall, slim, with a thick moustache. Crawford had no doubts regarding his colleague's abilities; coincidentally, Deans had joined the Flying Squad on the same day that the legendary Ghost Squad had been formed, just over a year previously, and he and Crawford – and indeed most of the team around him – had been working with this secret, undercover unit, carrying out arrests and observations. Therefore Deans had all the necessary qualifications for such a risky job: knowledge of clandestine operations, guile and courage.

Crawford took Deans to one side and put him completely in the picture, in particular explaining all the attendant risks; Deans immediately volunteered to be the decoy.

First, Deans completely familiarised himself with the way home taken by Mr Snell, so that when the time came there would be no hesitation in his route and he would appear to be acting completely naturally. Next, as information came in to Crawford, so it was passed on to Deans; the gang intended to attack and seize him as he left the footpath, tie him up, bundle him into a green van and rob him of the bank keys. He would then be taken to the bank by four members of the gang, the keys would be handed to other members of the team and he would be taken to the outskirts of Chingford, Essex, where he would be dumped in a lane. To this end, the services of Detective Sergeant Pirie from 'J' Division were called upon – he had already assisted on Ghost Squad cases – to try to pinpoint where it was that Deans would be abandoned after the raid. Similarly, Detective Sergeant Reid of 'S' Division was co-opted on to the Squad for his knowledge of the area in and around the home of Mr Snell.

Then, on Thursday, 6 February 1947, the snout contacted Crawford to say that the job was on for the following day.

★   ★   ★

At midday on Friday 7 February Mr Snell was asked to report to head office as a matter of urgency. Upon his arrival he was astonished to be greeted by the chief investigating officer of the Midland Bank, plus a team of detectives who explained the plan to him. Deans was given a suit and overcoat, very similar to Mr Snell's, plus horn-rimmed spectacles which resembled those worn by Snell – except that the lenses were made of plain glass – and a bowler hat. The hat certainly bore a strong resemblance to Snell's own bowler, except that this one had been reinforced with padding. Finally, Deans was provided with letters showing Mr Snell's name and address and two bunches of bank keys. The four £1 notes, the ten shilling note and the four half-crowns in his pocket were all marked. The bank's chief investigating officer went to the Kentish Town branch of the bank to inform Snell's deputy of what was happening, and Deans followed later, letting himself in at the side door of the bank.

It was dark as Deans left the bank, locked the door and set off towards the tube station. His departure was witnessed by two men who set off on foot following him. Their actions were, in turn, noted by Squad officers, who followed on after.

Showing Mr Snell's season ticket at the barrier at Woodside Park Station, Deans strolled off along the footpath leading to Holden Road. He knew the two men were following him but he was reassured by the sight of Woman Detective Constable Winnie Sherwin, posing as a housewife carrying a shopping basket. No shrinking violet, Winnie could give a good account of herself in a rough-house; when an abortionist had attempted to escape over the back wall following a raid on his house, Winnie had been waiting to flatten him with a right hook. Suddenly Deans spotted a green van parking underneath the railway bridge in Holden Road; there were two men inside it. Just then, a uniformed police constable cycled by; it was quite innocent, of course, since the officer had no idea of the drama which had been intended to be played out around him, but his presence was sufficient to put the gang off.

The whole scenario had been witnessed by Crawford, overlooking the scene from a house in Holden Road. The house possessed a telephone, and this was to be used to alert the majority of the Flying Squad team, secreted well out of the way at Camden police section house. But not tonight. Deans carried on to Snell's house in Westbury Road, opened the front door and walked inside.

One week later, the whole operation was carried out again. The same two men who had followed Deans the previous week were in the vicinity – they were William Ernest Hudson, aged twenty-four, a van driver and William Henry Stevens, aged forty-one, a labourer – but again (and for whatever reason – perhaps a dry run) nothing happened; once more Deans proceeded, unmolested, to Snell's house in Westbury Road.

The next occasion, Friday 21 February, was a bad night. Snow had been falling for twenty-four hours and had settled. In 1947 this was nothing unusual; in fact, the snow had started just prior to Christmas and there had been a transport strike, but by the time the dispute was resolved the trains were snowed in. They had just started running again; by March, they would come to a halt once more, due to the dreadful weather conditions. It was freezing cold, so much so that the sea froze off Margate and icebergs were seen off the Norfolk coast.

Therefore it was fortunate that the train which brought Deans for the third time into Woodside Park was actually running – fortunate for the gang, that is. Deans was again aware that he was being followed. He had spotted Stevens and another member of the gang, Victor Stanley Towell, aged twenty-seven, a costermonger, on the platform at Kentish Town Station. They got on the same train as Deans and alighted at Woodside Park Station. As he set off on his lonely walk, Deans noted a third member of the gang. This was James Frederick Cunningham, a thirty-four-year-old fitter from Walthamstow. Now, as Deans approached the railway bridge, there was the green van parked underneath it.

Two of the men passed him, he heard a voice say, "Right," and he felt a sickening blow to the back of his head, which sent the padded bowler hat spinning away. He had been hit by a sock containing three and a half pounds of wet sand; then four more blows descended on his unprotected head and he lost consciousness. It was a wonder his skull had not been fractured. The weapon, dropped in the snow, was later recovered by police.

Deans was picked up and flung into the back of the van, which roared away. The whole attack was witnessed by Winnie Sherwin and Len Crawford; but when Winnie telephoned to alert the occupants in the Squad car waiting nearby, the vehicle failed to start immediately, due to the freezing weather, and they lost precious minutes. Therefore she telephoned through to the Yard to circulate details of the van to the Squad cars at the Section House, plus other police cars in the area, adding that should the vehicle be seen, its whereabouts should be passed on to the other police cars but on no account was it to be stopped. She and Crawford were picked up and they went immediately to the area of the bank in Kentish Town, working on the assumption that the gang must turn up there. Crawford knew that as far as the gang was concerned time was of the essence; the raid had to be carried out as soon as possible before the 'bank manager' could be reported missing. But although there were very few vehicles on the roads in post-war austerity Britain, especially on a night such as this when the roads were treacherous with ice and snow, no trace of the van could be found. It was as though it had simply vanished into thin air.

★   ★   ★

Meanwhile, consciousness gradually returned to Deans in the back of the jolting van as it sped along. The scarf which he had been wearing was now tied over his eyes, his hands and legs were tied with rope, and as he groaned he felt something hard pressed into his side. "This is a stick-up," he heard one of the gang say. "Keep your fucking mouth shut or it's your lot." Since adhesive tape had been stuck over Deans' mouth, the directive was somewhat superfluous.

"Are you sure it's the right bloke?" asked another of the gang, and was reassured when he was told, "He's the geezer alright. He's got the keys in his pocket."

He had indeed; the gang relieved him not only of the keys but his wallet, watch, fountain pen and ring – plus the marked notes. Deans' condition was of some concern to at least one of the gang members, who felt his pulse and heart, put his ear to his nose to ensure he was still breathing, lifted the scarf from his eyes and shone a torch into them. "He looks bad," he said anxiously. "You hit him too hard, Jim." He was right to be concerned regarding Deans' condition; the policeman had received severe punishment to his skull, and the death penalty was still in place for murder.

But 'Jim' – James Cunningham – was unconcerned. "It doesn't matter," he replied. "No one saw us do it. We'll make our way to the bank by cab and bus. You doodle around for an hour and then dump him."

Two of the gang remained in the van; after some time, one of them said, "We'll dump the bastard here. No one will find him for a while." Deans was picked up, slung over the man's shoulder and dropped face down in the snow. He had no idea of his whereabouts – in fact he was in East Barnet, less than two miles from where he had been kidnapped – not that that mattered to him. He had sustained severe concussion, he was starting to experience the effects of exposure to the bitterly cold weather and once more he lost consciousness. The gang member was quite right; no one would find him for a while.

★   ★   ★

Meanwhile, no trace of the van had been found and, what was more, no trace of the gang. It was now forty minutes later than their expected time of arrival at the bank, and Crawford and his team were experiencing deep concern for Deans' well-being. Suddenly one of the suspects appeared. He looked about him cautiously, but all he could see was a courting couple, arm-in-arm. Satisfied, Richard Charles Beck, a nineteen-year-old window cleaner, walked up to the rear door of the bank, produced a set of keys from his pocket and inserted one in the lock. However, not all courting couples are as innocent as they seem, particularly on this occasion, when one of the star-struck lovers was Winnie Sherwin. Beck was promptly seized and affected astonishment when he was told he was under arrest for robbery with violence. "Me?" he exclaimed. "Not me! I was passing along here when two men stopped me and told me they would give me a hundred nicker to open the bank door for them. They gave me the keys," he added. It was not the most convincing explanation, and made even less so when he was searched and the second set of bank keys and Deans' watch were found. A number of answers were required immediately. A police observation van was nearby and Crawford used it as a makeshift interrogation room, with spectacular results. The yard rented by Cunningham in Walthamstow was found, as was the green van, its radiator still warm; a search of it revealed the adhesive tape, and three more of the gang were impolitely requested to give the whereabouts of Deans. As a by-line to this interview, the remaining two gang members were traced to Romford and arrested.

★   ★   ★

After an hour Deans had recovered consciousness and managed to untie the ropes around his ankles. He staggered to a house some distance away, where the occupier administered first aid and summoned medical assistance. Dr Charles Mervyn Scott later told the court, "Sergeant Deans was severely shocked from exposure to the cold on a wickedly cold night and he showed signs of concussion. His condition would be consistent with blows from a sand-filled stocking."

The gang appeared at Highgate Magistrates' Court the following day and on 13 March they were committed to the Old Bailey for trial. Just one of the gang denied the offence, but was found guilty, and on 27 March 1947 they had the misfortune to be sentenced by the Lord Chief Justice, Lord Goddard. All were sentenced to terms of penal servitude: Cunningham and Stevens to seven years each, Hudson to five years and Beck to four years. Towell and the sixth member of the gang, Henry Edward Jones, aged twenty-eight, a carpenter, were each sentenced to three years.

As the gang were led away, Goddard turned his piercing gaze on the well of the court and said:

> Stand up, Detective Sergeant Deans. The country – and London in particular – are most indebted to you for the extraordinary courage and devotion to duty you have shown in this case. You have added lustre to the already great record of the Force to which you belong. I shall make it my duty to call the attention of the Secretary of State to your most commendable conduct.

These generous words of praise were echoed by the Director of Public Prosecutions, and Deans was later awarded £15 from the Bow Street Reward Fund. Then, on 10 June 1947, Deans was highly commended by the commissioner. His commendation is worth quoting because it was an unusual citation, the wording of which I have never seen before:

> For extreme courage and devotion to duty in acting as a decoy, knowing that he would be attacked by six criminals who had planned to break into a bank. He was, in fact, seriously assaulted.

Crawford and ten of the other officers involved in the operation were commended by the commissioner for what was described as 'ability and enterprise'. Certainly in Crawford's case, that citation seems decidedly apt.

Three months after that, Deans was awarded the King's Police and Fire Services Medal. He was in good company; Bertie Rowswell, Norman Strange and Alberta Watts were gazetted for the same award on the same day.

Deans had been attending hospital at the time of his court appearance and afterwards returned there. In all, he was placed on sick leave for seven weeks, and although he returned to work, the effects of his injuries plagued him for years afterwards. He was presented with a silver cigarette case that Christmas by his admiring colleagues as a mark of their respect; he returned to Flying Squad duties, especially with Ghost Squad work, and on 8 February 1949 he was again commended by the commissioner 'for devotion to duty, while off-duty, and perseverance in the arrest of a violent criminal for shopbreaking'. A week later, he was promoted to detective sergeant (first class) and was retained on the Squad. More commendations followed until his seven years' service with the Flying Squad came to an end. He was posted to 'P' Division and then, two years later, promotion to detective inspector took him to 'N', then 'G' Division. Within a year came his last posting, to 'R' Division; industrious to the last, he notched up a total of eighteen commissioner's commendations before retiring with twenty-seven years' service. He enjoyed twenty years of retirement before he died at the age of sixty-nine. Were those injuries he sustained on the night of 21 February thirty-two years previously a contributory factor to his early demise?

I rather think they were.

CHAPTER 7

Winners & Losers

During the Blitz in the Second World War there was a very strong feeling that there should be an award for people from all walks of life who had demonstrated great bravery. The armed services were already catered for with the award of the Victoria Cross for the most exemplary bravery in the face of the enemy, but this was not available to civilians. Therefore, on 24 September 1940, His Majesty King George VI instituted the George Cross and the George Medal, for conspicuous gallantry in the face of the enemy and brave deeds generally. Both awards could be conferred on service personnel or civilians.

The George Medal – awarded for 'acts of great bravery' – is a silver disc 36mm in diameter, with the crowned effigy of the reigning monarch on the obverse; the reverse shows St George on horseback, slaying the dragon on the coast of England. The ribbon, 32mm wide, is crimson with five narrow blue stripes. Bars can be awarded to recognise further acts of great bravery, the letters 'GM' follow the recipient's name and, since 1977, posthumous awards have been permitted.

In the seventy years of its existence, over 2,200 George Medals have been awarded. Of these, eighty-four were awarded to members of the Metropolitan Police in recognition of their gallantry in connection with wartime activities. They were awarded sparingly enough, and the last was presented in June 1944; the next three, all at the same investiture, would not be conferred until seven years later. What follows is the story of how this came about.

★   ★   ★

Temple's Store was first opened in 1908. It was constructed of sheds and tents and was situated at the junction of Polesteeple Hill and Stock Hill, at Biggin Hill, Kent. Shortly afterwards, Temple's Store moved up to the top of Polesteeple Hill, at the junction with Hillcrest Road, and Valley Stores was established in 1914 next to it. A family home for the Temples was built next to the two premises, and their proud boast was they could 'supply your every want'. During the early hours of 28 September 1950, William Edward McGuire, a young thug from Bethnal Green, and David Cooney, both aged twenty, put their own liberal interpretation on the company's motto and broke into the premises.

★ ★ ★

For a twenty-year-old criminal, McGuire had an impressive pedigree; since the age of fourteen he had acquired thirteen serious previous convictions. Between the ages of fourteen and sixteen he was sent to Approved Schools; he absconded on seven occasions. Aged sixteen, he appeared at the Old Bailey charged with possessing an offensive weapon, assault with intent to rob, wounding and possessing a firearm. He was sent to Borstal, from where he escaped. During 1947 and 1948 he was convicted of other offences before again appearing at the Old Bailey, where he was convicted of robbery with violence, for which he was jailed for two years.

Impressive, yes, but this also demonstrated that in his short criminal career he had been caught on a large number of occasions. Unfortunately, his criminal enterprises had failed to imbue him with the resourcefulness of someone such as the gangland leader Billy Hill, who possessed a violent streak but also a great deal of criminal acumen. Vicious, McGuire certainly was, but what became clear was that he possessed a complete inability to see more than one or two steps ahead during the course of a criminal venture. After having been released from prison on 22 July 1950, McGuire was stopped by police in possession of some stolen cameras; instead of immediately making a dash for it, he handed over his identity card first, then ran. During the early hours of 21 September McGuire broke into a house in Northfields Road, Stamford Hill, where he stole £23 cash, plus a revolver and some rounds of ammunition. The same day, Cooney, his fellow shopbreaker in Kent, was released from a prison sentence – it will quickly become apparent to the reader that Cooney was as brain-dead as his accomplice – and six days later they decided to rob in broad daylight Laurence Joseph Doyle, an LCC rent collector, who, they had been told, would be in possession of £200. In the event, the robbery was so botched that had Mr Doyle not been knocked to the ground and kicked, the whole matter would have been hilarious. Attacked by dogs and chased by the occupants of a block of flats, the two young desperadoes scampered away, pausing only to pick up what they could of the rent collector's takings: four half-crowns and two florins – in other words, seventy pence. However, all was not lost. They decided to carry out a break-in somewhere in Biggin Hill, an area which Cooney said he knew. They caught a Green Line coach, arrived there at ten o'clock in the evening and decided to break into Temple's Stores. Billy Hill would have used a two- or three-car changeover to facilitate his getaway from a burgled premises, but an escape plan had not occurred to this witless duo. It was now so late that they had no means of returning to the East End of London.

★   ★   ★

The silent burglar alarm which fifty-three-year-old Thomas Temple, the company director, had installed in the shop premises sounded in his bedroom next door, and he immediately telephoned the police; then he telephoned his son and a relative who lived nearby. Just before one o'clock in the morning, the 'P' Division wireless car drew up outside the premises and Temple was there to meet them.

The driver was Police Constable 262 'P' John Kerr McCallum, who had joined the Metropolitan Police in 1932. He served the first fourteen years of his service on 'M' Division, where after three short years he had been qualified to drive wireless cars and had collected a commendation for the arrest of three shopbreakers. Having failed the sergeant's examination in 1938, he decided to concentrate on driving duties. Now, married with a child, the transfer to Bromley suited him, making travelling easier between the station and his home in St John's Road, Petts Wood. Within a year of his arrival at Bromley, he had made his mark with a further commendation for the arrest of two men for larceny. At forty-five years of age, he was not quite the oldest of the three officers who attended Temple's Store that morning; Police Constable 134 'P' Owen Percival Ashwin was six months older and had fifteen months more service. Standing one-eighth of an inch over six feet, Ashwin had spent all but just over a year of his service at Bromley. Just prior to the Second World War, he had been commended for 'close attention to duty and zeal' in a case of officebreaking; married, he lived at East Drive, St Mary Cray. He was the wireless car's RT operator, having passed the course six months previously.

The third member of the crew was the plain-clothes observer, Police Constable 404 'P' Ivan Stanley King. He had joined the police in 1947, shortly after demobilisation from the Royal Navy, having served as a Petty Officer from 1943 onwards. Aged twenty-four, he was married with a son and lived in Bromley; all of his short service had been spent on 'P' Division.

McGuire and Cooney were completely oblivious to the fact that not only was their unauthorised presence known to the owner, but also the police had arrived. McGuire had already found two pens in a drawer in a desk on the ground floor and had excitedly pocketed his spoils, and Cooney had found a cheque; they now made their way to the first floor, where they ransacked the safe, greedily seizing the accumulated takings for the Greater London Fund for the Blind and the Biggin Hill War Memorial Fund, bringing the value of their spoils to £4 in total.

Meanwhile, Temple and Ashwin went to the rear of the premises and, having entered through the rear door, Temple locked the door behind them and switched on the lights. Meanwhile, the other two officers, together with two members of Temple's family, Norman Joseph Gee and Reginald Alfred Temple, covered the outside of the premises. There were two staircases leading to the first floor, and Temple and Ashwin went separately up to the first level. As they met at the shop's office, they saw the two men inside the office; the first, McGuire stepped out of the office, produced the stolen revolver and fired at them. The shot missed and hit the framework of a showcase. Both McGuire and his associate Cooney now ran to the other side of the building, closely pursued by Temple and Ashwin, whereupon Cooney suddenly turned and rushed at Ashwin. There was a struggle, and McGuire, who was at the top of a staircase, turned and at a distance of less than ten feet fired, hitting Ashwin just below his throat. Firing two more shots at Temple, McGuire turned and ran downstairs, pursued by Temple; as McGuire reached the ground floor, he picked up a wooden display stand, smashed a plate glass window, and climbed through it on to the street. Temple knew the outside perimeter was guarded, so he quickly retraced his steps, only to discover the true extent of Cooney's stupidity.

Cooney had seen McGuire flee downstairs and must have heard the ear-splitting crash of the plate glass window being broken; therefore he might well have thought that (a) McGuire had escaped and (b) the escape route existed for him as well. Instead, he chose to believe that the sound of Temple's running footsteps ascending the staircase belonged to McGuire. Consequently, he leapt on top of Ashwin, who was now unconscious and no possible threat to anybody, and started punching him in the face, excitedly calling out, "Come on Bill, I've got the bastard!"

He was speedily disabused of this notion after Temple picked up a wooden flooring batten and hit him in the head, so hard that the wood broke after the third blow, causing the gallant Cooney to squeal pitifully, "Don't, Guv'nor – I ain't got a revolver!" Temple told him to stand in a corner with his hands on his head and administered what first aid he could to the badly wounded PC Ashwin.

Meanwhile, McGuire, still brandishing the pistol, was tackled by McCallum but managed to free himself and ran off. King, who had been on the flat roof to prevent any escape of the miscreants through the skylight, now joined McCallum in the street and together with Temple's two relatives they chased the gunman for a quarter of a mile. Just as the two officers had almost caught up to him, McGuire stopped, turned, and pointed the pistol at McCallum. "I've got a gun!" he shouted, "This is your lot!" and from a distance of just five feet pulled the trigger. There was a click – the hammer had fallen on a spent cartridge case – and McCallum grabbed hold of McGuire's right wrist – his gun hand – whilst King grabbed him by the left. There was a violent struggle, but with the assistance of Temple's relatives McGuire was relieved of his gun and his liberty. When searched, he was found to be in possession of seven rounds of .25 ammunition.

Ashwin, who had been severely wounded, was admitted to Farnborough Hospital and remained there for almost three months before eventually being discharged. It really had been a case of 'touch-and-go'.

The judge at Kent Assizes two months later obviously thought so, too. Mr Justice Travers Humphries was now coming to the end of his career as a judge, but it had been an illustrious one. In 1933 he had presided at the famous Leopold Harris fire-raising case, which lasted thirty-two days and was (then) the longest running trial at the Old Bailey. His summing-up had lasted three days and contained 100,000 words. The sentences he imposed ranged from nine months' hard labour to fourteen years' penal servitude, and the aggregate sentences amounted to 199 years. Then in 1949 he sentenced the multiple acid-bath murderer, John George Haigh, to death. The judge was no stranger to the imposition of severe sentences. He told McGuire:

> You shot at a police officer and you very nearly committed murder. You shot him in the chest; he was very, very ill and might well have died. I am glad to hear that the latest reports say that in the course of time, he is likely to recover but it is no thanks to you that you are not now being charged with the

crime of wilful murder. And if you had, you would have had no sort of defence. You were caught red-handed and you would have been hanged. At the age of twenty, it is a shocking state of affairs that all these things relate to you.

He then sentenced McGuire to fourteen years' imprisonment and was told, "Thanks, judge. Aren't you generous?"

Sentencing Cooney to a total of five years' imprisonment, the judge said:

You have pleaded guilty to robbery with violence and it has been said that this is the first time you have been convicted of using violence. This is true, but there is plenty of evidence that you knew McGuire was armed with the pistol, although there is none that you took part in the shooting.

Ashwin gradually recovered and on 15 January was able to resume light duties. Two weeks later he and his fellow officers were all highly commended by the commissioner and each was awarded £20 from the Bow Street Reward Fund. Then on 16 March 1951 the three officers – plus Thomas Temple – went to Buckingham Palace, where all of them were awarded the George Medal. Norman Gee and Reginald Temple were each awarded the King's Commendation for Brave Conduct.

In sentencing McGuire to a substantial (and well-deserved) stretch of imprisonment, Mr Justice Humphries made one small mistake; he also provided him with an identity by describing him as 'a desperado', and McGuire probably decided that he should live up to that description. Two years into his sentence he attacked a warder with an iron bar and was rewarded with twelve strokes of the cat-o'-nine tails, the loss of twelve months' remission of sentence and thirteen days on No.1 punishment – a diet of bread and water. Later, he climbed to the top of a cell block and pelted the warders with roof slates; they turned the fire hoses on him, and after an hour and a half he returned to the ground dripping wet but not, unfortunately, very much wiser. As has already been suggested, McGuire had no conception of the consequences of his actions, but as he was led off to the punishment block he was undoubtedly comforted by the thought that he was indeed a 'desperado'.

PC McCallum completed almost thirty-three years' police service; he resigned in November 1964 and enjoyed almost twenty years of retirement before his death, just before his eightieth birthday.

A year after he returned to light duties, PC Ashwin was again commended, this time for 'alertness and ability, leading to the arrest of four men for officebreaking'. He completed just under thirty years service and died two weeks before his sixty-eighth birthday.

Between being highly commended by the commissioner and his award of the George Medal, PC King was again commended by the commissioner, this time for 'initiative in a case of shopbreaking'. And yet within eighteen months of his investiture, he voluntarily resigned. He had served less than five years, and whilst his conduct was, of course, described as 'exemplary', he did not receive a pension, just a gratuity of £79 6s 0d – by today's standards, just over £1,600.

On the sixtieth anniversary of the break-in at Temple's Stores, there was a ceremony at Bromley police station, at which Borough Commander Charles Griggs commemorated the gallantry of the three officers and Mr Temple. As well as his richly deserved George Medal, Thomas Temple also received the 1950 Binney Award. The building where Temple's Stores stood was demolished in the 1960s and is now occupied by Roundway shops. But the thoroughfare where his stores once traded has been re-named Temple Street – a fitting epitaph for a very brave man.

CHAPTER 8

An Unwelcome Visitor

n mid-March 1954 a genuine Portuguese passport was handed to the British Consul in Lisbon, and its bearer politely asked for a visa to enter Great Britain. He was, he informed the British representative, a commercial traveller, and he was duly given permission to land and conduct business in England for a period not to exceed two months. Several weeks later, at a preliminary hearing, the St Pancras coroner raised serious concerns about whether the visa was in order and suggested that enquiries be made of the British authorities in Lisbon. This resulted in Norman Dodds, the Member of Parliament for Dartford, posing some rather pointed questions to Sir Hugh Munro-Lucas-Tooth, the Secretary of State for the Home Department, during a House of Commons debate on 15 April 1954. But it is debatable whether anything was wrong with the issue of the visa. The man was a Portuguese citizen, having been born there, and he had no criminal record in Portugal. When he arrived at Liverpool on the liner *Hildebrand* on 19 March, his passport and visa caused no concern to the immigration officer, to whom the traveller honestly declared his possession of $1,650, and a check revealed he had no criminal record in England. The traveller had been baptised Justine de Almeida; that was the name which appeared on his passport, and he was forty-nine years of age. When it suited him, the little visitor could be charismatic and plausible, and it is likely that some of this charm was exercised on the immigration officer, who really, with hindsight, should have carried out a thorough search of the swarthy foreigner. If he had done so, he would have discovered that de Almeida was in possession of a 6.35mm Mauser automatic pistol and ammunition. First manufactured in 1910, this was one of 61,000 such weapons produced. Known as a 'pocket pistol', it was just five and a half inches in length and when it was fully loaded, with a bullet in the chamber, held ten rounds of ammunition. Fired into a pine block at a distance of ten yards, a bullet would penetrate two and a half inches into the wood. Not that that was of the slightest interest to de Almeida, because the pistol was simply a tool of his trade. He had a criminal history involving firearms stretching back thirty years, and he was as mad as a hatter.

* * *

Taken to the United States with his family when he was seven years old, de Almeida was admitted to an industrial school three years later, as a neglected child. His criminal career had commenced in 1914 at the tender age of nine, and from then until the time of his deportation he notched up twenty convictions, which included theft and assault. In 1925 he was sentenced to from seven to ten years' imprisonment for armed robbery. Paroled after serving eight years of his sentence, within a month he was found in possession of a pistol and received a further two and a half years' imprisonment. Following his release, de Almeida was at liberty for just two years before being arrested, once again for armed robbery. On this occasion he was sentenced to twenty-five years' imprisonment, but in 1943 he was found to be insane and sent to a mental institution. Released ten years later, in December 1953 he was deported to the land of his birth, Portugal.

Because Portugal and Britain and a great number of other countries world-wide were members of Interpol, an organisation which assists member countries to identify and trace the whereabouts of dangerous and persistent criminals, it would have made a great deal of sense if the United States of America had informed Portugal of de Almeida's record. Had the USA been a member of Interpol, no doubt they would have done so; but the head of the Federal Bureau of Investigation (FBI), the insecure and deeply suspicious J. Edgar Hoover, had withdrawn his country from membership of Interpol in 1952. In depositing a bundle of laundry on Portugal's frontier, the USA had neglected to inform the authorities just how dirty it actually was.

No one knows precisely what de Almeida did or where he went during the five days following his arrival at Liverpool. The journey to London was straightforward enough; from Liverpool (Lime Street) he would have caught a train to Manchester (Piccadilly), and from Manchester (Central) in less than four hours he would have arrived at Marylebone. But when he turned up at Lisson Grove, Marylebone, London on 24 March 1954, the $1,650 was gone and he had just £8 18s 8d of his own. No doubt that was what prompted him to carry out a robbery at 39 Lisson Grove, the address of Wehrles Ltd, a jeweller's shop.

Just before closing time at 5.30 that evening, the shop's assistant, twenty-six-year-old Edward Ernest Mansfield, had gone to a nearby café, where he saw the proprietor, Pietro Boni, and purchased a sixpenny jug of tea. As Mansfield – married, with a three-year-old daughter – returned to the shop, de Almeida followed him into the premises, locked the door behind him and held up Mansfield and the proprietor, fifty-six-year-old Marcus Wehrle. Married with two sons aged eighteen months and three years, Wehrle had planned to move house from Kingston to Beckenham the following week, to a house which he had bought for the sake of his children. Now the men were forced into the workroom at the rear of the shop and the gunman used Wehrle's tie to bind Mansfield's wrists behind his back. Then something happened – and clearly it would not have taken much – to cause de Almeida to shoot Wehrle straight between the eyes, killing him instantly, and then to shoot Mansfield, also in the head. The following day was Mansfield's wedding anniversary; instead of celebrating it, he lay in hospital, where he died twelve days later. After shooting the two men, de Almeida thrust Wehrle's wallet, containing £19, into his pocket, then ran out of the rear of the premises; but his escape route was blocked by walls on one side and a ten-foot corrugated-iron gate.

The two shots were heard quite clearly by a thirty-nine-year-old van driver, Walter Davis Kingston, a customer who was about to enter the shop to collect a wristwatch, as well as a number of other witnesses, one of whom was Mrs Florence Wood, who lived in a flat above the jeweller's. She was just about to get her children's tea when she heard banging, scuffling and confused noises coming from the shop below. There was a moment's silence and then she heard a man groan, "Oh!" She rushed downstairs, saw her neighbour Emily Bridgeman and told her, "I think someone's being done in, downstairs." The women went into the Post Office next door, where one of the girls employed there telephoned the police.

It was clear something was very wrong, and Mrs Constance Raoul of Lisson Grove knocked on the shop window, hoping to scare the raiders away. She then went up to the roof and looked down into the yard at the rear. There she saw a crouching figure and thought it was Marcus Wehrle; she shouted, "Mr. Wehrle, we're coming to you!" But in fact it was de Almeida whom she was addressing.

The first police car to arrive was driven by Police Constable Leonard Geoffrey Bocking (known always as "Jeff"), five feet eight, slim and a native of Docking, Norfolk. He had volunteered for the Royal Air Force within six months of his eighteenth birthday, achieving the rank of sergeant, and after completing his wartime service had joined the Metropolitan Police. His seven years' service had been spent on 'D' Division and he was married with a four-year-old son.

Seconds later, a wireless car drew up, whose RT operator was Police Constable George Alexander Sinclair. At twenty-eight, the same age as Bocking, he had joined the Royal Air Force exactly two weeks after him and had served as a flight sergeant. He joined the Metropolitan Police seven months after Bocking, and they served on the same division. Sinclair, who had married a year previously, was a bright recruit, having achieved very high marks in his police examinations; an industrious one, too. Five months previously, he had been commended by the commissioner for effecting the arrest of a lady who was described as 'a cunning female thief'.

Having been apprised of the seemingly fraught situation, Police Constable Douglas Percy Miller, Bocking's RT operator, guarded the front door of the premises. Bocking, Sinclair and Police Constable James Morrison, the driver of Sinclair's vehicle, went to the rear of the premises, via the home of Mrs Emily Bridgeman of Lisson Cottages, and climbing through her bedroom window they found the back door of the shop open. There they discovered the bodies of the two men; PC Morrison telephoned for assistance and an ambulance. Sinclair searched the shop premises and Bocking carried out a search of the yard at the rear. Suddenly Mrs Bridgeman looked into the yard and at the bottom of some steps, in a doorway next to the jeweller's, saw a crouching man holding a pistol. She told her husband, who in turn looked down to see Bocking standing at the top of the steps, his back to the gunman and unaware of his presence. Joseph Bridgeman shouted a warning, and Bocking turned to see de Almeida crouching, ten steps below him. "And then," said Mr Bridgeman, "I saw the bravest thing I can ever remember. One of the policemen (Bocking) saw where I was pointing and gave a little acknowledgement with his hand as if to say, 'OK, chum, I've got it.' Then, slowly and deliberately, as calm as you please, he began to walk down the steps." As Bocking approached de Almeida, Mr Bridgeman later told reporters, "The copper said in an almost pleasant way, quiet and smiling, 'What are you doing down there?'"

There was no reply, and there was absolutely no doubt whatsoever in Bocking's mind that this man was the murderer. As he drew nearer, so de Almeida raised his right hand and, as Bocking later told an inquest, "I was about two steps from the bottom when I saw he had a gun. I leapt and grabbed his right wrist. There was a struggle."

Sinclair had heard the commotion as he was searching the shop and now he rushed into the yard and down the steps. "Look out, he's got a gun," shouted Bocking and grabbed de Almeida's arms from behind. Sinclair was now facing the gunman, and there was a shot. Sinclair grabbed the weapon but was unable to free it from de Almeida's grip; he punched him hard in the stomach several times before getting hold of it. Dragging Sinclair to the ground, de Almeida pulled his hand away and reached for his coat pocket; Sinclair, believing he might have another weapon, searched him. There was no other firearm, only Marcus Wehrle's wallet. Then de Almeida said simply, "I've been shot." And so he had; this was the shot which the officers believed he had fired at them. "That," said Bocking, "was meant for me." A later examination of de Almeida's 'pocket pistol' revealed that three shots had been fired from it: one each for the unfortunate Mr Wehrle and his assistant and one for himself.

Taken to St Mary's Hospital, de Almeida died within minutes of his admission. An inquest was opened and adjourned, and then on 28 April a full inquest was held with a jury at St Pancras Coroners' Court before Mr Bentley Purchase. During the intervening period a scrupulous investigation had been carried out by Detective Superintendent Jack Manning, and the jury had no problem concluding that de Almeida had murdered Wehrle and Mansfield and that he himself had died accidentally. After returning the verdicts, the foreman of the jury added, "We would like to congratulate the officers who went about their duties in this courageous manner."

On 1 June 1954 the commissioner highly commended both officers for 'outstanding courage and tenacity', and two weeks later they were awarded £15 each from the Bow Street Reward Fund. Four months later, both were awarded the George Medal.

★   ★   ★

Bocking concentrated on driving fast police vehicles; he qualified as a Class I driver which meant he could drive for the Flying Squad. During a posting to B6 Department (Traffic), he became a 'strapper' for the Squad – deputising for the regular Squad drivers who were sick or on leave. It was whilst he was performing this duty that he became involved in the case of John Marson, an armed prison escapee, that resulted in one of his passengers, Detective Sergeant Peter Woodmore, being one of two recipients of the George Medal and three others receiving the British Empire Medal for Gallantry. In addition, he was part of the

Flying Squad team who in 1966 transported several of the Great Train Robbers to different prisons following a security scare. In 1968 Bocking was officially co-opted on to the Squad, where he remained for the rest of his service. He was highly thought of by the detectives and the other drivers on the Squad. Former Squad driver Mick Gray remembered him as, 'Nice ... quiet', as did another driver, Peter Ansell, who served with him on 10 Squad but had no idea whatsoever that he had been decorated with the George Medal. Fellow driver Gordon Reynolds told me, "He never mentioned the circumstances of how he was awarded the medal. He was nice, very quiet, but I got the distinct impression that he was not the sort of person you'd care to upset!" Bocking retired on 1 May 1977, having served (with the inclusion of 101 days' war service) exactly thirty years. As well as the George Medal, he had another badge of distinction. He was a member of 'The Caterpillar Club'. Membership of that organisation depended on the applicant showing that his life had been saved by the use of a parachute when jumping from a damaged aeroplane, which was what had happened to Bocking during his wartime service with the RAF. The name of the club came from the combination of silk, originally used in the manufacture of parachutes, and the silken thread used by caterpillars to act as a brake on their descent to the ground. The motto of the club, unsurprisingly, is: 'Life depends on a silken thread'.

Jeff Bocking returned to his roots and purchased a property in Dersingham, Norfolk. He worked for the clothing company Jaeger in a security capacity until state retirement age. His son Steven told me that he never spoke about the award of the George Medal. In later life he suffered from Alzheimer's and Parkinson's Disease and was admitted to a nursing home where he died, of pneumonia, on 9 December 2007. At the time of writing, his widow Gwen is in very poor health, having suffered a series of strokes.

★   ★   ★

Sinclair had a taste for thief-taking and became an aid to CID. Appointed detective constable on 7 March 1955, he was posted to 'L' Division, where he learnt his trade as a detective, picking up one commissioner's commendation for 'ability and determination in arresting two violent criminals' and ten days later another for 'ability in arresting a gang of active criminals'. Promotion to detective sergeant in 1961 later took him to the first of two postings to the Flying Squad (with a posting to C11 in between), and as he rose through the ranks, to two postings to the Regional Crime Squad. He received more commendations, including for 'courage and determination in arresting two active and dangerous criminals' and 'persistence and ability leading to the arrest and conviction of three criminals for robbery'. He reached the rank of detective superintendent, having been commended on eleven occasions, before retiring on an ill-health pension aged fifty; he died just before Christmas 1992.

★ ★ ★

The de Almeida case was a matter which could have been so easily avoided; the senseless slaughter of two decent men. Should the British Consul in Lisbon have issued a visa to de Almeida? On the facts presented to the British representative, there was no reason why not. Should the authorities in the United States have informed their Portuguese counterparts of the deportee's appalling record, including his mental instability? They most certainly should, and the fact that they did not was possibly because, having got rid of that unsavoury specimen, they did not want to run the risk of Portugal refusing to take him. What of the immigration officer at Liverpool? It is easy to be wise after the event, but the fact is that here was a Portuguese national in possession of American currency amounting to a whopping $1,650, equal by today's standards to £8,400. One would have thought that alone should have been sufficient to cause the most complacent customs officer's eyebrows to assume the shape of crescent moons and to merit both an explanation and a more thorough search of his luggage.

Perhaps the immigration officer might have been spurred into action if one of de Almeida's fellow passengers had had a quiet word with him. As Charles Samuel Porter later told the inquest, he was surprised when de Almeida produced the automatic pistol while they were on the high seas. "He said to me at the time," admitted Mr Porter, "'This should stop anybody at five yards.'"

CHAPTER 9

The Beast of Croydon

A series of physical and indecent assaults on women commenced in Croydon, South London in November 1954. The attacks appeared to be the work of the same man: aged about thirty, five feet ten tall, with brown hair, physically very strong and with the lower part of his face masked.

All the attacks took place in the same area: Fairfield Footpath, one and a half miles in length, running between Fairfield Road and Chichester Road, close to the busy A2039 Park Hill Road. To the west of the footpath was a recreation ground and to the south of that area, Coombe Cliff, a large house and grounds with a reservoir nearby. Between these busy thoroughfares, the footpath was a gloomy area, lit by infrequent gas-lights. There was no pattern to the attacks; they could happen at any time and they were becoming increasingly more violent. Aids to CID patrolled the area, but of the attacker there was no sign. When plain clothes and uniform patrols ceased, the attacks recommenced, and all within a quarter of a mile of Croydon police station – it was as though the attacker was baiting the police to come and arrest him.

At that time, there were five women officers stationed at Croydon; all volunteered to act as decoys, in pairs and alone, in uniform or plain clothes. And then on 20 February 1955, the attacker, partially clothed, leapt out from some bushes at a twenty-five-year-old married woman who lived close to Fairfield Road and had almost reached home. When she told him to get away, he punched her violently in the face; as he forced her to her knees, her screams were mercifully heard by a man walking nearby, and her attacker made good his escape.

The decoy patrols were stepped up. One of the women police officers was WPC 325'Z' Kathleen Flora Parrott, married with a ten-year-old son. She was the thousandth woman to join the police and at that time she had four years' service. The officer with whom she regularly patrolled was Woman Police Sergeant 38 'Z' Ethel Violet Bush, who had joined the Met in 1946 following wartime service with the Women's Auxiliary Air Force. Single, she had been promoted to sergeant in 1953 and posted to Croydon police station; both women were aged thirty-nine.

It was inevitable that at some time, unless the man was caught, one of the women would be attacked, yet still they patrolled that terrifying thoroughfare. In fact, both women would be subjected to attacks of appalling ferocity.

The first was WPC Parrott. Finishing duty at 10.30 on the night of 7 March 1955, she changed out of her uniform and commenced her walk home, the most direct route being along the footpath. "It's changed a lot, now," she told me, fifty-five years after the event, "but then there was a lot of shrubbery and high walls." She had almost reached Chichester Road when she heard the sound of running footsteps behind her and a man grabbed her from behind, his forearm jammed across her throat; as the pressure increased she began to lose consciousness. She dropped her handbag and shopping bag, screamed and lashed out blindly with the torch she was carrying at her attacker, who told her, "I won't hurt you if you stop screaming." He then indecently assaulted her, but WPC Parrott fought back, managed to break free from the choking grip, turned and faced the man. Seeing that he was masked, she ripped the cloth from his face and got a good look at him; she was certain she would be able to recognise him again. Surprised at her actions, the man ran off.

The Divisional Surgeon examined WPC Parrott at Croydon police station; there was considerable bruising to the sides of her neck, consistent with great pressure being applied, as well as injuries to her face, thigh and knee. The injuries were severe enough for her to be confined to her bed for three and a half weeks, and although additional women patrols commenced the very next night, supported by male officers in plain clothes, no further attacks occurred. And yet, within a week of returning to duty after five weeks' sick leave, WPC Parrott resumed the decoy patrols. When I asked her why, over half a century later, her reply was unequivocal: "I wanted that so-and-so in prison."

During the early evening of Saturday 23 April, WPS Bush and another woman officer were on routine patrol on the footpath in uniform and were about to return to Croydon police station for their refreshment break, when they spotted a man hiding in some bushes; as Miss Bush told me fifty-five years later, "I thought – that's him!"

He was also seen by WPC Parrott, who informed two male officers and set off on a lone patrol, with one officer ahead of her, the other set to follow the suspect. But the man vanished, so the officers returned to the police station and set up a plan. WPS

Bush changed into plain clothes and set off to Fairfield Footpath. An hour and a half had now elapsed since the initial sighting of the man, but as Miss Bush commenced her solo, terrifying patrol, there were half a dozen CID officers, plus a dog handler and WPC Parrott, secreting themselves at intervals along the route, behind walls and in the shrubbery.

As WPS Bush set off along the footpath, so she noticed a shadowy figure emerge from the area of the recreation ground; now she knew beyond doubt that the man intended to attack her. All would depend on the officers being able to intercept him before serious injury could be inflicted. As the man crept forward, so he passed WPC Parrott who was hiding behind a fence; in the light of one of the very few gas lamps she saw his face and immediately identified him as her attacker of six weeks previously.

With enormous presence of mind, WPS Bush continued to walk along the footpath, assuming an air of nonchalance that she did not feel, yet was completely convincing. Then the man ran up behind her and when he was a few feet away bent down and picked up a large Y-shaped tree branch. He was seen by Police Constable Hillier to hit WPS Bush an atrocious blow on the back of her head, wielding the branch with both hands. As the officers raced towards the couple, Miss Bush turned and grabbed hold of the man's jacket to detain him until help arrived, but he punched her in the face so hard that Police Sergeant Leslie Morgan, a dog-handler who had been secreted behind a wall to avoid being seen by the suspect, thought that a pistol had been fired. As he pushed his police dog 'Skip' over the wall and followed it, his hand came into contact with broken glass cemented into the top of the wall, badly lacerating it, and he fell on top of the dog, disabling it; as he then stumbled over the prostrate form of Miss Bush, the man made good his escape. Twenty officers flooded the area and commenced a meticulous search, but of Miss Bush's attacker there was no sign.

WPS Bush was conveyed to the Mayday Hospital, Croydon, where Dr A. Silverstone inserted eleven stitches into the wound on the back of her head. After observation, she was conveyed to a nearby nursing home and thence to the Metropolitan Police Nursing Home at Hove, where she remained for two weeks. It was the end of the investigation for her. Now, at ninety-four years of age, she recalls few of the fine details of the incident, although as she wryly told me, "I remember, he had a good strong swipe."

But on that Saturday evening, the investigation was far from over. Detective Sergeant James Smith found the Y-shaped piece of wood, still wet with blood, and WPC Parrott found something even more interesting. On the footpath, close to the attack, she picked up a fountain pen and pencil set. Shortly afterwards, Woman Police Constable 466 'Z' Marion Jones paraded for night duty. She had been part of the decoy patrols ("They seemed to go on forever," she told me, in 2010) and now she was instructed to go immediately to the Mayday Hospital to see if the pen and pencil belonged to WPS Bush. "I had the most difficult job getting to see her, because the matron impressed upon me how ill she was," Mrs Jones told me, "but after I explained how important my enquiry was, I did get to see her. I showed her the pen and pencil, but she said, 'No, they're nothing to do with me.' I rushed back to the station, because if they didn't belong to her, they must have belonged to her attacker." Meanwhile, officers had regrouped at Croydon police station, and from their combined descriptions suspicion fell upon a man who lived in Dunley Drive, New Addington, approximately three miles from the scene of the attacks, a man who had three previous convictions.

His arrest was carried out by Detective Sergeant Fred Fairfax, who two years previously had been the first Metropolitan Police recipient of the George Cross. At five feet nine, the stocky former commando captain was hugely disinclined to heed the vociferous denials of William George Barnett, a twenty-nine-year-old labourer. Like the cunning detective he was, Fairfax showed the pen and pencil set to Barnett and his wife, and casually asked, "Who do these belong to?" Mrs Barnett, indicating her husband, exclaimed, "Oh! That's what I gave to him for Christmas!" It was the beginning of a long, slippery slope for Barnett.

WPC Parrott was one of seven people who attended an identification parade, and although all of the participants in the parade had the lower part of their faces masked, as she told me, "I recognised him immediately." So did every other witness in the parade, but despite this, after he was formally charged, Barnett replied, "No, not me."

Later, however, Barnett asked the officer in charge of the case, Detective Sergeant Albert Charman, "Can I see the woman?" Asked why, Barnett replied, "I am sorry. I want to apologise to her for all I've done. I just couldn't stop it and I'd like to tell you." In part of the written statement which followed, Barnett said:

> I do not mean to do harm to anybody but something just comes over me at times. I have tried to stop myself ... Last night was the first time I have ever used anything on a woman.

I picked up a bit of wood and cracked her on the head and ran off. I wish I could stop it but something just comes over me.

Barnett admitted all of the attacks on the footpath, and when he was committed for trial to the Old Bailey from Croydon Magistrates' Court, WPS Bush, just released from the convalescent home, was allowed to sit whilst she gave her evidence. Asked if he had anything to say, Barnett replied, "All I can say is, I am sorry for the women, not for myself because I am no good in this world. I am a beast on God's earth. But I am very sorry for the harm that I have done and for what I have made them endure and listen to this morning." The chairman of the Bench, Mr Brian Still, stated:

The court would like to pay a tribute to the courage and devotion to duty of the women police officers, especially WPS Bush and WPC Parrott. They voluntarily exposed themselves to the risk of serious injury which was in fact sustained by WPS Bush. Their conduct was in the very best tradition of the police and their courage was of a very high order. We would like to commend them and hope that their senior officers will take note of this commendation.

Their senior officers did; both women received a high commendation from the commissioner for their courage and when they appeared before the Chief Metropolitan Magistrate, Sir Laurence Dunne, who presented them with £15 cheques from the Bow Street Reward Fund, he said, "If anyone can imagine a finer a story in the history of the Metropolitan Police, I shall be pleased to hear it."

Barnett appeared at the Old Bailey on 16 May 1955 and pleaded guilty to wounding WPS Bush with intent to cause grievous bodily harm, actual bodily harm to WPC Parrott as well as indecently assaulting her and attempting to render her unconscious with intent to commit an indecent assault, plus assaulting the twenty-five-year-old housewife; in addition, he asked for three other cases to be taken into consideration. Telling Barnett, "What emerges from this appalling series of offences is that no woman is safe while you are at large," the trial judge, the Common Serjeant, Sir Anthony Hawke sentenced him to a total of ten years' imprisonment and then called the two women officers before him and told them:

I cannot imagine higher courage than you showed along that footpath with full knowledge, with your eyes open, that you might be, as Sergeant Bush was, the victim of a horrible and violent assault. The conduct of the police is always a matter of which we in this country can be proud. I think this country is entitled to be proud of you two officers. I think you have done a very great and gallant thing.

The same day, the *Evening Standard* proclaimed, 'The courage of two policewomen' and the *Star*, quoting Barnett, stated, 'I have been a beast'. With the flair which newspapers possess, Barnett became known as 'The Beast of Croydon'.

On 22 November both officers were presented with the George Medal at Buckingham Palace by Her Majesty Queen Elizabeth II, who told them, "I am very proud of you both." In the fifteen years since the medal had been struck, this was the first such award to women police officers.

Incredibly, the Fairfield Footpath still held no terrors for WPC Parrott; in the same month as she was awarded the medal, she arrested a man for indecent exposure there, whilst she was off duty; she received another commendation. But although she passed her sergeant's examination, she never was promoted; after just five years' service she resigned to devote more time to her family. WPS Bush continued her career, working at West End Central, Bow Street, Southwark and Brixton police stations until her retirement in 1971. However, the story does not end there.

★   ★   ★

Barnett was released from prison in 1962 and he moved to Cosedge Crescent, Waddon, Surrey, far, far closer to Fairfield Footpath than he had lived before – less than a mile away. But there was no repeat of the type of offence for which Barnett had been imprisoned – until September 1971. Then a fifty-one-year-old housewife was waiting at a bus stop in Croydon when a car pulled up and the driver, Barnett, asked her, "I'm going to Purley – is that any use to you?" The woman accepted the lift, but after a short distance Barnett stopped in a particularly lonely area and got out of the car, telling her that he wanted to relieve himself. When he returned, Barnett dragged the woman out of the car feet first, pulled off her underwear whilst holding her upside down, then threw her on to the ground and brutally raped her. "That was nice, wasn't it?" he sneered, before getting back in the car and driving off, leaving the terrified woman in that deserted spot.

The woman reported the matter to the police, but like her counterparts of sixteen years previously she decided to do a little decoy work herself. And three months later it paid off. As she stood at a bus stop, Barnett again drew up and offered her a lift. He did not recognise her but she identified him and declined the lift; as he drove off, she noted the registration number of the car.

Barnett predictably denied the allegation when he was questioned by detectives; "I get all I want with my girl," he inelegantly replied. But when his briefcase was searched and pornographic literature and photographs were found, as well as items of women's clothing, Barnett's composure began to crumble; and when he appeared at the Old Bailey in March 1972, he pleaded guilty to rape. "Give me a chance to marry the girl I love," Barnett pleaded to the judge, Mr Justice Nield, adding, "I will never get into trouble again. I ask you on bended knees." Although 'the girl', who identified herself as Mrs Violet Masters, told the judge that she knew of her paramour's criminal past, and it was also said that Barnett supported his elderly mother, it did not save him from jail.

Barnett was sentenced to five years' imprisonment, a rather lenient punishment bearing in mind the severity of the attack and his previous convictions. Even though seventeen years had passed since his ten-year sentence had been imposed, when the newspapers reported, 'Beast of Croydon in jail again', the case was still fresh in everybody's minds in the area. But even that was not the end of the story.

*   *   *

In December 2005 the eighty-one-year-old Barnett gave a newspaper interview, in which he described his thrilling adventures as a Royal Naval Beach Commando during World War Two to the *Croydon Advertiser*, under the heading 'My Secret War'; as these things do, it attracted attention. In fact, the interest which was generated sent the reporters back to Barnett's door one month later to confront him with facts which had not been disclosed during his last interview.

"Women had been hurt and the police needed a scapegoat," he whined. "They fitted me up. I went to prison for a crime I didn't do. After I came out, a man came up to me and said he'd done it. But I never told anyone," he added indignantly, "that would be grassing."

With some justification, the reporter enquired about the confession, the plaintive apologies at court, the pleas of guilt. "I was drugged," replied the chain-smoking Barnett. "You say anything when you're drugged, don't you? I didn't know what I was saying."

Leaving aside Barnett's pen and pencil being found at the scene of the attack, and the seven positive identifications, the idea of Barett being injected with a drug which prompted his oral and written confession at the police station, its effects lasting until committal proceedings several weeks later and through to his appearance at the Old Bailey two months after the attack, might provoke much excited comment amongst the most eminent toxicologists; alternatively, Barnett's suggestions could be dismissed as the ramblings of an elderly and manipulative pervert.

Miss Bush was furious, stating, "I don't want him to get away with this. The fact that he is now saying he is a saint and not a sinner, is just awful." Mrs Parrott was similarly unimpressed. "When I look back on it," she said, "there is something sad about a man who can lower himself in that way."

After Barnett was sentenced for rape, one of his workmates said, "We knew him as a quiet fellow, who liked to dress up as a clown and make children laugh at parties."

The children's laughter was not shared by a number of unfortunate women – including two very gallant women officers – who had the misfortune to encounter Barnett. To them, he was simply 'The Beast of Croydon'.

CHAPTER 10

The Deptford Terror

T he George Cross – 'for acts of the greatest heroism or of the most conspicuous courage in circumstances of extreme danger' – has already been fleetingly mentioned, and it ranks next to the Victoria Cross – 'for valour'. Both medals can be awarded to the armed forces for acts of the highest bravery. However, the Victoria Cross is reserved for armed forces personnel only, while civilians can win the George Cross.

The plain silver George Cross, 48mm high and 45mm wide, hangs from a 38mm dark blue ribbon. On the obverse there is a circular medallion in the centre, depicting St George and the dragon, surrounded by the words 'FOR GALLANTRY'. On the reverse, in the centre of the cross, the name of the recipient and the date of the award are engraved. The cross is attached by a ring to a bar ornamented with laurel leaves through which the ribbon passes. The recipient is permitted to use the letters 'GC' to follow his or her name. It can be awarded posthumously, and although bars to the award are permitted, none have been awarded to date. The cross was intended to replace the Empire Gallantry Medal (first struck in 1922), and the holders of this award were invited to exchange their medal for the George Cross. Holders of the cross are entitled to an annuity, which at the time of writing amounts to £1,495. The cross has twice been issued collectively, firstly by King George VI in 1942 to the people of Malta for their heroism during sustained air attacks; secondly to Northern Ireland's Royal Ulster Constabulary (RUC) in 1999 by Her Majesty The Queen in recognition of the bravery of the Province's police force during the thirty years of an unrelenting campaign of terrorism. Anyone who has worked with them – as I have – knows that the honour was thoroughly deserved. Unfortunately, two years later a supine British Government caved in to political demands and cravenly renamed the RUC the Police Service of Northern Ireland.

In all, just over 160 George Crosses have been issued and four have been awarded to London police officers. The first was awarded in 1953, thirteen years after the cross had first been struck; and the second, five years later, was presented to an aid to

CID who was one of the three-man crew of a 'Q' Car. The vehicles were the Metropolitan Police's divisional counterpart of Flying Squad vehicles. Anonymous, fast cars, driven by a Class I or Class II uniformed driver in plain clothes, the cars were crewed by a CID officer and an aid to CID. First introduced in 1934, the cars patrolled the division to which they were assigned, on the lookout for criminals, and were in radio contact with the Yard.

But on the evening of Saturday 29 March 1958, as 'P' Division's 'Q' Car, a big Wolseley 6/80 saloon, drove through the darkened streets of Bromley, Kent, little appeared to be happening – until 7.55 pm when the radio crackled into life to inform the crew that there were intruders at Genden.

★ ★ ★

Genden was a large detached house, situated on the junction of Bickley Park Road and St George's Road, in Bickley, Kent. A driveway in Bickley Park Road allowed access to Genden, and surrounding the property (and extending down St George's Road) was a weatherboard fence over six feet high.

The owner was an American company director, Frederick Pickles, and earlier that evening he had secured and left the premises. In addition, Mr Pickles had set his burglar alarm, installed after the house had been broken into previously. It operated on a record/telephone method direct to the local telephone exchange and was undetectable to an intruder.

Within four minutes of acknowledging the call, the 'Q' Car arrived at Genden; two of the crew, Detective Constable Bill Moody and the driver, Police Constable 203 'P' Harold Wanstall, ran into the front garden of the house, circling the outside of the premises in opposite directions. Meanwhile, the aid to CID, Police Constable 558 'P' Henry William Stevens, a thirty-year-old former member of the Fleet Air Arm with five years' service with the police, ran into St George's Road to cover the perimeter fence. Having run some thirty yards along the road, he suddenly saw a tall thin man, dressed in a dark trilby hat and a grey overcoat, appear on top of the fence. The man was approximately five yards away from Stevens when he jumped down on to the footpath. His face was clearly illuminated by a street gas lamp, and Stevens shouted, "I'm a police officer – stop!"

The man ran off down St George's Road towards a footbridge which crossed railway lines 100 yards away, with Stevens, a slim, fit, six-footer in hot pursuit. As the man crossed the road he was illuminated by a second gas light and, with Stevens gaining on him, he half turned, pointed a gun at the officer and shouted, "Stop, or you'll get this." But Stevens disregarded the threat and was almost within striking distance of the man when there was a flash and a loud report from the gun; Stevens felt a severe blow to his mouth and his face lost all feeling. He threw himself on the gunman from behind, grabbing the pistol from his hand and at the same time grasping him round the neck. By now, the two men were at the iron railings by the railway bridge and Stevens forced the gunman against them. "All right, I'll give in," gasped the man. "I've had enough."

Stevens, who by now was exhausted and traumatised, instinctively relaxed; the man took the opportunity to stretch out his hand behind him and grab Stevens' genitals. The excruciating pain caused him to release his hold on his assailant, who ran off back along St George's Road towards Bickley Park Road. Although Stevens was feeling extremely weak and disorientated – he could feel broken teeth inside his mouth – he nevertheless continued the chase. After the man had run forty or fifty yards along St George's Road he stopped, inexplicably, and started to retrace his original route towards the railway bridge. As he approached Stevens and tried to pass him, Stevens confronted his assailant. With blood running down his chin on to his shirt front and jacket, Stevens said, "You bastard. I'll know you again, wherever you go. I'll get you." The man dashed by, but as he did so Stevens lunged at him and grabbed hold of his collar, at the same time calling out for assistance. He was utterly determined not to let go, even though by now he was in a very bad way indeed. The man dragged him along and then escaped by wriggling out of his topcoat and jacket. Stevens collapsed. As he struggled to his feet, he saw the man run across the footbridge and disappear into the darkness. Again Stevens took up the chase, but his quarry had vanished.

Meanwhile, Moody had discovered a window which had been broken open at the rear of Genden, when he heard Stevens calling for assistance. Wanstall also heard Stevens' shout and climbed over the fence into St George's Road, where he saw his colleague grappling with a man some seventy yards away. The man disappeared over the footbridge, and by the time Wanstall arrived at the bridge there was no sign of him. Stevens was bleeding copiously from the mouth and was on the point of collapse. Moody (who, en route, had picked up the black trilby hat worn by the gunman) also collected his topcoat, jacket and pistol and summoned assistance to organise a search of the area, while Wanstall rushed Stevens to Bromley Hospital. Dr John

Samuel Tweedale Cox MB, BS discovered that Stevens was suffering from a penetrating wound to the left side of his lower lip; the lateral incisor and the canine tooth on the left side of his lower jaw were both broken, and there was also a penetrating injury to the left underside of Stevens' tongue. Within an hour Dr Cox had operated, removing what he described as 'a mass of metal' from Stevens' tongue – it was, of course, a flattened bullet – and extracting fragments of teeth and metal from his lower jaw. With masterly understatement, he described Stevens' injuries as 'being consistent with having been shot'.

Detective Inspector Harold Bland, in charge of the CID at Bromley, now arrived at Genden. He was no stranger to crimes involving shooting at police officers; nine years previously, he had been awarded the last King's Police and Fire Services Medal ever to be issued, for arresting a man who, whilst attempting to escape from a police car, had shot at Bland, the bullet passing through his clothing.

Now he took possession of the gunman's clothing and a .22 revolver, which contained one spent bullet and other live ones in the chamber. When he later examined the gun, he saw that the bullet which had been fired was of the longer type, whilst the remainder were of the short type. In addition, the rim of the bullet adjoining the spent cartridge had been struck by the revolver's hammer point but had not discharged. It thus appeared that a further attempt had been made on Stevens' life. Bland also searched the discarded jacket and, amongst other items, he found a pair of scissors.

And that, for 29 March, was that. Quite enough for one day.

★ ★ ★

The following morning, David Caulfeild-Stoker, the owner of 'The Firs', a house in St George's Road, was walking near the iron railings by the railway bridge when he found a muddy cotton glove on the ground. He handed it to DI Bland, who had arrived with other detectives to carry out a further examination of the scene of the burglary and the surrounding area. A Ronson table lighter was also found lying in the mud in the vicinity of the railway bridge. Both the lighter and the scissors found in the discarded jacket pocket were identified by Mr Pickles as his property, and the hat and topcoat worn by the gunman were positively identified by Harold Arthur Lewis, of 'Uplands', 23 Shawfield Park, Bromley. His house had been burgled ten days previously, and property including his coat and hat had been taken.

On Monday, 31 March DI Bland visited a tailor's business, Sidney Charles, at 36 Deptford High Street. The owner examined the gunman's discarded jacket and declared that he had made the jacket, part of a single-breasted, two-piece suit made in 'Braetwist', a two-fold worsted cloth. The customer who had personally collected this suit on 3 June 1957 was well known to Mr Charles, who had been making his suits for a considerable time. His name was Ronald Leonard Easterbrook.

Easterbrook had been known to the police since 1947 and was referred to locally as 'The Deptford Terror'. He thoroughly disliked being crossed in any way and possessed a pathological hatred of police officers, equalled only by his love of firearms. The tall, thin offender was a former Borstal boy, who had received his sentence for housebreaking, theft and attacking a police officer with a length of lead-filled rubber hose. A further confrontation with the law was reported in the *Kentish Mercury* of 13 June 1953, which reported that Police Constable 216 'R' Roy Hobbs had had to move on a group of youths on two occasions for causing a disturbance in Deptford High Street. Easterbrook, the ringleader, took umbrage at the officer's insistence and, handing his jacket to one of the group, said to PC Hobbs, "Get out of it, I'm good enough for you, any day. I'll soon do you." What might have happened next is anybody's guess, because PC Hobbs was a tough veteran of the Second World War, but PC 506 'R' Kellet arrived in a patrol car and the young man was arrested for threatening behaviour. Easterbrook later told the local court that PC Hobbs "had got a vivid imagination and got the needle", but the Magistrate, Mr Stevenson, fined him twenty shillings, telling him that the officer had acted in a perfectly reasonable way "and tried to shut you up, but you wouldn't take the hint."

Just how much the officer had 'got the needle' and how little Easterbrook had failed to take the Magistrate's prescient advice are matters for conjecture, but following this encounter, PC Hobbs, by now an aid to CID, arrested Easterbrook for warehousebreaking. Hobbs was commended and Easterbrook was sentenced to twenty-one months' imprisonment. This was followed by a four-year sentence for stabbing a man with a knife. At the time of his attack on Henry Stevens, Easterbrook should have been keeping a low profile. On 23 August 1957 he and his brother Thomas had been drinking in the Star and Garter, New Cross Road, SE8, when a confrontation had occurred between them and William John Mills, a labourer. Ronald Easterbrook, a small glass in his hand, walked over to Mills and said, "You've knocked my gin over me, you cunt." Mills started to apologise but he was instantly attacked;

Easterbrook smashed the glass on the counter and cut Mills badly in the face. Frank Henry Dunn, a casemaker, intervened and was attacked in turn by Easterbrook, who slashed his cheek open. The two brothers then fled. Out of all the customers in that crowded bar, only one came forward as a witness; the barmaid was so terrified that she vanished, never to return. Both the injured men, who had lost a considerable amount of blood, were examined at Miller General Hospital, SE10. Dunn had sustained a deep, three-inch cut across his right cheek and required eleven sutures. Mills had suffered two main injuries: an irregular incised wound in front of his ear which had severed the temporal artery, and a half-inch long cut above the other wound; these required six and three sutures respectively. Both men were scarred for life.

An hour and a half later Thomas Easterbrook was arrested at the family home at 6 Holden House, Deptford Church Street, SE8 by Detective Sergeant Len Mountford, a very tough customer and a former Flying Squad officer. Of Ronald Easterbrook there was no sign, but Mountford took possession of his jacket and shirt which bore bloodstains. Since that time, Ronald Easterbrook was circulated as being 'wanted'; when his brother appeared at the Old Bailey on 8 November 1957 he was acquitted on both charges of causing grievous bodily harm.

In the meantime, Henry Stevens was visited in hospital by DI Bland. He was carrying a number of photographs of criminals and without saying a word he showed them to Stevens; as soon as Stevens saw the 'mugshot' of Ronald Easterbrook he immediately identified him as his attacker.

And Easterbrook? He had been staying in Albacore Crescent, Lewisham, under the name of Ronald Leonard, but had left on Saturday, 29 March 1958. And on Monday 31 March Joyce Maud Wicks, the manageress of the Goodwood Hotel, 61–67 Queensborough Terrace, W2, welcomed a new guest to room 24. He signed the register as R.L. Joseph of 44 Brookdale Road, Brockley, but he was better known to the authorities as Ronald Easterbrook. Although the police were carrying out the most painstaking of enquiries in order to find him, Easterbrook managed to elude them for the next ten days.

★   ★   ★

The CID officers from Bromley police station were not the only policemen interested in tracing Easterbrook. Scotland Yard's top crime-busting arm, the Flying Squad, were also hearing whispers of information about him, one being that he had acquired another gun and that any police officers who were rash enough to try to detain him would receive five of the bullets, the last being kept for himself. In addition, through their informants, the Squad had discovered where Easterbrook was holed up.

The raid, early on the morning of 10 April, was led by Flying Squad officer Detective Sergeant Peter Vibart. This very tough ex-soldier had served in the Metropolitan Police for twenty-two years and by that time had been commended by the commissioner on no less than thirty-four occasions. With the Goodwood Hotel surrounded, and having obtained the master key, Vibart, together with Detective Constable John 'Polly' Perkins and other officers, crept up to the third floor. But when Vibart inserted the key into the lock of room 24, he discovered the door would not open; Easterbrook had taken the precaution of barricading it. Vibart smashed the door off its hinges, and as he and the other officers dashed into the room Easterbrook sat up in bed in the corner of the room. "We're police officers!" shouted Vibart, and Easterbrook, who had a pistol under his pillow, started struggling violently to reach it. This was a mistake, it being one matter to shoot, cosh, stab or slash an adversary and quite another to confront an unarmed police officer as tough as Vibart, who punched Easterbrook very hard indeed on the chin, whereupon all resistance ceased.

Perkins handed a .455 calibre Colt automatic pistol to Vibart, which was later identified as being one of six firearms stolen from the artillery museum at Woolwich some six months previously by means of a storebreaking, and then discovered that the pistol was unloaded. Telling Easterbrook in rather formal police parlance, "We are all police officers and I believe you to be Ronald Leonard Easterbrook who is wanted for the attempted murder of a police officer at Bickley on the 29th March, by shooting him," Vibart cautioned him and received the reply: "Fuck the copper. If that had been loaded, you would have got it as well." Vibart searched the drawers of a dressing table and found a small canvas holster and a hatchet, also a single cotton glove.

DI Bland interviewed Easterbrook at Bromley police station an hour after his arrest. After being told that he would eventually be charged with Stevens' attempted murder, Easterbrook replied, "I know it's down to me. I bought the gun and the one you found tonight from a man for a pound. He had eight. I've had it. You carry on. You've got my jacket. If I come the old story it was nicked from me, it still boils down to the same. You can do what you like."

Bland later showed Easterbrook the hat, jacket and overcoat and said, "These were left behind by you when you ran away after the shooting. The overcoat and hat are the proceeds of a case of housebreaking at Bickley." Easterbrook replied, "That's my jacket. I don't know anything about the overcoat and hat. I'm saying my jacket and trousers were nicked from me on the morning when the job was done."

Bland then showed the prisoner a number of other items. He said, "This gun is the one you used on the PC. The knife, pen, torch and scissors were in the jacket pockets. The lighter was found in the road where you struggled with the PC. The scissors and lighter had been stolen from the house, Genden, which you had broken into."

Easterbrook replied, "I bought that gun as I told you. There was one round in it then. I weeded some more bullets at a fun-fair at Southend and loaded it up. The knife, pen and torch are mine and were nicked with my suit and the gun."

"Where," asked Bland, "do you say your suit was stolen from?"

"I'm not saying," replied Easterbrook. "If I told you where, somebody else would be in for trouble. What can I lose? I am sticking to it; that jacket, gun and other things were nicked from me. If you ask where I was when the job happened, I was in a pub on my own where I knew nobody and nobody knew me."

Bland showed Easterbrook the muddy left-hand cotton glove found in St George's Road and also the other right-hand cotton glove, saying, "This other glove, which matches it, was found among your other stuff in your room at the hotel." At that Easterbrook shrugged his shoulders dismissively. "There's hundreds like them."

Later that morning Easterbrook appeared at Bromley Magistrates' Court and was remanded in custody; on 24 April 1958 committal proceedings took place. He was charged with shooting at Henry Stevens with intent to murder him, breaking into Genden, Uplands and the Artillery Museum and inflicting grievous bodily harm on William Mills and Frank Henry Dunn. Evidence was called to support these charges, and at the conclusion of Bland's evidence Easterbrook replied, "I have nothing to say," adding, "There is not a word of truth in it."

Evidence was also given by Dr Lewis Charles Nickolls from the Yard's Forensic Science Laboratory that when he examined the revolver which had been used to shoot Henry Stevens, it was in some respects defective, because although it could fire single shots it would not fire a second round without pushing back the trigger, rotating the cylinder and cocking the hammer. This also explained the indentation on the rim of the bullet next to the spent one which had shot Stevens.

When Stevens gave evidence, he produced this gun, and showed his wound to the Magistrates; with his evidence complete, the Chairman of the Bench, Mr J.C. Gibbs, addressed him as follows:

> You acted with great bravery and great determination and I have not the slightest doubt your colleagues are aware of this and that the attention of the commissioner has been drawn to it. But the Bench would wish to say that there are others who are concerned – your fellow citizens – who must be relieved and proud to think that men like you and your colleagues are on duty at night as well as in the day time to protect them, I think that should be said.

With that, Easterbrook was committed in custody to stand his trial at the Old Bailey, which he did on 12 May 1958 before the Honourable Mr Justice Ashworth, who had previously been a junior treasury counsel. He was a no-nonsense judge, who six years later would be the last ever to utter the sentence of death, on Peter Allen and Gwynne Evans at Manchester Assizes, the last murderers to hang in England.

Easterbrook had already aired a number of defences: he had not shot Henry Stevens, nor had he broken into Genden. Then, changing his story, he alleged that both offences were the fault of the anonymous man who had stolen his suit on the morning of the shooting, whilst he, Easterbrook, had been at an unknown pub where he knew nobody and nobody knew him. And the savage glassing of Messrs Mills and Dunn? His brother had been responsible, he stated, knowing that his brother had been acquitted and therefore could not be tried twice for the same offence.

But now, in a complete turn-about, Easterbrook placed himself right at the scene when he pleaded guilty to shooting Stevens with intent to cause grievous bodily harm or to resist his lawful apprehension, and also to the burglary at Genden. He pleaded not guilty to a charge of shooting with intent to murder and two charges of receiving stolen property – the discarded hat and coat and the pistol found in his possession at the time of his arrest.

David Karmel QC, assisted by junior counsel John Hall, two experienced barristers, appeared for the defence, but unbeknown to Easterbrook he had an ally right in the heart of the enemy's camp. Travis Christmas Humphreys was born in 1901 and in 1924 he was both called to the Bar and formed – unusually for a barrister – the London Buddhist Society. In 1950 he had been appointed Senior Treasury Counsel, and it is unlikely that a more

incompetent barrister – and certainly a more controversial one –
ever drew breath. He appeared for the prosecution in the
contentious murder trials which resulted in the hanging of Ruth
Ellis and Derek Bentley and successfully prosecuted in the case
of Timothy Evans, where it was later discovered that Reginald
Christie had been responsible for the crimes (plus a few more) for
which Evans had been hanged. When the jury failed to agree on
a verdict in the case of Donald Hume, charged with the murder
of Stanley Setty, Humphreys, rather than seek a retrial on the
most compelling of evidence, blithely offered no evidence and
accepted a plea of Hume's being an accessory after the fact. After
serving his twelve-year sentence (and three months prior to the
Easterbrook trial) Hume just as blithely admitted to the *Sunday
Pictorial* that he had indeed committed the murder and then went
to Switzerland, where during the course of an armed robbery he
shot and killed a Zürich taxi driver. Humphreys would go on to
become a judge at the Old Bailey in 1968; police officers
collectively loathed him for his attacks on their character* and his
weak-kneed sentencing. It was as though he was trying to make
amends for his previous appalling oversights; but when he gave a
rapist two suspended sentences in 1975, the Lord Chancellor had
to defend him in the face of a House of Commons motion to
dismiss him. The National Association of Probation Officers lent
their support, but since Humphreys made a habit of handing out
probation orders left right and centre to some of the most vicious
armed robbers, it must be assumed they had a vested interest.
However, a great many people – most of them police officers –
breathed a sigh of relief when he resigned the following year.

So now, with Humphreys appearing as prosecuting counsel, the
trial got underway. It did not take very long, firstly because
Humphreys immediately offered no evidence on the charge of
receiving the stolen pistol, and secondly because Easterbrook had
abandoned his former assertion made at the Magistrates' Court
less than three weeks earlier that "there was not a word of truth"
in DI Bland's deposition. Indeed, there was a great deal of truth
in it. Since Easterbrook had admitted shooting Stevens, the

---

* The author endured one such attack on his veracity from Judge
Humphreys; this was after the prisoner in the dock had pleaded guilty to
robbery and wounding, where the elderly victim had been slashed with
a knife. The defendant, who a few months previously had been placed
on probation for two years for robbery by Judge Humphreys, was once
again placed on probation.

question was, did he intend to murder him? No, Easterbrook told the jury. He had only intended to hit the officer with the revolver, he said, telling them, "I always carry a loaded gun." The gun had gone off when he tripped, and Christmas Humphreys completely missed the point that if this had indeed been the case, Stevens would have probably been shot in the foot, rather than the mouth.

When the jury returned after four hours' deliberation, they found Easterbrook guilty of receiving the hat and coat but were unable to agree on the charge of shooting with intent to murder. Since a unanimous verdict was at that time necessary, the judge discharged them. However, at the end of the day's proceedings, the judge called Henry Stevens in front of him and commended him with the following words:

> Stevens, I would like to say this to you, and I am quite sure the jury, though they have not agreed upon their verdict on count one, will completely endorse what I have to say, and indeed, I am sure counsel for the defence will, too: in my view your conduct was of the very greatest gallantry and really is a performance of which you might be rightly proud and I hope your senior officers will take account of it.

The next day, evidence was heard in respect of the two cases of grievous bodily harm at the Deptford pub, and the jury found Easterbrook guilty in both cases.

It was then that the unofficial third member of the defence team played his master-stroke. Even though there was a mass of evidence to swear in a new jury to retry Easterbrook on the charge of shooting Henry Stevens with intent to murder him, Christmas Humphreys offered no evidence, and Easterbrook was formally found not guilty.

Before passing sentence, Mr Justice Ashworth addressed Easterbrook as follows:

> In my view, you are a wicked and dangerous man, and I feel it is my duty to send you away for a long time. If you had been convicted of shooting with intent to murder the sentence I am about to pass would have been even longer. This was a vicious affair involving a police officer. You are a lucky man that Providence intervened to save you from a charge of capital murder. If I am any judge of such matters it might well have resulted in your conviction and that might well have been the end of you. You seem to have no respect for persons, law or property.

He then sentenced Easterbrook to ten years' imprisonment for shooting Stevens, four years each for the Deptford pub slashings and twelve months' imprisonment each for the burglary at Genden and receiving the hat and coat from the housebreaking; all sentences to be served concurrently.

"I will bet money I will never finish it," said Easterbrook defiantly, although inaccurately, and as he was taken down to the cells he added for good measure, "I would like to congratulate the police on maintaining a high standard of collusion and perjury." Having due regard for his own standards of truthfulness throughout the affair, it was a remark considered by many as being a bit rich.

Stevens returned to work and he, Vibart (who had been promoted to the rank of detective inspector) and Perkins were highly commended by the commissioner for outstanding courage and devotion to duty. Six weeks after the commendation, the three officers each received cheques for £15 from the Bow Street Reward Fund, from Sir Laurence Dunne, the Chief Metropolitan Magistrate.

The third supplement to the *London Gazette*, No. 41528, dated 17 October 1958, announced that Stevens would be awarded the George Cross and Vibart and Perkins the Queen's Commendation for Brave Conduct. On 25 November 1958 at Buckingham Palace, to commemorate his truly breathtaking gallantry, Stevens received the Cross from Her Majesty, Queen Elizabeth II.

Henry Stevens served two tours with the Flying Squad and retired from the Metropolitan Police in 1983 with the rank of chief inspector, thirty years to the day after he had joined. He had been commended on fifteen occasions for outstanding police work and his character was described as 'exemplary'.

Of course, that was not the end of the story; but with a criminal of Easterbrook's capabilities, it seldom is, is it?

★   ★   ★

Serving his ten-year sentence, Easterbrook decided upon a path of non-communication with staff and inmates alike; therefore a fellow prisoner was surprised when Easterbrook actually spoke to him, although less so at the content of his address: "When I get out of here," stated Easterbrook, emphatically, "all I want to do is kill a copper." It was not through want of trying that he failed.

Following his release, Easterbrook drifted in and out of crime, but although he still displayed his hatred for authority on a grand scale, he could not be described as a particularly successful criminal. In the spring of 1981, following an unsuccessful armed raid on a cash-in-transit vehicle, he decamped and was arrested in a café by uniformed officers. He tried to grab a bag at his feet before he was overpowered; inside the bag was a loaded handgun. Interviewed by Flying Squad officers, Easterbrook stated that he had tried to grab the gun, but not to resist arrest, oh no. It was to commit suicide rather than go back to prison, and since there was no evidence to contradict this studied piece of hokum, it was accepted by the prosecution; for conspiracy to rob and possessing a firearm Easterbrook was sentenced to eight years' imprisonment.

He was released in February 1986 and eighteen months later he participated in a robbery – in fact, he would later say, he was 'talked into it' by a police informant – on 23 November 1987. He was in company with Tony Ash, who had twenty-one convictions dating back to 1955 and who was described as 'a big softy' by the third member of the team, Gary Wilson, a twenty-four-year-old criminal with eleven previous convictions, including one for robbery. After carrying out an armed robbery at Bejam's Store, Woolwich and stealing £10,411, the three men got into a Mercedes and drove back to Sunbury Street, where a stolen BMW saloon awaited them. Unfortunately, so did the Flying Squad and the PT 17 Firearms Unit. As Ash got out of the car, gun in hand, he was called upon by Inspector Dwight Atkinson to surrender. Ash refused to drop his gun, and Easterbrook, who was lying on the back seat of the car, opened fire with a Smith & Wesson .357 Magnum, shooting Atkinson in the leg; he then fired five more shots. The police returned fire. Easterbrook, wounded in the shoulder, was desperately trying to reload his gun as he was arrested, but Ash was dead.

Easterbrook would later ridiculously suggest that no barrister would accept a case where the accused claimed he was defending himself against a police 'shoot to kill policy' – when any one of a host of left-wing lawyers would undoubtedly have offered their services for free. But in conducting his own defence at the Old Bailey, Easterbrook unintentionally presented himself as a figure of fun. I know – I witnessed it. He was given an enormous amount of latitude by the judge, Mr Justice Turner, as Easterbrook knew full well he would be; alas, all to no avail. Wilson (who, two days before the trial began, attempted to escape from Pentonville Prison) was sentenced to seven years' imprisonment. The jury were not informed of this attempt, nor were they informed that Easterbrook had endeavoured to escape during the trial by using explosives to blow his way out of the prison van; but on 30 November 1988 he was found guilty of robbery, shooting a police officer with intent to cause him grievous bodily harm and firearms offences. It was thirty years after he had been convicted of shooting Henry Stevens and, notching up his eleventh conviction, he was sentenced to four concurrent life sentences. The judge commended the officers, especially Inspector Atkinson who fifteen years previously had been awarded the Queen's Commendation for Brave Conduct, for his actions in assisting in the arrest of a bank robber who had fired shots at the officers who pursued him.

Although it would be a prison sentence without end for Easterbrook, he was in his element. A classic whiner and self-proclaimed victim, Easterbrook pulled every manipulative string possible. All through his criminal career he stated he was prepared to kill himself rather than face another prison sentence – except that he never did. Incarcerated, he went on hunger strikes to end his life – except that he always recovered sufficiently to take solid food. Refusing to communicate with anybody, he was still prepared to do so when it suited him. Protesting against his conviction and sentence, claiming he had been denied legal representation, he took his case to the Appeal Court, the Criminal Cases Review Commission and the European Court of Human Rights. After a Home Secretary set his life sentence at twelve and a half years he was offered parole but heroically (and because victims of criminal injustices do not accept hand-outs) Easterbrook chose to remain in jail, where, inside and out, he was almost hysterically worshipped by his band of followers. "Ronnie is a man with three hearts," solemnly if illogically proclaimed one of his fans, a view of Prisoner No. B88459 not shared by police. As a former Flying Squad officer commented, "My impression of Easterbrook was that of a reckless, extremely dangerous and unsuccessful career criminal. I think he was more cowardly than vicious and certainly not as professional and calculating as the type I was more accustomed to dealing with. His story of attempting to commit suicide showed a degree of criminal cunning when faced with situational adversity."

Easterbrook died in Gartree Prison on 10 May 2009, the day before his seventy-eighth birthday. For a man who hated the police so much, it would have been the unkindest of cuts to have reminded him that he was directly responsible for so many of them receiving awards for courage, including the highest civilian award that it is possible for the sovereign to bestow.

CHAPTER 11

No Head for Heights

The miner's daughter from Twechar, Dumbartonshire, had wanted to join the police since the age of sixteen. She had been involved in a car crash, and was impressed with the authority of the police constable who arrived and took particulars of the incident. Short in stature, she confessed to having no confidence, so she went to gymnastic classes and eventually reached a height of five feet five and one quarter. Aged just twenty, former typist Margaret Shaw Cleland travelled down to London to join the Metropolitan Police; coincidentally, the sergeant who had interviewed her for her new job had been the constable who recorded the details of the car accident four years earlier. She would later say that previously, if she was short-changed in a shop, she would be too nervous to go back to rectify matters. But all that would soon change; within months of joining, when a man attacked her, she grabbed hold of the scarf round his neck and all but garrotted him, before carrying out his arrest. And what was more, Margaret was quite unequivocal about not having a head for heights; but her courage, forty-three feet above street level, her razor-sharp reactions as a gymnast and her strong hands would soon be put to the test; none would be found wanting.

*　*　*

It was a chilly afternoon as Woman Police Constable 232 'E' Cleland set off on patrol from Gray's Inn Road police station on 4 March 1964. Her career had commenced on 'Y' Division at Wood Green police station in 1960 but she had been very unhappy in the local police section house – a woman sergeant, a strict disciplinarian, had made her life a misery – and after a short ten-month posting she had been transferred to 'E' Division in the heart of London's West End and had thoroughly enjoyed her two and a half years there. She was comfortably settled at Ede Section House, Mare Street, Hackney and had taken part in undercover and plain-clothes duties; just seven months previously, she had been commended by the commissioner for her initiative and devotion to duty in connection with offences under the Licensing

Acts. But no such excitement was anticipated as Margaret walked the beat and a chill wind blew across Gray's Inn Gardens on that quiet Wednesday afternoon; it never is. However, just over a quarter of a mile away to the west in Marchmont Street, the problems of a thirty-one-year-old Cambridge garage owner, who was with his twenty-two-month-old son, were spiralling out of control and about to reach breaking point.

Thomas French had spent the previous night in a Bloomsbury hotel with his baby son Stuart. His wife Irene, eight years younger than him, had left him three weeks previously and he was desperate to find her. French had eaten lunch in a café in Coram Street and had fed the baby from his plate. Barbara White, a sixteen-year-old waitress who served him, later said, "The little boy was crying a lot."

A little later Miss White left the café, and as she reached the junction of Coram Street and Marchmont Street a voice called out, "You know me, love, don't you?" She looked round; then she looked up. Over forty feet above her, on the flat roof of a building scheduled for demolition, was the man to whom she had served lunch. Thomas French was sitting astride a single iron railing, about two feet above the surface of the roof; in his arms was his baby son. A card fluttered down from the roof; it was picked up by sixteen-year-old Annette Harris, who was passing. "It asked me to phone a number to see if the man's wife had been traced," she later said. In fact, Miss Harris tried to telephone the number on the card but was unable to get through; instead, she sensibly dialled 999. Two ambulances and two fire tenders arrived; so did a clergyman, as well as several hundred onlookers. The fire brigade called on members of the public to assist them in stretching out a huge net in the street below. Meanwhile, Thomas French was becoming more and more distressed; he shouted that he had been evicted from his flat, he chain-smoked and he called out that he would jump from the roof with the baby.

And then, within fifteen minutes of French first being seen on the roof, at 4.10 that afternoon, the crowds in the street below fell silent, because they saw WPC Margaret Cleland walking out on to the roof. She took off her cap in an effort to put French at his ease and when she heard his voice she realized he was a fellow Scot; in fact, his family came from Tollcross, Glasgow, just sixteen miles from her home in Twechar. She called out, "Will you let me speak to you, Jock?" and her accent was so broad that 'Jock' almost sounded like 'Joke' – but there was nothing remotely amusing about the situation; the guard rail upon which French was sitting was insecure, and he was becoming so agitated that at any moment he could have overbalanced – or jumped – and fallen with the baby to the street below.

Between the steeply pitched slate roof and the parapet was a foot-wide gully, and it was along this channel that Margaret started to advance steadily towards French. With the cold wind blowing through her wavy auburn hair, she began quietly and earnestly talking to the desperate man, telling him not to let his baby son die; but as French wept, he gestured wildly and swayed backwards. The crowd in the street gasped; a woman in the crowd cried, "Oh, merciful Mother of God, save the baby!" and the sobbing child called out, "Mamma!"

Margaret offered a bar of chocolate for the child, then a bottle of milk, but as she edged closer French screamed that he would jump. "It's not the first time I've been fed up with everything," Margaret told him quietly. "I've just sat down and thought it out." French showed her a photograph of his wedding and said he was trying to find his wife. By now, two hours had passed since French had ascended to the roof, and the crying baby gave Margaret the excuse she needed to suggest to French that the baby was cold. Seeing the child's discarded coat, she asked, "Do you mind if I pick up this coat and put it on the baby?" She had got within six feet of French; now, holding out the coat, she had advanced to within four feet and knew it was now or never.

Margaret placed the coat around the child's shoulders on top of his light-blue siren suit with pixie hood and, as French lifted his arm from the child to assist her, she dived forward, grabbed the child and at the same time with her other hand seized hold of the sleeve of French's coat. Throwing herself backwards, she wrenched the baby from French's grasp, pulling French in towards the roof. Cradling the baby in her arms, she fell sideways on to the pitched roof. The crowd forty feet below gasped at the sheer courage of her actions; then Benjamin John Eagle and Maurice Alfred Charles Jewby, both ambulance driver attendants, dashed forward and seized French, who was lurching towards the parapet; their actions would later result in both of them being awarded the Queen's Commendation for Brave Conduct.

Amidst cheers from the crowd, Margaret descended to the street where she was hugged by one of the women onlookers. "I felt like kissing her," said Margaret.

Strapped to a stretcher, French was taken first to St Pancras hospital (and later, Friern Barnet hospital), where he received the treatment which he so badly needed; the baby was initially taken into care, and no charges were proffered by the police. Irene

French was traced to a supermarket in St Aubin, on the Channel Island of Jersey; separated from a senior aircraftsman who was arrested on suspicion of having absented himself from the RAF, she sobbed, "Please bring my baby to me – I can't live another moment without him."

★   ★   ★

Flowers piled up on the counter at Gray's Inn Road police station, recruiting for policewomen doubled overnight and Margaret received eight proposals of marriage. Her parents, John and Margaret Cleland, were enormously pleased. Speaking from their home at Merryflats, Twechar, her mother said, "I am very proud," adding, "when she was young, Margaret was always very daring." This was the twenty-three-year-old who later told the first of many press reporters, "I'm dead scared of heights!"

The incident had certainly attracted the interest of the press. The following day, the headline of the *Daily Mirror* was 'Don't let your baby son die', and the *Daily Express* revealed, 'Terror on the Roof' with the subheading 'Policewoman saves baby', together with the most dramatic photographs. The news flashed around the world. The *Boston Herald* informed its readers of 'A desperate man, a baby's life, a long hour in London'. The *Waco News Tribune* in Texas showed the moment Margaret seized the baby with the subheading 'Dad's leap with baby foiled' and the *Evening Outlook*, Santa Monica, California informed its readers, 'Policewoman risks life, saves baby'. On the other side of the world, New Zealand's *Christchurch Star* revealed, 'Policewoman rescues baby from death in London drama'.

Showing a photograph of a relieved *agent* WPC 232, surrounded by smiling, admiring members of the public, the French press reported:

"I was terrified of falling," remembers Margaret. "I was on the edge of the roof; the weight of the child could have caused me to fall." Suddenly police officers and paramedics, who had been waiting at a distance on the roof, rushed past and succeeded in grabbing French just as he was about to jump. The incident had lasted for over one and a half hours, but eventually, both the father and the child were saved.

The heroine, Margaret, has been a police officer for three and a half years. It has been her dream to be a police officer since she was a child. During the rescue, she only lost her composure once: when the crowd, who had been watching in

Coram Street welcomed her with tremendous applause. "I just did my duty," she later told journalists.

Three weeks later, Margaret was awarded a commissioner's high commendation for 'outstanding courage and perseverance' and on 12 May she was awarded £20 from the Bow Street Metropolitan Magistrates' Court Reward Fund by Mr K.J.P. Barraclough, who described her as 'a very brave young woman'.

But when three months later Margaret discovered that she was to be awarded the George Medal, she admitted she was 'stunned'. "I don't know why they've done this," she told reporters. "I've already had a £20 reward – I never expected anything else." Margaret's mother stated, "This is the proudest day of my life," and now, discharged from hospital, Thomas French praised her as well. "It was a very brave thing," he said. "She saved my son's life and mine, too."

All good things come to an end. Having collected her medal from the Queen at Buckingham Palace and just before Christmas, on 20 December 1964, Margaret Cleland voluntarily resigned from the Force. She had served with the Metropolitan Police for just four years and twelve days. Due to her brief service, her Certificate of Conduct was shown as 'very good'. But on her Central Record of Service this was crossed out. Instead, it was amended to read 'exemplary – by direction of the commissioner'.

Margaret's early departure from the Metropolitan Police was at the behest of her father. Margaret's mother had suffered poor health all her life; now, her father asked Margaret to return to Twechar to help look after her. Margaret must have proved to be a most competent nurse; speaking to me in 2010 at the age of seventy, she remarked wryly, "She died last year – she was ninety-one!"

Within six months of returning to Dumbartonshire, she rejoined the police as part of that county's constabulary and there she worked as a woman police constable for two years. A daughter was born in 1967 as the result of a relationship which sadly failed to last. Margaret was later employed as a civilian at the front counter of one of Lanarkshire Constabulary's police stations; it was there she met her future husband, one of the constabulary's serving police officers, and they married in 1977. Her spouse was not one of the original eight suitors who proposed marriage following the events which won her the George Medal, and that was a pity. It was, as Margaret told me, 'a most unhappy marriage', which came to an end when her husband died of cancer in 1988. She now lives alone, still in Scotland, close to her daughter and her daughter's family and still close to her roots.

Following his discharge from Friern Barnet hospital, Thomas French was reunited with his wife and he returned to his garage at Station Road, Waterbeach, Cambridgeshire. Susan Raif, who knew the Frenches prior to the marital breakup, described Thomas French as being 'a really nice, kind chap'. She last saw him in the late 1960s when he was running a stall at Cambridge market. Stuart French, now a forty-eight-year-old office worker, told me in 2010, "Having initially been put into care, we had to go to court in Cambridge for me to be officially returned to my parents," and the family was increased by two daughters. In 1980 French sold the garage business and moved to Linwood Road, Cambridge; Irene French died of an aneurism in 1990, and Thomas French followed her to the grave when he died of cancer in 2007.

And in 1965, the year following Margaret's departure from the Metropolitan Police, Gray's Inn Road police station closed for operational purposes. During its sixty-seven-year existence, it had produced some outstanding police officers – but few as courageous as Margaret Cleland.

CHAPTER 12

The Ride of Death

I t is easy to be wise after the event; all of us have been in that position. And yet this incident started off so well – a sharp-eyed police officer had spotted a parked-up Mini bearing false number plates in Drayton Road, Leytonstone during the early hours of 15 July 1965. Either 'Juliet One-one', the 'J' Division 'Q' Car, or the night-duty CID, or both – unmarked cars each containing three officers in plain clothes – ought to have been alerted. In consequence, an observation would have been set up – two aids to CID in a nondescript observation van close to the suspect Mini, and either the CID car or the 'Q' Car, or both, in the vicinity, with all of the vehicles in radio contact with each other. In this way, as soon as a suspect went to the Mini, the aids could alert the other police vehicles and jump out of the observation van in order to arrest the offender; then the 'Q' Car or CID car could quickly drive to the scene, if necessary, to block in the suspect vehicle. If it appeared that the suspect in the vehicle was likely to escape, the police car could ram it, or (and this scenario was far more likely) in the event of a peaceful arrest convey the prisoner to the police station. I know, because I was involved in an exactly similar situation. It is a simple strategy, and it works.

But not in this case. It was thought far better to start knocking on householders' doors in the vicinity of the stolen car in the middle of the night; apart from seriously annoying the neighbourhood, this ran the risk of alerting the car thief to the presence of police if he lived in the vicinity – as indeed he did. As six o'clock in the morning arrived, so the night-duty handed over their outstanding matters to the early turn shift; and still the CID had not been alerted. An hour later, the crew of 'Juliet Two', the marked police Area Car, came on duty; this included the observer, a uniform officer wearing plain clothes. Knowing him to be a very keen officer, the duty officer drove him to Drayton Road in his private car and left him there in it, at some distance from the suspect vehicle, taking the car keys with him and walking back to Leyton police station in Francis Road. So that was the situation: a lone officer in plain clothes, with no means of pursuit and with no means of communication; personal radios would not make an appearance in the Metropolitan Police for another three years. Nobody knew if one suspect or four would approach the car. This was an ill thought-out scenario, set for disaster; and the fact that PC Barrett was not killed or crippled was due to his courage, his enormous determination and a great deal of good fortune.

★   ★   ★

The bravery of Police Constable 365 'J' John Henry Barrett was never in question. His National Service had been spent with the Royal Military Police, serving mainly in Gibraltar, before he joined the Metropolitan Police in 1956. Most of his service had been spent at Leyton, and Barrett was married with two young children, a girl and a boy. His first commendation came within eighteen months of joining; whilst on holiday with his wife in Clacton, he went to the aid of a police constable who was being attacked. He was commended again in 1964 for vigilance and ability when carrying out two arrests and the following year he was commended for another arrest off-duty: a man had left a stolen car with false plates outside the house of Barrett's mother-in-law in Clapton, to be used in a robbery the following day. Now, five weeks later, Barrett was about to become involved in another incident oddly reminiscent of the case for which he had just been commended, involving a stolen car with false number plates parked outside a house.

After an hour of waiting, Barrett saw a man – John Michael Stannard, aged twenty-three – emerge from a nearby house and make his way towards the Mini. A fitter's mate, Stannard had a busy sideline; not only had he stolen the Mini, he had also stolen two other cars – a Humber and a Morris – as well as an outboard motor and navigational equipment valued at £900 from a yacht moored in the River Hamble, Southampton.

As Stannard inserted a key into the lock on the driver's door, so Barrett ran over to the car; but by now, due to the distance involved, Stannard was in the driver's seat and had started the engine. Barrett showed his warrant card and shouted that he was a police officer, but Stannard put the car in gear and drove straight at him. To avoid being run down, Barrett dived on to the bonnet of the car and hung on to the rain channels on either side of its roof. Stannard accelerated away, and for the next five minutes, at speeds of 30 mph, did his best to dislodge Barrett, who was shouting at him to stop; Stannard swerved from side to side across the road, braking sharply then accelerating fiercely, and on two occasions crashed into parked cars. He banged Barrett's fingers through his open window to try to break his grip, shouting, "Get off or be knocked off!"

There was never any question of Barrett drawing his truncheon to smash the windscreen; with the lunatic way in which Stannard was driving, it was all he could do to retain his grip on the car. Had Stannard succeeded in breaking his hold on the car, Barrett would have slid off underneath the wheels, with undoubtedly fatal consequences.

Astonished early-morning pedestrians turned and gaped as this ride of death was enacted through the side-streets of Leytonstone, and Barrett shouted out to them to call the police; as he told me forty-five years later, "I think at least one of them must have done."

As the car entered Queen's Road, Stannard shouted, "Get off, or I'll do you!" and then, with the car travelling at 30 mph, he braked suddenly and leapt from the car, which freewheeled down a slope and hit a tree. The sudden impact caused Barrett to be thrown free; he landed in the roadway on his head and shoulders. Badly dazed, he got to his feet; he had seen Stannard run off into a side road and now he followed but lost sight of him. He enlisted the aid of some newspaper delivery boys to keep watch for any movements of the suspect, and then assistance from Leyton police station started to arrive. The arrest was later carried out by Police Constable Aubrey Crabb from West Ham police station; Stannard was found cowering in a garden shed, close to the scene.

Barrett was taken to hospital, but incredibly he was not detained and was allowed to go home. Matters changed considerably that evening when he was rushed back to hospital, suffering from concussion. Altogether, he spent one month on sick leave; he later spent ten days recuperating at Hove convalescent home. However, the effects of the impact he had sustained would last for years, with headaches and mood swings.

In the meantime, Stannard had confessed his misdeeds, and during the course of their enquiries the CID arrested Lionel Borges, a twenty-five-year-old chef who had been implicated in the various thefts. The investigation was conducted by the marvellously eccentric Detective Sergeant Arthur Baigent, who, apart from his astonishing social gaffes, was best remembered for his report of a burglary where entry to the premises had been effected by cutting through a corrugated iron roof. After half a dozen unsuccessful attempts to spell 'corrugated' correctly, Arthur simply gave up and wrote 'crinkly tin'.

But he had more success with Borges, who stated, "This has been worrying me for a long time. I would have got everything cleared up but I didn't want to split on Stannard." Stannard had been charged with the attempted murder of Barrett, but in November 1965 at the Old Bailey the jury was directed to find him not guilty of this offence by the trial judge, Mervyn Griffith-Jones. Giving evidence, Stannard had piteously told the court that he had panicked, he had never intended to do Barrett any harm, "and at no stage did I ever drive fast." Convicted of causing Barrett bodily harm by 'wanton and furious driving', the judge told Stannard:

> This was the most wicked conduct to a police officer doing nothing but his duty and doing it thoroughly well. That conduct could have resulted in serious injury, if not death to that police officer.

After jailing Stannard for a total of eighteen months and Borges for twelve months, the judge told Barrett, "Your conduct is worthy of the highest commendation," as indeed it was.

He was highly commended by the commissioner in December 1965 and a month later was awarded £20 from the Bow Street Reward Fund. Four months later he was gazetted to be awarded the British Empire Medal for Gallantry, which was presented to him at County Hall by Earl Alexander of Tunis.

The British Empire Medal (BEM) had originally been instituted in 1922, both for 'meritorious service' and for gallantry, at which time it was known as the Empire Gallantry Medal (EGM). The EGM was superseded in 1940 by the George Cross and the George Medal, but its successor, the BEM, was still awarded for gallant acts which just failed to reach the criteria required for the George Medal. From 1940 until 1974 (when the BEM was replaced with the Queen's Gallantry Medal) 128 awards were made to Metropolitan Police officers, including a bar to the award. The silver medal was 36mm in diameter, with an effigy of a seated Britannia on the obverse looking towards the sun to her right, encircled with the words 'For God and the Empire' and at the bottom the words 'For Meritorious Service'. On the reverse, the royal cipher was surrounded by a crown, incorporating the words, 'Instituted by King George V'. A straight clasp attached to the medal with laurel leaves secured the 32mm wide rose-pink ribbon, edged with thin pearl-grey stripes. The recipient was permitted to add BEM after his or her name, the medal could not be awarded posthumously and the fact that it was awarded for gallantry was denoted by a silver oak leaf emblem worn on the ribbon.

★   ★   ★

Prior to this incident, Barrett had applied to become a dog handler, but despite his exemplary record of off-duty arrests, he was told selection for a course could take as long as seven years. However, following the investiture Barrett was very quickly given a course and, as he wryly told me, "I could have had a dog and a horse as well." In total, he had three dogs – Zola, Khan and Bodie – and remained on 'J' Division for the rest of his career, where he carried out a great deal of useful work.

In 1971 Barrett and another officer rescued an elderly woman who had attempted suicide by putting her head in a gas oven. As well as being commended by the commissioner and receiving a resuscitation certificate from the Royal Humane Society, he was feted at a reception given by the Mayor of Waltham Forest. In 1975 he was again commended by the commissioner and the judge at Snaresbrook Crown Court for his action in a case of robbery and firearms offences; and ten months later again, both by the commissioner and Snaresbrook Crown Court, for arresting five people wanted all over England for forging Post Office savings books. In 1977 he was on foot patrol with his dog one Sunday afternoon and, leaving the dog to keep watch, Barrett climbed over a gate into an enclosure which housed several garages. He discovered a number of car parts taken from Transit vans which had been stolen and broken down for spares. It led to the arrest of thirteen persons and another (and final) commendation for Barrett.

Barrett retired after twenty-five years' service to the house in Woodford where he has lived for all of his married life. He has been married for fifty-two years and has four grandchildren, one of whom is a police constable at Limehouse police station; Barrett's brother was also a police officer and his son is a police sergeant, also at Limehouse.

After his retirement Barrett opened an art gallery, but after thirteen years it had to close when he was afflicted with a virus which paralysed him from the waist down. Now aged seventy-four, he still drives and manages to walk, albeit for very short distances, with a stick.

Given Barrett's amazing courage and fortitude, as someone who had survived 'the ride of death', it would take more than paralysis to stop him.

CHAPTER 13

A Dangerous Man

I n 1812 Lady Caroline Lamb denounced her former lover Lord Byron as being 'mad, bad and dangerous to know'; the same description could equally have applied to Maxwell Thomas Pigott, a century and a half later. The difference was that Byron delivered a stinging rebuke to her ladyship (described as 'brutal, even for the heartless period in which it was written'), and he had his chums to back him up. Pigott was not so fortunate; few people – judges, police officers, his victims or fellow criminals – had a good word to say for him. Even today, over thirty years after the events which brought him to prominence, only a small select few at New Scotland Yard know the details of what might or might not be his current identity or whereabouts. He may or may not be in this country, and his features may have been altered by plastic surgery – if that is the case, it would have been a prudent move, since he incurred the displeasure of his former associates who placed a price on his head, an underworld contract for his demise.

* * *

When Detective Sergeant Henry – always known as Harry – Charles Clement was asked to run the 'B' Division 'Q' Car in 1965, he was given the courtesy of being allowed to choose his own crew. The driver was easy: Police Constable 480 'B' John – known as Jack – Methven, a local officer with great experience of the area and a Class I driver. The choice of aid to CID, Police Constable 396 'B' Dennis Meade Boyse Bartlett, raised a few eyebrows, simply because of his inexperience – he had only been an aid for nine months – but Clement, a former sergeant during his six years with the Grenadier Guards and the veteran of a previous tour with the Flying Squad, was unerring in his judgement of men. "I knew instinctively he was made of the right stuff," he told me many years later, and he was right; twenty-six-year-old Bartlett might have had only three years' total service in the Metropolitan Police, but prior to that he had served for five years as a second mate in the Merchant Navy.

On Monday, 6 September 1965, the crew of the 'B' Division

'Q' Car were on patrol when thirty-five-year-old Clement, who had been based at Chelsea police station for the previous twelve months, received an R/T call from the local Area Car, 'Bravo Two'; as a result, PC Methven turned the car towards the Cromwell Road, a thoroughfare containing a number of hotels, including at No. 111, the Ashburn.

On their arrival, Clement saw the two police officers from the Area Car talking to the hall porter; also present were two other men, Maxwell Thomas Pigott and William White, and all the men walked up to the first floor and entered room 37. Because Clement was not fully conversant with what was being discussed, he introduced himself to the group and asked what was going on. The hall porter replied that he thought he had recognised Pigott and White as being responsible for a theft at the hotel some two or three weeks previously and showed Clement the hotel register, in which one of the men had given his address as 'Montreal, Canada'. Both men said that they would wait until the manager returned to the hotel, when their identity could be verified.

However, PC Bartlett had slipped away and made enquiries of his own; he discovered that Pigott had been charged with housebreaking at Chelsea police station on 27 July and on 5 August he had been committed to the Inner London Sessions for trial. Despite strong police objections, he had been given bail. Bartlett had a quiet word with Clement, who unequivocally stated to the suspect: "Your name is Pigott. You should have attended the Inner London Sessions today, and there's a warrant in existence for your arrest. I'm arresting you and taking you to Chelsea police station."

At that, twenty-two-year-old Pigott thrust his hand into his jacket pocket, and Clement immediately grasped his wrist, turning it towards his body. Forcing Pigott's hand from his pocket, Clement saw a yellow 'Jif' plastic lemon, a favourite with housewives in its natural form and also with robbers, in its adapted form – filled with ammonia. Clement shouted to the two uniform officers to hold White, whilst Bartlett seized Pigott's left arm. White broke away from the officers, jumped on to the bed and assumed the fighting stance so beloved of followers of martial arts films. As the officers advanced towards him, White suddenly reached into his jacket pocket, withdrew another plastic lemon and, unscrewing the cap, shouted, "Move, move, or you'll get this in your eyes, you bastards!" He immediately started squirting the contents at the police officers, and with the acrid stench of ammonia filling the air Clement shouted that acid was being sprayed and that everybody should clear the room. White was now squirting the ammonia at the head of Clement, who sheltered his face behind Pigott whom he was still holding, and for the second time Clement shouted for the others to get out of the room. He then pushed the struggling six foot of Pigott across the bed towards White, and as he did so White squirted ammonia straight into Clement's eyes.

The pain in Clement's eyes was unbearable, and he made his way towards the door to get out, while ammonia was still being sprayed at his head and neck. Managing to open the door, he staggered on to the landing and fell to the ground, unable to see. He was convinced that all the officers had left the room, but he was wrong; the two uniform officers had left but not Bartlett, who fought on alone; ammonia was squirted into his eyes, he was savagely struck on the head with an axe, hit with a stool and viciously kicked into unconsciousness. Pigott and White then ran to the fourth floor of the hotel, broke into a room and scrambled out through a window. More police had been alerted, the men had been chased, and fifteen more officers arrived, some with dogs.

Now the fugitives broke into room 409 of the adjacent Frobisher Hotel, where the twenty-two-year-old receptionist Julie Gardner was washing her hair. Alerted by her screams, the hall porter, Stuart Anderson, dashed upstairs and pulled the terrified young woman from the room. "Two men ran past me," said Anderson, "and one squirted me with something from a lemon." The men kicked in the door of room 420, climbed out of the window and on to a ledge.

Clement, meanwhile, put up a call on the car radio, and then became conscious of the presence of an unknown lady, whom he always described as "possibly of Kensington or Chelsea and who smelled wonderful, held me, pulled my head down to her bosom and said, 'My poor darling, what have they done to you?'" Clement savoured the moment only briefly; the next thing he heard was a man's voice calling out, "Stand back, lady," and with that, he received a face-full of water; now he could at least vaguely see out of one eye. Muttering thanks to his anonymous benefactor, he ran into the Cromwell Road, where he saw several police officers and heard one shout, "There they go, along he parapet." Clement ran into the yard of the Adelphi Hotel, 127 Cromwell Road, and then a voice called out: "They've come down; they're in here!"

Still with very limited vision, Clement dashed into the hotel and through the glass doors into the lounge; in the room were two police officers and Derek Harding, the hotel's accountant. Also present were White, who was holding the axe which he had used with devastating effect on Bartlett, and Pigott, in the centre of the room, spraying ammonia from two plastic 'Jif' containers and screaming, "Get back, get back!" With that, a battle royal commenced.

White flung the axe at Clement; he jumped clear, the axe missed and smashed into one of the glass doors. Pigott threw a coffee table at Clement who threw one back, hitting Pigott in the legs. White then retrieved the axe, flung a table at the window and climbed on to the window sill. Pigott was still squirting ammonia at Clement, who picked up a heavy cuspidor on a stand and flung it at Pigott, striking him on the head. Pigott screamed and fell to his knees, still squirting ammonia, but was subdued by other officers, who dragged him from the room.

White found his escape route was cut off – he had been confronted by police officers outside – and now he turned and jumped back into the lounge. Screaming, "I'll kill you, I'll kill you!" he rushed at Clement. As the accountant, Mr Harding, commented later, "One man put up a tremendous fight. He was swinging his hatchet in real earnest, he was really having a go."

White certainly was 'having a go'; as Clement closed with him, so White swung the axe. The blow went over Clement's left shoulder and, locked together, the two men fell over a table then on to an armchair, which toppled over, bringing the fiercely struggling men crashing to the floor. With Clement on top, White kept trying to hit his back with the axe, but Clement pressed his head into White's upper arm. Salvation, in the form of Police Constable Methven, then appeared. Drawing his truncheon, Methven struck White several times on the head, and as Clement later drily recorded, "White dropped the axe and ceased to struggle."

It was all over. As well as Clement's and Bartlett's debilitating injuries, Police Constable Wall had been hit with a chair and had a possible fracture of his hand; Police Constable Amey (one of the crew of 'Bravo Two') had also been assaulted. All were conveyed to St Mary Abbot's hospital, Kensington, for treatment.

Press photographs at the time show Clement, wearing dark glasses, being assisted across the road by a colleague; fortunately, he sustained no lasting damage. Unfortunately, as it eventually transpired, the same could not be said for Bartlett.

★   ★   ★

Four days later, Pigott was sufficiently recovered to appear at the Inner London Sessions, which was where he should have been on the morning of his confrontation with Clement & Co; had he been there, he would undoubtedly have saved himself a great deal of trouble. He pleaded guilty to housebreaking and false pretences and asked the court to take into consideration ninety-five other offences, comprising housebreaking, receiving stolen goods, false pretences and credit by fraud. For his first conviction he was sentenced to four years' imprisonment.

On 4 November 1965 Pigott and White appeared before His Honour Judge Bernard Gillis QC at the Old Bailey. Both men pleaded guilty to two charges of housebreaking, with Pigott pleading guilty to wounding Bartlett and White, not guilty to a miscellany of other charges. The trial commenced, but on the third day both men asked for the remaining charges to be put to them again and offered pleas which were acceptable to the prosecution. In addition, the men had been an industrious pair of housebreakers. Whilst Pigott had been on bail, following his initial arrest on 27 July, he and White had carried out what was later referred to as 'an absolute spate of housebreakings', usually at good-class hotels, and it was clear that the men were proficient in entering rooms with the use of celluloid and false keys. Also found in their possession was a doctor's stethoscope, which, when placed against a hotel room door, indicated whether or not the room was occupied. Pigott had booked into a room on 16 August at the Ashburn Hotel, giving the name 'Michael Johnstone', and it was this identity which had been queried by the hall porter on 6 September and which led to the mêlée and the pair's arrest. Both men now asked the court to take fifty-eight other offences into consideration: forty-nine cases of housebreaking, five cases of larceny and four cases of receiving. The value of the property (most of which was recovered) amounted to £4,939 5s 2d.

For the two cases of housebreaking and wounding Bartlett with intent both men were sentenced to a total of six years' imprisonment. For throwing a corrosive fluid with intent at both officers they were both sentenced to seven years' imprisonment, and for causing actual bodily harm to another officer Pigott was sentenced to two years' imprisonment; all the sentences were to be served concurrently, making a total of seven years' imprisonment. Before they were led away to the cells, Judge Gillis called the officers before him and told them:

The court has heard in the course of the evidence an account of the manner in which these officers were executing their duty in circumstances and conditions of great peril and great violence. In my opinion, all these officers conducted themselves both courageously and in accordance with the highest tradition of their service. I desire to commend each of them. Especially I desire to commend, in addition to what I have already said, the exceptional bravery of Police Constable Bartlett and Sergeant Clement.

The prosecution counsel, Mr Brian Leary, undertook to pass his Lordship's comments on to the appropriate authority, and so he did; Clement, Bartlett, Methven, Wall and PC Evans from 'F' Division were highly commended by the commissioner for 'outstanding courage and determination, resulting in the arrest and conviction of two dangerous criminals armed with offensive weapons whereby each officer sustained personal injury'. Six weeks later, Clement and Bartlett were each awarded a cheque for £20 from the Bow Street Metropolitan Magistrates' Reward Fund, and on 16 August 1966 the *London Gazette* informed the officers that they were to be awarded the British Empire Medal for Gallantry.

It was a time of great satisfaction for Clement, coupled with enormous sadness. Four days previously, Clement, now serving with the Regional Crime Squad, had been called to Braybrook Street, Shepherds Bush. The crew of the 'F' Division 'Q' Car, 'Foxtrot One-one' – Detective Sergeant Christopher Tippett Head, Temporary Detective Constable Stanley Bertram Wombwell and the driver, Police Constable Geoffrey Fox – had been murdered there. Clement was one of three officers deputed by the detective chief superintendent to wrap the bodies where they lay in the road and place them on the grass verge. He grieved for the officers who had been so mercilessly gunned down. He had taught Head beats when they were in uniform at Walham Green, Fulham, later working with him as an aid to CID, and had served as a detective constable on 'F' Division, from where he knew Fox. Of the three killers who were later caught, only the ringleader, Harry Maurice Roberts, is still behind bars.

* * *

Clement was delighted to discover that his British Empire Medal would be presented to him by Field Marshal The Right Hon. The Earl Alexander of Tunis, KG, GCB, OM, GCMG, CSI, DSO, MC, CD, PC (UK), PC (Can), who was one of his heroes. Mentioned in dispatches on no fewer than eight occasions, this gallant soldier immediately identified Clement as a former guardsman; it was the icing on the cake for Harry Clement.

Unfortunately – and undoubtedly because of the severe and sustained injuries he had received – Bartlett's personality underwent a change. Appointed detective constable, he was posted to the Yard's Interpol office – understandably known, because of the non-dynamic nature of the department's activities, as 'Sleepy Valley' – but although, as Clement later told me, "Senior officers, to my personal knowledge, leant over backwards to help him," it did no good. Bartlett had been a good, keen, intelligent officer, but after fifteen months at Interpol he was posted to 'L' Division, south of the Thames, and ten months later he voluntarily resigned. Aged twenty-nine and having served six and a half years in the Metropolitan Police, he left with a small gratuity and no pension. "My view, that was shared by others," Clement told me, "was that Dennis could have gone on to senior rank, for – until the axe injury – he was made of the right stuff."

In the same year that Bartlett resigned, Clement received an urgent call on his RCS radio to return to the Yard immediately. There he was issued with a service revolver and ten rounds of ammunition; Pigott had escaped from Wormwood Scrubs Prison, was believed to be in possession of a firearm and was swearing vengeance against Clement.

Pigott did not immediately appear, but the following year a detective constable from Brighton was investigating a long-firm fraud; he went to an office and asked the occupant if he would mind accompanying him to the police station to answer some questions. The man was affability itself, but when he got to the office door he remarked that he had forgotten something and went back to his desk. There was something about the man that put the young detective on his guard, and as Maxwell Thomas Pigott (who by now was understandably using an alias) reached inside a drawer, so the officer kicked it shut with Pigott's hand inside. The desk drawer proved to contain an automatic pistol, and at Lewes Assizes Pigott was sentenced to a total of six years' imprisonment. Following his release he started associating with East End hit-man Alfie Gerrard and one or two other notorious characters; then Pigott took a further step up the ladder of criminality.

*   *   *

In the meantime, Clement got on with his life and career. He visited a Harley Street eye specialist, Mr Marzetti Shaw, who told him that his left eye resembled 'the surface of the moon' – where the ammonia had burnt minute craters. Mr Shaw was a member of a family of advocates: his brother Erwin was a respected solicitor and his other brother a formidable judge. The ophthalmologist later told Clement that he had mentioned the case to his brother and had suggested that the imposition of more severe sentences in cases of this nature might be appropriate. Sadly, for the violent offenders who had the misfortune to appear before the hard-line Sir Sebag Shaw PC, this prophesy turned out to be only too true.

Another incident occurred at this time which stuck indelibly in Clement's memory. The Beatles had each been awarded the MBE in 1965. There were a number of people who thought that 'The Fab Four' should not have been honoured, since they believed them to be just a bunch of cocky, talentless youngsters. Such outraged citizens regarded the awards as a sop from a gutless government, and many recipients of similar awards returned their own medals, including a Second World War veteran who possessed a row of twelve. They were, of course, in the minority, because the vast majority of the country was in the grip of an adoring 'Beatlemania'. But in 1969, when John Lennon returned his medal with an accompanying, insolent note to the Queen stating that it was 'as a protest against Britain's involvement in the Nigerian-Biafra thing', the protesters who had been furious when the awards had been bestowed on the Beatles in the first place, became incandescent with rage; and Harry Clement was one of them. Striding out into the garden of his home, Clement threw his medal away into the darkness – it is possible that strong drink took a hand in this arbitrary decision – and stalked back into the house.

★   ★   ★

On 7 May 1970, David Knight – member of a notorious family of scoundrels, including club owner Ronnie Knight, who was then married to the actress Barbara Windsor – was stabbed to death in the Latin Quarter nightclub, Leicester Square, by the barman, Alfredo 'Eyetie Tony' (or 'Italian Tony') Zomparelli. Opinions differ as to why this confrontation came about; the Knight family claim that they went to the club to demand an explanation of why David had received a severe beating whilst drinking in the Angel, Islington. The opposing faction allege that the Knights were attempting to muscle in on the club, owned by the West End gangster Albert Dimes. But whatever the truth of the matter, David Knight was dead and Zomparelli escaped. Six months later he gave himself up, pleaded guilty to manslaughter and was sentenced to four years' imprisonment; but that was not enough for Ronnie Knight, who wanted revenge.

None of this yet had anything to do with either Harry Clement or Maxwell Thomas Pigott – who was now calling himself George Bradshaw. Circumstances, however, would shortly change.

★   ★   ★

Meanwhile, Clement was promoted to detective inspector, then detective chief inspector and was commended by the commissioner for the arrest of a gang of international drug traffickers and for courage in effecting the arrest of four men for conspiracy to rob. He was also awarded a certificate from the Society for the Protection of Life from Fire after he and his Flying Squad driver, Police Constable Gordon Reynolds, repeatedly entered a burning house and rescued two children aged three and four, who were trapped with their father on the first floor.

★   ★   ★

Released from prison, Zomparelli was murdered on 4 December 1974. He had been playing the pinball machine at the Golden Goose amusement arcade, Old Compton Street, when two men entered the premises and four .38 bullets were fired into the back of Zomparelli's head, killing him instantly. Naturally, the prime suspect was Ronnie Knight, who was arrested but released after he was found to be impressively alibied; and there, for the time being, the matter rested.

In 1977 Bradshaw – alias Pigott – was arrested for a series of robberies and for using a firearm with intent to resist arrest, and in February 1978 he was sentenced to ten years' imprisonment. However, a year into his sentence, Bradshaw decided to try to broker a deal by turning supergrass, and the bait that he offered was a tempting one. He was moved from the austerity of Wormwood Scrubs Prison to the relative comfort of Twickenham police station, where he commenced his lengthy de-brief. It was at this time that Harry Clement, now a detective superintendent, walked into the office of Detective Chief Superintendent Bob 'Tug' Wilson and glanced at a photograph on his desk. It depicted Pigott, and Wilson hastily snatched it up and slammed it face-down on the desk, saying Clement should not have seen who it was. Clement replied with some asperity that this was the man who had attacked him in 1965; telling him he was aware of that, Wilson swore him to silence because of what Bradshaw had had to say.

Bradshaw had named 105 criminals who had been involved in armed robberies, and in 74 separate statements under caution he had detailed other serious offences which he had committed; but the jewel in the crown was that he had participated in the murder of Alfredo Zomparelli. He alleged that Nicky Gerrard – son of the notorious Alfie – had been paid £1,000 for the killing by Ronnie Knight, and Bradshaw had earned £325 for keeping lookout. And if £1,000 seems a little miserly for a gangland hit, there were fringe benefits attached to the contract; it appeared that Nicky Gerrard had been having an adulterous affair with Zomparelli's wife (soon to become a widow), a former stripper named Rozanna.

Now, on 17 January 1980, Bradshaw appeared at the Old Bailey and pleaded guilty to the murder of Zomparelli. In addition, he pleaded guilty to arson at the Directors Club, Drummond Street, Camden, between 8 and 11 June 1976, robbing Michael North of £10,000 on 21 January 1976, robbing Edward Rootes of £25,000 on 9 June 1976 and shooting David Cahill with intent to cause him grievous bodily harm on 19 August 1974. He also asked for a further 107 offences to be taken into consideration.

Richard Du Cann QC for the prosecution told the court, "The assistance given by the defendant towards solving serious and organised crime can only be described as invaluable," but Mr Justice Comyn stated that the courts could not be bargaining places for informers. He remarked, "There can be no fixed tariff for informers – a tariff for a grass, a lower tariff for a plus-grass and a lower tariff still for a supergrass."

In sentencing him to life imprisonment for the murder, six years for the robberies, five years for the arson and four years for the shooting, all of which would run concurrently and concurrent to Bradshaw's existing ten-year sentence, Mr Justice Comyn told him: "Yours is a terrible and terrifying story of years of grave and wicked crime, often involving the use of firearms. You know you will be a marked man for the rest of your life." However, when Ronnie Knight and Nicky Gerrard were both acquitted of the murder, Bradshaw, who was said to have shot or injured fourteen people and had amassed a quarter of a million pounds during his criminal career, was viewed as an unreliable witness, and his desirability as a supergrass tempted his handlers no longer. Instead, he spent ten years in Wakefield prison on Rule 43 – or, as it is known in prison parlance, 'behind the door' – and following his release he slipped below the radar and vanished. His whereabouts to this day – save to a chosen few – are unknown.

* * *

With just under twenty-eight years' service, Clement retired as a detective chief superintendent. He moved a long way away from his native London and now immerses himself in charity work. And long after his retirement he received an unexpected present. One evening his wife handed him a small case; inside it was his missing British Empire Medal with the oak leaf for gallantry. Following his fit of pique all those years previously, his wife and daughter had searched the garden by torchlight until they found it and hid it away, until the most propitious time came to reunite it with its owner.

Three Tough Customers

When nineteen-year-old David William Barnard purchased a .38 Smith & Wesson revolver, together with six bullets, he was up and running for business. He already had a criminal record – two appearances before the Juvenile Courts and two convictions as an adult – and he was also suspected of housebreakings. But possession of a firearm meant that he had gone one step up in the criminal pecking order; he was about to enter the realms of armed robbery.

Dressed from head to toe in black, Barnard entered a moneylender's office, Morris Kent Ltd, Singer Street, Finsbury, on the morning of 16 September 1964; and when the manager, Stanley Tepper, refused to hand over cash without the necessary checks being made, Barnard fired one shot at almost point-blank range, grazing Tepper just below the hairline and causing blood to pour down his face. Fortunately, Tepper managed to escape out of the back of the premises, and following a police enquiry Barnard was found asleep in a council flat in Warwick Grove, Clapton. The revolver with four live rounds in it was under his pillow. He admitted the offence and also a housebreaking which he had committed following the abortive robbery. Two months later he appeared at the Old Bailey and pleaded guilty to assault with intent to rob, possessing a revolver with intent to endanger life, the housebreaking, and he asked for ten other cases of housebreaking to be taken into consideration. Barnard was sentenced to a total of twelve years' imprisonment, and the trial judge, Mr Justice Milmo, told him:

Judges have to harden their hearts when dealing with those, whether young or old, who carry guns. You are pathetically young but you are hardened in crime and are a thoroughly dangerous criminal. It is no fault of yours that you are not charged with capital murder. Society has to be protected against people like you.

The Court of Appeal (Criminal Division) later reduced the sentence to one of eight years' imprisonment, but a thoroughly dangerous member of society had at least been put away; that is, until 6 June 1966, when Barnard was one of four prisoners who escaped from Wormwood Scrubs. Three of them were soon recaptured, but Barnard stayed at liberty for five days. He was caught through a mixture of his stupidity and sheer bad luck. A car hired under an assumed name which had been used in a spate of housebreakings was discovered parked outside a basement flat in Green Lanes, Harringay. Barnard was in the basement flat, and that showed his stupidity. His bad luck was that he was about to be confronted by three very tough detectives.

★   ★   ★

Detective Sergeant Laurence Scott was tough by any standards; just one quarter of an inch under six feet tall, he was once described by his daughter as 'having no fear'. That was a complete understatement. Born in 1920, Scott had enlisted in the Army in 1940 and in 1942 had volunteered for the 21st Independent Parachute Regiment; with the rank of corporal, he had taken part in operations in Italy, Norway, Palestine and Holland – the latter in the ill-fated 'Operation Market Garden'. He fortunately avoided capture following intensive fighting and escaped across the Rhine to Nijmegen – fortunately, because Laurence Scott was known by his birth name, Laurence Solomon, and with his Jewish origins he was under no illusions as to his fate had he been captured. Scott was also aware of Hitler's infamous *Kommandobefehl* of 1942, in which he ordered that all allied troops on 'so-called commando missions in Europe' who were captured were to be 'slaughtered to the last man', adding ominously, 'It does not make any difference whether they are dropped by parachute'. Of the 10,000 men parachuted into Arnhem, fewer than 3,000 got out. Of those who were not killed in the fighting, 5,000, including 3,000 wounded, were taken into captivity. The fact that many of them survived may have been due to humane German officers disregarding Hitler's orders, or simply to a need for the German forces to conserve ammunition.

Joining the Metropolitan Police ten days after demobilisation, Scott – he changed his name by deed poll in 1950 – served on 'Y' Division as a uniformed police constable and an aid to CID, before appointment as detective constable took him to 'E' Division. He was promoted to the rank of detective sergeant (second class) and in August 1963 he received his third – and final

– posting to 'Y' Division. He had been commended on nine occasions, and now he settled into 'Y' Division's Wood Green police station. It was not then a detective inspector's station; Scott was in charge of the CID. He had married within one month of joining the police; now he had two children, a boy and a girl. Bob Robinson, then an aid to CID, remembered him as 'avuncular ... a pipe smoker', and Roy Medcalf concurs. "He was like a mother hen," Roy told me. "He looked after the troops and if ever there was any trouble he always took full responsibility."

Detective Sergeant Douglas Frank Albert Davies was another tough character; a wartime Royal Marine, he had also served at the Admiralty and after being demobilised in time for Christmas 1945 he joined the Metropolitan Police on New Year's Day, 1946. After twenty years of service, Davies had served on the Flying Squad and had accumulated twelve commendations, including awards for the arrest of fifteen men for conspiracy, larceny and receiving, two murders and the arrest of two youths who had caused malicious damage by the use of explosives. Now aged forty-two, Davies was married with two sons and, with his posting to 'Y' Division, was junior to Scott in service.

The wild card in the pack was Detective Sergeant Alexander Anthony Eist. Much the same height as Scott and Davies, Eist had joined the Merchant Navy at the age of sixteen one week after hostilities had ceased, and sailed the seas for three years before joining the Metropolitan Police in June 1948. He served in the East End of London on 'H' Division, where he spent ten years as a police constable, an aid to CID and a detective constable. He was brought to notice quickly; within a year of joining he was awarded a commissioner's commendation for 'devotion to duty while off duty and alertness in a case of receiving'. Coincidentally, his next two commendations were also for receiving. In 1958 he was posted to the first of three tours with the Flying Squad which would last a total of eight years. Eist was courageous – in 1950 he was awarded a bronze medal by the Royal Life Saving Society – and he was industrious, too. He had been commended in cases of assault with intent to rob, arson, riotous assembly, a case of conspiracy to rob, the arrest of four men for robbery and the arrest of three active lorry thieves. The latter type of offence appeared to be a speciality of Alec Eist's. Although he appeared to have very good sources of information as to when a lorry was going to be stolen, Eist seldom participated in the actual arrests. He would certainly prepare the application for the informant's reward after the arrests, but then, following a successful operation in respect of a stolen lorry where at least some of the consignment had been recovered and the arrested lorry driver was volubly protesting his innocence, Eist, always a loose cannon, would award himself some unofficial leave. This he would spend at Newmarket racecourse – until he absented himself once too often. His non-attendance was brought to the notice of Detective Superintendent Tommy Butler, the operational head of the Squad. Butler, a martinet who regularly worked a sixteen hour day and who castigated his officers if they dared to request a legitimate day off, would tolerate none of Eist's antics. He kicked him straight off the Squad and into Wood Green police station.

These were the three police officers whom David Barnard was going to threaten with a loaded rifle. He was making a big mistake.

★   ★   ★

At 2.30 on the afternoon of 11 June 1966, police officers were quietly surrounding the house in Green Lanes, purely because of the suspicious vehicle outside which had been linked to the housebreakings – nothing more. Davies went to the front door and spoke to a woman who answered his knock. Scott and Eist took up their positions at the sides of the house, and Scott, looking through the letter-box in the basement door, saw a man emerge from a room. As Scott called out that he was a police officer and that the man should open the door, the man returned to the room and then re-emerged, this time carrying a rifle, and ran across the passageway. Scott immediately kicked open the basement door, ran into the premises and through into the back garden. He was joined by Davies and Eist, who immediately recognised the man to be Barnard. They were fully aware that he was a highly dangerous, escaped prisoner; this was reinforced by the fact that Barnard was sitting on a wall at the end of the garden and pointing the rifle at them. Despite his warning the officers that he would shoot, they nevertheless advanced on him, whereupon Barnard jumped from the wall into the adjoining garden, which belonged to Wix House, an old people's home. He was pursued by Scott and Eist, with Davies attempting to cut off his retreat; as Barnard shouted, "I'll shoot if you come any nearer!" he jumped over another wall. Scott and Eist followed and now, picking up flower pots, they pelted Barnard with them. At the end of the garden Barnard once more threatened the officers, carefully raising the rifle to his shoulder and pointing it directly at Scott, who was the nearest. Without hesitation, Scott brought him to the ground with a rugby tackle, and during the furious struggle which followed, Eist and Davies joined in to disarm Barnard. The rifle in his possession had three .22 bullets in the magazine and one in the breech ready to fire. After the arrest Davies went back to search the suspect vehicle outside the premises, whereupon a caller to the house attacked him; during the ensuing struggle, both men fell eight feet into the basement area, and with the assistance of Detective Constable Bernard Whittaker and Police Constable Bernard Finch (both of whom were later commended by the commissioner) the man was overpowered and arrested. In addition, an eighteen-year-old girl at the house was arrested for possession of cannabis resin.

Barnard was committed for trial from Tottenham Magistrates' Court, where the Bench warmly congratulated the three officers on their courage, and on 21 July at the Middlesex Area Sessions Barnard pleaded guilty to possessing a firearm with intent to resist arrest and was sentenced to five years' imprisonment, consecutive to his present sentence. The Chairman, Mr Ewen Montague QC, praised the officers, telling the court:

> The officers exhibited a heroism which even in the glorious annals of the Metropolitan Police was really of an outstanding nature. To proceed towards this young man who had already been known to use a firearm was to exhibit courage of the very highest possible degree.

On 2 September 1966 the commissioner highly commended the officers, and on 7 October Scott, Eist and Davies were each awarded certificates and cheques for £20 by the Chief Metropolitan Magistrate, Sir Robert Blundell at Bow Street, to mark their 'outstanding courage and devotion to duty'. The following February, the *London Gazette* announced that Scott would be awarded the George Medal and Davies and Eist the British Empire Medal for Gallantry.

Scott received a congratulatory letter from the Home Secretary, Roy Jenkins, and a hand-written one from the commissioner, Sir Joseph Simpson; but following the ceremony at Buckingham Palace, Scott admitted that he felt embarrassed about the distinction between his award and the medals awarded to Eist and Davies. "I feel a bit upset about it," he told the *Daily Express*. "But it is a great honour – one which belongs to my division of Wood Green which has a lot of brave men in it, already." However, Davies disagreed. "Let's face it, we were all in a difficult spot," he said. "But it was Laurie Scott who went after the bloke in the first place and he stood just that much more chance of getting killed." And after that, it was back to work.

★ ★ ★

Just prior to the investiture at Buckingham Palace, Douglas Davies had been promoted to the rank of detective inspector and posted to nearby Holloway police station. He was awarded another commendation for his work in a case of manslaughter and armed robbery and later was posted to 'S' Division until promotion to detective chief inspector took him to Stoke Newington, where he spent the last two years of his service. Admired by Bob Robinson as being 'quiet and deep', Davies retired after almost thirty-two years' service.

★   ★   ★

Alec Eist was, to put it mildly, a controversial character. The stolen lorry-loads still appeared as if by magic; on one auspicious occasion he sent some aids to CID to arrest a man driving a lorry, only for them to be mightily surprised to discover that the lorry had not yet been stolen. A year after the announcement of his award he was promoted to detective sergeant (first class) and returned to the Flying Squad, which was now under the overall control of Tommy Butler, who, it can be imagined, kept a close eye on Eist's comings and, particularly, his goings. Opinions about him varied; one of his contemporaries described him as 'charismatic', another as being 'as bent as a corkscrew'.

Yet another described Eist as being 'a likeable rogue' and went on to say, "he used his charm and people skills to become a successful detective. Alec knew a lot of villains and they were people from whom he gained his information – and it was quality information." With regard to Eist's initial expulsion from the Flying Squad and his weakness for horseracing, he undeniably had some good winners – which would explain why he was invariably flush with money and why some of his colleagues felt that this must be a sign of corruption rather than legitimate income. But, as I was told, "Alec was recovering more than all of the Flying Squad put together and it was not long before he found his way back. If he had a bent side, I never saw it."

Reg Dudley, who was convicted of a double gangland killing (and who was later cleared on appeal), described himself as a fence and he would not have concurred with those sentiments. "I also had a close relationship with a bent detective, Alec Eist," he said. "My friends knew if they were in trouble, for a few grand, channelled through me, Alec would do what he could to make evidence 'disappear'."

When James Earl Ray was arrested in London (and later convicted of the murder in Tennessee of Dr Martin Luther King Jr) it was Alec Eist who spent some time with him in the cells at Cannon Row police station, a session which produced a rather surprising confession, which became the subject of some heated speculation at the House Assassinations Committee in November 1978. It was later alleged by Ray's attorney that the committee had allowed perjured testimony from Eist without permitting him time to investigate it; and in a breathtaking piece of inadmissible evidence he informed the committee that he had received a telephone call from a London barrister who told him that Eist 'had been fired from Scotland Yard after being charged with theft and perjury and was later found guilty of corruption'. Hopefully the committee did not accept this outburst as evidence, because it was not true.

What was certainly true was that Eist's astonishing, roller-coaster career continued after his *tête-à-tête* with James Earl Ray; promoted to detective inspector, he was posted to 'D' Division and then in June 1972 was attached to the Regional Crime Squad, where he assisted in investigating the Wembley Bank Robbery, which unearthed Bertie Smalls, the first supergrass, and also caused fresh controversy when £25,000 from a criminal's safety deposit box went missing. However, Eist was commended by the commissioner, the Director of Public Prosecutions and the trial judge at the Old Bailey for his 'outstanding diligence and detective ability' in the case, and with that came promotion to detective chief inspector and a posting back to the Flying Squad. But time was running out for Eist; this posting lasted a bare nine months before he was transferred to Holloway. The Holloway posting was even shorter – seven months – before he was sent to 'J' Division. Eist, several other officers and a solicitor were arrested and stood trial for allegedly arranging alibis for two London thieves. However, Eist was acquitted and was awarded costs, so James Earl Ray's attorney's friendly London barrister got that wrong, as he did when he stated that Eist was sacked. However, Eist was returned to uniform and given a job as officer investigating collisions involving police vehicles. How are the mighty fallen! He lasted there less than three months before he was given an ill-health pension, suffering from a disease involving obstruction of the airways and from depression.

It was a poor ending for the detective whom many thought to be the finest middleman when it came to negotiating with criminals. He took a pub at Six Mile Bottom in Hertfordshire and died of a heart attack on 27 January 1982. "Did you hear that Alec Eist died?" I asked a police colleague, the day following his demise. "Alec? He ain't dead," was the contemptuous reply. "He's middling in limbo!"

But saint or sinner, adored or reviled, Alec Eist was undeniably a brave man. And when, twenty years after his death, his medals were auctioned at the Dix Noonan Webb auction house, Piccadilly; they sold for £1,200, four times the estimated price.

*   *   *

If there were mixed views regarding Alec Eist, none existed about Laurence Scott. He was deeply admired, not only for his gallantry but for his man-management skills. He made one unsuccessful attempt to pass the examination for inspector and after that he remained a detective sergeant (second class) – widely known in the vernacular as 'a second-hand'. His favourite retort was, "I'm the oldest second-hand sergeant in the Met," and at the time when the rank was going to be abolished, he sent a birthday card to the commissioner, Sir Robert Mark, saying, "Don't forget the second-hand sergeants!"

He duly received a telephone call from the commissioner's staff officer, who demanded to know, "How did you know it was the commissioner's birthday?"

"Because I'm a detective," blandly replied Scott, but obviously the commissioner caused a little detective work to be carried out, because he discovered that he and Scott shared the same birthday. On their combined birthday in 1974 Mark sent the following note:

> Thank you for your very kind good wishes on our joint birthday. They are warmly reciprocated. I don't forget the devoted and proficient second class (not second hand!) CID Sergeants in division, or indeed, any members of the Force in the front line and I am always open to suggestions of how their lot can be improved.

"He was a character, a clown," recalls Roy Medcalf. "The plan drawer at Wood Green had a Lagonda; Laurie used to get him to drive it down Wood Green High Road, with Laurie standing on the running board!"

Bob Fenton QGM, as a new detective constable, remembers Scott fondly. He had compiled a 'Soup Report' – outlining the facts of a case where a defendant had been committed to the Crown Court for sentence. Scott read the report. "And he thought it so good," recalls Fenton, "that he told me he was going to award it a Green Shield Stamp. He did; he stuck it on the report and sent it off!"

Det. Supt. Arthur Askew KPM
in 1934

The arrest of Frederick Westbrook

DDI Bob Higgins and others, following
Westbrook's arrest

DC Edward Snitch GM

PC George Dorsett GM & Bar

DS William Deans KPFSM

PCs John McCallum GM, Owen Ashwin GM & Ivan King GM

PC George Sinclair GM

L–R: Gwen Bocking, Steven Bocking, PC Geoff Bocking GM & Mrs. Bocking's mother, Olive Warby

WPC Kathleen Parrott GM & WPS Ethel Bush GM, in 1955

Ethel Bush in 2010

Kathleen Parrott aged 93

Henry Stevens GC,
aged 80

Stevens' medals

WPC Margaret Cleland GM – rooftop rescue

Margaret Cleland on the rooftop

Margaret Jackson née Cleland – September 2010

PC John Barrett BEM, receiving his award from Earl Alexander of Tunis

DS Harry Clement BEM, receiving his award from Earl Alexander of Tunis

L-R: DSs Laurence Scott GM, Alec Eist BEM & Douglas Davies BEM

Laurence Scott at the Arnhem reunion, 2004

Laurence Scott's medals

Terry McFall GM (left),
Anthony Gledhill GC

'Papa One' – driveable no longer

L-R: DC Phillip Williams GM,
DS Raymond Adams BEM,
DC Reginald Jenkins BEM

Phillip Williams congratulated by the Commissioner, Sir John Waldron KCVO

L-R: PC Keith Giles BEM, SPS Arthur Garner GM, the commissioner & PS Brian Parsons BEM

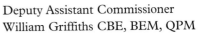
Deputy Assistant Commissioner
William Griffiths CBE, BEM, QPM

PC Rodney Phillips BEM in 1970

TDC William Griffiths in 1970

Ernie Pawley GM, talking to Her Majesty, The Queen Mother

L-R: Alexander Callender QGM, PC Michael Hills GM, James Beaton GC, CVO, Ronald Russell GM, Glenmore Martin Queen's Commendation for Brave Conduct, TDC Peter Edmonds QGM & Brian McConnell QGM

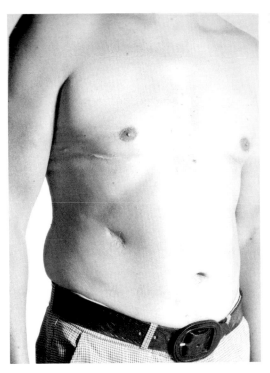

Pawley's bullet wound – taken 1979

Derek Hall QGM,
October 2010

King's Police Medal

Queen's Police Medal

George Cross

George Medal

Queen's Gallantry Medal

British Empire Medal
for Gallantry

"I was on a Noddy patrol* in Wood Green and I arrested several youths in a Mini who were armed with knives and on their way to commit a robbery in Tottenham," recalled former Police Constable Derek Bradley. "Laurie took over the investigation and got me a commendation at the Crown Court. I always found Laurie one of the nicest people you could wish to meet and always willing to help us young PCs."

Scott retired on 25 October 1976, having served thirty years and forty days; but his service to the public did not end there. He immediately took up a position as a civilian CID clerk, sadly a now defunct post. For the next eight and a half years, the CID office at Wood Green ran like clockwork with Scott at the helm as a type of super-office manager. But eventually this came to an end when Scott reached the age of sixty-five and retired. At his leaving party he said, "It is much more difficult today than when I was a young CID officer. There are so many stresses and it is difficult enough as it is." He had been a keen fund-raiser for the Hornsey Handicapped Centre and was the founder member of the 21st Independent Parachute Company Club.

He retired to East Barnet with his wife Peggy (who sadly predeceased him in October 2007), but whenever possible he attended the annual Arnhem reunion in Holland. In 2004, the sixtieth anniversary of the battle, the Scott family duly attended and thoroughly enjoyed the celebrations. As they got off the coach at Victoria, Bob Robinson, who in retirement had become a London taxi driver, heard a woman call out, "Can you help my father, please?" He got out of his cab to assist an old veteran wearing a distinctive red beret and suddenly exclaimed, "If it isn't my old detective sergeant, Laurie Scott!"

Scott died peacefully on 31 August 2010. The funeral service, held at New Southgate Crematorium on 9 September, was heavily attended. Delivering the eulogy, Bob Robinson looked at the coffin and, referring to the taxi-ride home six years previously, remarked, "I kept the fare and tip you gave me – sorry!" There is no doubt that the intrepid Laurie Scott would have appreciated those sentiments!

---

* A Noddy was a lightweight Velocette motorcycle, so called because riders on patrol were unable to salute inspectors and above but were required to acknowledge their presence by nodding to them.

CHAPTER 15

Officers Under Fire

S omewhere in England there is a man who is now approaching state retirement age. To his friends and family there is no mystery about his identity, but I simply do not know his name; nor did many people when, as a fourteen-year-old schoolboy, he stepped into the witness box at the Old Bailey on 30 January 1967. He was referred to simply as Master 'A', his address was not disclosed and what he had to say, which he delivered with great composure, prompted the trial judge, Mr Justice Hinchcliffe, to remark later, "Master 'A' seemed to me to be a bright boy, full of good sense. And as a result of his action, what might have been a serious robbery did not take place." He later awarded him £15, a sum well worth having, when one considers that it was then the equivalent of the weekly starting wage for a police constable under the age of twenty-two.

Master 'A' had been with his father, who was working in a building at Creekside, London SE8, during the early afternoon of Thursday, 25 August 1966. Looking out of the first-floor window, he saw parked in the street below a two-tone (grey and blue) Wolseley saloon – the registration number was 567 BJD. Sitting inside the vehicle he saw three men – a driver, a front-seat passenger and a third man sitting in the rear of the car. The boy idly watched them but was then bemused when the front-seat passenger started to struggle into a suit of overalls. To the boy's concern, he then saw the man produce a shotgun and finally a cosh; holding it in one hand, he started to smack it into the palm of his other hand, as though testing it for effectiveness. It also appeared that he was about to pull a mask over his face. The boy told his father, who immediately telephoned the police.

Master 'A' then ran downstairs and out into the street as a police car drew up in response to the 999 call, and he told the officers that the car had just driven off towards the junction with Creek Road. This was the start of a terrifying car chase, covering seven miles and lasting sixteen minutes. Shots would be repeatedly fired by a group of desperate and thoroughly professional criminals at two very resolute, unarmed police officers, who stared death in the face. This is what happened.

★   ★   ★

The crew of area car, call sign 'Papa One', drove out of Lewisham police station at seven o'clock that morning on routine patrol. They would drive through the areas of Lewisham, Brockley and Deptford contained in that sector of 'P' Division, on the alert for sightings of crime and ready to provide a fast response to any emergency calls received from Scotland Yard's Information Room – or 'MP' as it was referred to during radio transmissions. The driver, Police Constable 196 'P' Anthony John Gledhill, eased the area car out into Ladywell Road; the vehicle he was driving was a Wolseley 6/110, with a powerful 3-litre engine, capable of a maximum speed of 102 mph. The car could accelerate from 0–60 mph in 13.3 seconds, which was respectable enough, given that it was fitted with a Borg-Warner automatic gearbox; this model was much loved by advanced police drivers because of its comfort, dependability and handling.

Gledhill had joined the Metropolitan Police in 1957, straight from the ranks of the police cadets, and was posted to Lee Road police station. Within six months he was married; twelve months later he had been awarded his first commendation, for keenness and persistence in effecting the arrest of three housebreakers. In August 1964 he received a second commendation, this time for alertness and valuable assistance in a case of murder, and five months after that he qualified as a Class III driver at Hendon Driving School. Now aged twenty-nine, just over five feet nine and stockily built, Gledhill was as keen as mustard.

The RT – or radio-operator – was Police Constable 784 'P' Terence Frederick McFall, and he too had been a police cadet before joining the Royal Military Police. After three years service in Germany, he had joined the Metropolitan Police a year after Gledhill; he was also married and, like Gledhill, had two children, a boy and a girl. The same age as each other, the two men had been firm friends since Gledhill had transferred to Lewisham from Lee Road police station some eighteen months earlier. They had crewed 'Papa One' on a regular basis and had carried out some impressive arrests.

The third member of the crew was Police Constable George Webb. Whilst Gledhill and McFall were in full uniform, Webb (himself a uniform officer) was the plain clothes observer. In the event of suspicious activity being reported to the car, the observer could be dropped off to carry out unobtrusive observations and make arrests. And that was Webb's intention on this particular day; a theft suspect who had been dismissed from his employment at a factory in Creekside was due to return at 1.30 that afternoon to draw his wages. Webb asked to be dropped off at the factory beforehand so that he could wait for the suspect, make the arrest and then call for the area car to transport them to the police station. Just then, there was an RT call for all cars to be on the lookout for a lorry, the driver of which was thought to be armed, in the immediate vicinity of 'Papa One'. Webb was dropped off at the factory, and McFall jokingly remarked to him, "That's right, George, you stay here and we'll go and get shot at." Not to be outdone, Webb laughed: "Just my luck; I bet you'll get some action now." And with that, the crew drove off and scoured the area for the lorry – which was never found and was, in any event, unconnected with the events that would shortly follow. It was while the crew of 'Papa One' were waiting for Webb's call that they received the RT call to the suspect Wolseley in Creekside. They were unaware of it at the time, but the very factory where Gledhill and McFall had dropped off their colleague was to be the target of an armed robbery as the wages arrived.

Following the conversation with Master 'A' – the boy also mentioned that whilst he was watching the men he had heard a bang and seen blue smoke rising from the Wolseley, which suggested (incorrectly, as it transpired) that the shotgun had been discharged – Gledhill drove off towards Creek Road; but as he reached the junction the suspect vehicle turned into Creekside, so suddenly that it almost struck the Area Car. In fact, five men were in the car. The driver was William Henry Cooper, aged thirty-six. Wearing a brown trilby and glasses, Cooper had commenced his criminal career in 1946 and had thirteen previous convictions, including offences of larceny, assault, occasioning actual bodily harm and malicious damage. He had had previous dealings with the Flying Squad and exactly five months previously had failed to appear at Old Street Magistrates' Court in respect of two cases of assault on the police, so he was now currently circulated as being wanted. Next to him in the front passenger seat was John Roger McVicar, also circulated as being wanted; in his case for escaping from Wakefield Prison precisely four months earlier where he was serving an eight-year sentence for robbery. With five previous convictions dating back ten years, McVicar was rightly considered to be extremely violent and highly dangerous.

Three men were in the rear passenger seats; sitting behind McVicar was William Gentry, aged thirty-four, a criminal with fourteen previous convictions, and next to him was Frederick James Davies, aged thirty-three and with ten previous convictions. On the offside behind the driver was another man, who escaped arrest.

Shoving the quadrant into reverse, Gledhill quickly backed the car into a side street, then roared off in pursuit of the Wolseley, whilst McFall depressed the transmission button on the RT microphone and sent the first of many messages: "MP from 'Papa One' – Urgent message. We are chasing suspect car 567 BJD. It's well loaded, and going like the clappers along Creekside."

With the headlights full on, blue light flashing and the two-tone horns blaring, the Area Car tore into Deptford Church Street, its speed reaching 50 mph, and then right into Giffin Street. A light shower had made the road surface slippery, and both pursuer and pursued bounced off the kerb as they turned the corner. Across the busy junction with Deptford High Street they sped, along Douglas Way and then right into Amersham Vale. As they roared past the police station, Gentry leaned out of the rear window of the Wolseley and fired two shots from a Bayard 7.65 mm automatic handgun. "God, they're firing at us!" gasped Gledhill, and his words were heard across the airwaves in Information Room. Both bullets missed the pursuing police car by a fraction, one striking the back of a private car parked outside the police station.

The Wolseley turned left into Edward Street and Gentry fired again; once more the shot missed, and as McFall wryly told me, over forty years after the event, "Tony and I were now slouched low in our seats which could easily give the impression to those seeing us that the Met had drastically lowered the height restrictions!"

Not that there was anything remotely amusing about the situation at the time, especially when almost immediately after Gentry's shot he ducked back into the car to provide space for McVicar, who now leant almost all his upper body out of the front passenger window, raised a sawn-off shotgun and, taking careful aim, fired. The shot hit the windscreen of the police car but it stayed intact. As the Wolseley approached the junction with Sandford Street, it swerved right into Woodpecker Road and Gentry fired two more shots; later, passers-by discovered two spent 7.65 mm cartridge cases on the pavement. At Scawen Road, McVicar again took careful aim and fired the shotgun, the shot once more rattling against the Area Car's windscreen, and this was followed by Gentry and the other man on the offside of the Wolseley firing shots from their pistols, both of which missed. As the Wolseley tore into Evelyn Street, McVicar fired again, the shotgun pellets again hitting the windscreen and peppering the bonnet. The gunmen's car roared into Lower Street towards Surrey Docks, and both back seat passengers, nearside and offside, fired a total of three shots; one hit the windscreen, and then the Wolseley swerved left into Gomm Road, which led to Southwark Park. As they drove through the park gates, the Wolseley followed a sharp right-hand bend and vanished from sight; but just before it did so, Gledhill saw the vehicle's brake lights flash and on an impulse brought the Area Car to a halt. To the left, the park with mothers and children; to the right, St Olave's Hospital. Had the Wolseley stopped perhaps to carry out an ambush, to get the officers in range of the guns? Gledhill inched the car forward, in time to see the Wolseley roar away. With what was soon to occur, it appeared his suspicions were well founded. The two cars ran on into Southwark Park Road, and as the Wolseley turned into Jamaica Road Gentry fired again and missed, and at Major Road the offside passenger also fired at the pursuing police car. "Get someone with guns down here, for God's sake!" said McFall, who had been giving a street-by-street commentary to Information Room. The two cars now thundered south along Drummond Road, a long stretch of carriageway, until a lorry drove across the junction with Southwark Park Road. The Wolseley braked and Gledhill saw smoke billowing from its tyres and brake-drums, but it was too late; the gunmen's car was travelling too fast, it smashed into the lorry and that was the end of the pursuit. Fourteen shots had been fired at the Area Car, and Gledhill had reached speeds of 80 mph in pursuit of the Wolseley, which had often travelled on the wrong side of the road and against one-way traffic systems. It was only slightly amazing that no one – police, pedestrians or other road users – had been killed or seriously injured. However, it was by no means the conclusion of the drama; this only represented the end of round one.

★   ★   ★

The four doors of the Wolseley were flung open, the five men leapt out and McVicar, his sawn-off shotgun held at waist height, advanced menacingly towards the police car; Gledhill slipped the car into reverse and slowly backed away. McVicar then stopped, turned and ran back to the other men, who split up – McVicar and Davis headed for the bridge under the railway line between London Bridge and South Bermondsey, whilst Gentry and the other two men ran off into Raymouth Road, where there were a number of businesses underneath the railway arches. The officers cautiously followed the men – Gentry, they could see, was still holding a pistol – and then suddenly the men darted into a yard used by Gosnell Brothers, a transport company. Neither Gledhill nor McFall knew this area, and it was quite likely that the men had found an escape route through the premises into the vicinity of Galleywall Road, which was the area towards which McVicar and Davis had run.

'Papa One' drove slowly into the yard, but this was the moment the gunmen had been waiting for. They leapt out, led by Gentry, his face covered in blood as a result of the crash, who pushed his pistol through Gledhill's open window, pressed it against his temple and shouted, "Get out, else you've had your fucking lot!"

★   ★   ★

In the meantime, the crew of Area Car 'Mike Four' were about to be treated to the business end of McVicar's sawn-off shotgun. They had arrived at the head of Galleywall Road in time to see McVicar and Davis running towards them. Pointing the sawn-off at Police Constable 515 'M' Bill Williams' face, McVicar screamed, "Do you want some of this?" Without waiting for an answer, McVicar then ran off, and Williams and Police Sergeant 66 'M' Paul Officer grabbed hold of McVicar's companion, Davis. "Got one outside Shuttleworth Biscuits and Spar," 'Mike Four' almost casually informed Information Room. A sawn-off shotgun was later found in nearby Anchor Street, with one used and three live cartridges, together with discarded overalls and driving gloves, and police units were homing in on the fleeing McVicar on the railway lines. But McVicar was not caught; not that day.

★   ★   ★

Slowly, their hands raised, Gledhill and McFall got out of the Area Car. Gentry still had the pistol aimed at Gledhill's head at point-blank range, then Cooper and his companion ran off into Raymouth Road, back in the direction from which they had come. "I've got their fucking motor!" screamed Gentry to them, but either the two running men had had quite enough of driving Wolseleys for one day, or – and this is a possibility – they believed that police officers were about to be murdered in cold blood and wanted to disassociate themselves from the act by being as far away from the scene as possible.

Once he was in the driver's seat of 'Papa One', it was obvious that Gentry was unused to driving a car with an automatic transmission; he experienced the utmost difficulty in putting the police car into reverse; in addition, he was staring fixedly at Gledhill and still pointing the pistol at him through the open window. But eventually he did find reverse and the car lurched backwards; now Gentry would experience the same difficulty in putting the car into 'drive'.

Meanwhile, it was clear to McFall that if Gentry was going to escape in the sequestrated police car, he would be driving south along Raymouth Road. Out of view of Gentry, who was concentrating his attention on keeping Gledhill at bay and putting the police car into 'drive', McFall ran towards a lorry further down the thoroughfare which had stopped to make a delivery at one of the businesses in the arches. His intention was to get the lorry driver to block the road with his vehicle to stop Gentry escaping, before he returned to assist his comrade.

Gledhill, meanwhile, was anxiously looking back down the road, towards the junction with Southwark Park Road – where were the police vehicles carrying firearms who had declared over the radio that they were on their way? Thirteen days previously, the three-man crew of 'F' Division's 'Q' Car, 'Foxtrot One-one' had been murdered in cold blood by three gunmen. Two of the 'Q' Car murderers had been caught but the third member, Harry Maurice Roberts, was still at large. The armed units on their way to 'Papa One' were local officers, many of whom were barely trained in the use of their .38 Webley & Scott pistols – and similar officers were also hunting Harry Roberts who, thanks to guerrilla skills learnt with the British Army in Malaya, was currently on the run and would remain so until two months later when he crawled out of his hideout in Thorley Wood, Hertfordshire, begging police officers not to shoot.

However, the murders had prompted the commissioner, Sir Joseph Simpson KBE, to demand that the Force be issued with up-to-date weaponry and that officers be properly trained in its use. A training course for a dedicated firearms unit would be set up in January 1967; but that day had not yet arrived, and neither had the 7th Cavalry-style rescue for which the crew of 'Papa One' had been praying.

And now, frustrated by his inability to put the automatic transmission into 'drive', Gentry (still pointing his pistol at Gledhill) made a fatal mistake. He turned his head to look at the quadrant to see why the car was not moving forward – he had neglected to pull the lever into the position marked 'D', but now he did so. At that moment, Gledhill realized he would never again have a better opportunity; he dived forward through the open window and grabbed hold of Gentry's right wrist – his gun hand – in a grip which he hoped would never be broken. "Terry, help, help!" he shouted, and McFall heard him – he raced back to the car which, now in gear, shot forward, dragging Gledhill with it. Still he would not relinquish his grip on Gentry's wrist, and the car accelerated towards McFall, who drew his truncheon with the intention of smashing the windscreen, somehow forcing the car to stop. Suddenly there was a tremendous 'bang!' – possibly due to the stresses which 'Papa One' had been subjected to – and the front offside tyre burst; this amazing and unexpected sight was actually witnessed by McFall. The sudden loss of stability caused the Area Car to career across the road out of control, and the front offside wing crashed into some parked cars. The impact caused Gledhill to fall to the roadway, his left hand cut and bleeding, and 'Papa One' ran head-on into a truck parked outside Macquire and Murray's builder's yard. By now McFall had wrenched open the front passenger door, launched his six feet one-and-a-half inches into the car and delivered the first of many blows with his truncheon on any area of Gentry's body which made itself available; Gledhill got up from the roadway and ran to the driver's door but Gentry thrust it open, once more knocking Gledhill to the ground. Jumping from the car, Gentry fled into the builders' yard, pursued by the two officers, and looked around wildly for an avenue of escape. Sadly for him, there was none, and now poor, frightened Gentry, who only minutes before had been heroically pumping bullets at two unarmed police officers, pointed the gun at the same two advancing officers and screamed, "I'll kill you bastards if you move!" But they did move; and Gentry fired. The bullet passed between the two officers; Gledhill felt the wind of it pass before it smacked into the wall of a block of flats behind him. Then Gentry pulled the trigger again; this time there was nothing but a click. With that, both officers launched themselves at Gentry, Gledhill hanging on to his gun arm and McFall thrashing him with his truncheon. Gledhill wrenched the pistol from Gentry's grasp and hit him with it so hard that the butt shattered. On his way to the ground, Gentry vainly attempted to reach into the pocket of his overalls containing his Bayard 7.65 mm automatic, which fortuitously was later found to be empty. The weapon which Gledhill had seized was a Harrington & Richardson .32 revolver; three of the bullets were spent. Gentry had been battered into unconsciousness, and as the kneeling police officers gasped for breath they noticed that they had been joined by an elderly workman. Standing over Gentry's prostrate body and holding a length of twelve-inch metal stench pipe aloft, he calmly remarked, "Don't worry mate, if 'e moves, I'll drop this on 'im."

★   ★   ★

Assistance now arrived, and since Gentry no longer represented a threat, McFall became concerned for his wellbeing; he dressed the injuries on Gentry's head with a bandage from the first-aid box which was later replaced with a plaster by the ambulance crew who conveyed them all to Guys Hospital for treatment. Gentry – bearing in mind that three of the gunmen were still at large – received his treatment under the supervision of armed police officers. En route, they saw the wreckage of another area car, 'Mike One', which had crashed at speed in an effort to come to their assistance. A number of police cars experienced similar incidents, but this was not the only reason for other police vehicles failing to reach them; some were anticipating the escape routes which would be taken and were setting up roadblocks, whereas the gunmen were virtually driving around in circles in the vicinity of Southwark Park Road in an effort to throw off their pursuers.

After receiving treatment in hospital the officers were taken to Tower Bridge police station, where an incident room was in the process of being set up under the supervision of Detective Superintendent Charles Moynihan. The great and the good came to offer their congratulations; the Assistant Commissioner (Crime) Peter Brodie OBE, QPM warmly thanked two of 'his chaps' (as he liked to refer to his men), as did Area CID Commander Bob Acott DFC, a veteran detective and former Flying Squad officer.

And after a long talk and a few drinks, it was time for Gledhill and McFall to go home. After the euphoria of emerging from such a fraught situation, battered and bruised but still alive, the congratulations of their colleagues ringing in their ears, it was a time for sober reflection. It had been less than two weeks since the murder of the crew of 'Foxtrot One-one'; it was a matter on every police officer's mind, none more so than Tony Gledhill's and Terry McFall's. They, too, had stared death in the face and, perhaps by divine intervention, had survived.

Since the abolition of the death penalty a few years previously, robbers knew they had little to lose. The penalty now for murder – life imprisonment – was the same as the penalty for robbery. Whereas coshes, ammonia sprays and pickaxe helves had been the staple impedimenta for robbery – as had jam, smeared on brown paper, to be smacked into the victim's face – firearms were now the order of the day. What did it matter if a victim or police officer was murdered? Even if you were arrested, there was no death penalty involved – and escape was always an option. McVicar had already proved that, and he would do so again.

Although Gledhill and McFall had exhibited great gallantry, both would admit to being thoroughly frightened by their experience – and there is no better example of a brave man than one who will acknowledge that. But for both men now it would be a sleepless night, the first of many in which they fearfully awaited the early hours of the morning and the certain arrival of the demons of memory.

* * *

On the following day, 26 August, Gledhill and McFall were picked up by police car and driven to Tower Bridge police station, where they would work for the next two weeks and where the investigation was already underway. As they entered the incident room, there was the buzz of conversation, the click of typewriters and ringing of telephones. Everyone was going all-out to identify and track down the three remaining gunmen, witnesses were being traced and interviewed, exhibits were collected and the various scenes of crime were being forensically examined and photographed.

It had initially – and reasonably – been thought that the bang heard by 'Master A' and the blue smoke seen coming from the Wolseley in Creekside had been as a result of McVicar's shotgun being fired. This was not the case; a spent 7.65 mm cartridge case was found in the roadway where the car had been parked. And apart from 'Papa One's' windscreen and bonnet being peppered with shot from McVicar's shotgun, one shotgun pellet was found, lodged in the radiator grille.

Less than three weeks later, the first arrest of the three wanted men was achieved; but it was not due to the investigation team. The Flying Squad had a tip-off that on the morning of 15 September a robbery was going to occur somewhere south of the Thames, with a security van as the target. A committed robber named Tony Baldesarre was going to be involved, and his flat at Nine Elms was put under observation. In mid-morning there was a report that a security van had been attacked by armed men in nearby Mitcham but that the gunmen had fled without stealing the money. The Squad headed for Nine Elms, to be told by the watchers that their target and three men had entered the flat. Shortly after the Squad arrived, three of the men left the flat and headed for the lift. As the lift doors opened on the ground floor, the unarmed Flying Squad officers were confronted by the men, one of whom was John McVicar.

The three men were arrested, but McVicar attacked the officers holding him and broke free. However, as Detective

Sergeant Dave Dixon told me, "McVicar reckoned without one of the officers, who had represented Britain as a sprinter in the Commonwealth Games." This officer easily caught him, and Detective Sergeant Nicky Birch quite easily subdued him. A search of the flat revealed both the existence of an impressive amount of firearms and ammunition and the presence of Tony Baldesarre, who unsuccessfully tried to convince the Squad officers that he had been home all morning.

On 22 September Gentry and Davis were committed for trial to the Old Bailey from Marylebone Magistrates' Court, and the chairman of the bench, Mr W.B. Frampton, complimented both Gledhill and McFall, saying, "I would like to add my own commendation to both these officers for their bravery."

On 7 October Gledhill, McFall and other witnesses positively identified McVicar on an identification parade at Wandsworth Prison as being the front seat passenger with the shotgun in the Wolseley.

In the meantime, the officers working from Tower Bridge police station had, through the use of information received, discovered that at a certain time, on a certain day, William Henry Cooper would be arriving at a North London school to pick up his child. "The psychology was that he wouldn't be in possession of a gun when he went to meet the child," I was told by William Hucklesby, then an acting detective inspector, and this proved to be the case. Cooper gave up without a struggle. On 24 November he was positively identified by three witnesses as being the driver of the Wolseley.

★　★　★

Number One court at the Old Bailey was packed on the morning of 30 January 1967. In the dock sat the four defendants, in the well of the court was an array of bewigged barristers and their instructing solicitors, and presiding was the trial judge, Mr Justice Hinchcliffe. To the charges of attempting to murder the crew of 'Papa One', using firearms with intent to endanger life, conspiracy to rob and miscellaneous firearms offences, the four prisoners pleaded not guilty, and the trial commenced.

The courtroom was hushed when the two officers gave their dramatic account of the chase and identified the various weapons used. Then it was the turn of the defence. McVicar and Cooper denied being involved in any way whatsoever with the offences; Davis presented a somewhat pathetic excuse as to how he came to be arrested; but Gentry's defence was nothing less than breathtaking. On the morning of the arrests, he said, as he was about to commence a gardening job – this explained why he was wearing overalls – he was bundled into a car and kidnapped by four men whom he knew (although not their names or addresses) to whom he owed money. When the men produced masks and firearms, Gentry was naturally horrified and told his captors of his concerns, but his trepidation was cruelly ignored. Just then, the police chase commenced and several of the men discharged firearms at the police; when one ran out of ammunition, he handed the pistol to Gentry and told him to put it in his pocket, which he did. After the Wolseley crashed, Gentry panicked and ran off with two of the men, one of whom thoughtfully passed him a revolver, which he accepted. Gentry now realized that if he was caught the police would unkindly accuse him of being involved, and therefore he attempted to take the police car in order to escape. The shot fired at the two officers in the builder's yard? Naturally, the gun went off accidentally, said Gentry.

After a two-week trial all the men were found not guilty of attempting to murder the two officers, but then, despite the most compelling evidence, criminals are so seldom convicted of that particular offence. Instead, they were found guilty of possessing firearms with intent to endanger life, conspiracy to rob and firearms offences.

Before passing sentence, Mr Justice Hinchcliffe addressed the prisoners as follows:

> Those who fire shots at the police, or make use of loaded firearms when police are in the course of their duty, or seeking to make an arrest, cannot expect mercy. Sentences must be passed which will punish, and which will deter others who may be minded to commit similar offences. All of you have criminal records, but the offences of which you have been convicted are much more serious than any you have committed hitherto. I have no doubt of the risk you ran when you decided to make use of firearms to commit a robbery and/or to resist or prevent your lawful apprehension.

He then sentenced Gentry to a total of seventeen years' imprisonment, McVicar to a total of fifteen years' imprisonment and Cooper and Davis each to a total of thirteen years' imprisonment.

Calling the two officers before him, the trial judge told them:

I think your conduct in dealing with these armed bandits is beyond praise. Both of you displayed courage of a high order, and you carried out your difficult duties in a way that has earned you the respect and admiration of all right-thinking persons. I commend you both and I direct that this commendation be sent to the appropriate authority.

The case later went to the Court of Appeal (Criminal Division). In dismissing the appeal, the Law Lords also commended McFall and Gledhill. A few months later, McVicar appeared at court in respect of the attempted robbery of the security vehicle, the offence for which he had been arrested by the Flying Squad; he was sentenced to eight years' imprisonment, consecutive to his previous sentence, a total of twenty-three years.

Prior to the trial, both McFall and Gledhill applied to join the CID as temporary detective constables; they were accepted and both remained on 'P' Division. On 10 March 1967 (coincidentally, Gledhill's birthday) both officers attended Bow Street Magistrates' Court, where the Chief Metropolitan Magistrate, Sir Robert Blundell, presented each of them with a certificate and a cheque for £20, saying:

The learned Justice's comment was sent to the Commissioner of Police and in due course has reached this court where it was considered by myself and my colleagues and we decided without hesitation that indeed, this was a case of quite exceptional courage.

On 28 April 1967 *Police Orders* recorded that both officers had been highly commended by the commissioner for 'outstanding courage and devotion to duty whereby they sustained personal injury', together with Sergeant Officer and PC Williams, the crew of 'Mike Four'. In addition, six members of the investigating team at Tower Bridge were commended by the commissioner for 'determination and detective ability'. One month later it was announced in the *London Gazette* that Gledhill would be awarded the George Cross and McFall the George Medal.

Both officers were accompanied to the investiture at Buckingham Palace by their wives and children. McFall's son Andrew was aged three and his daughter Jacqueline, five. Now Mrs Jacqueline Ashley-Collins, she recalls, "I remember my lovely little sky blue outfit and my lacy socks ... I remember Buckingham Palace and the long corridors with red carpet ... I remember Andrew wanting to go to the toilet and the Queen in a lilac satin dress."

Gledhill's son Stewart was five and his daughter Rachel three; they noted with delight at the end of the ceremony the appearance of a Yeoman Bed Hanger (a member of the Queen's bodyguard) with white hair and a beard, who appeared in his red ceremonial uniform. "There's Father Christmas!" Rachel exclaimed, which brought a smile to the Queen's face.

Following the investiture, during which Her Majesty the Queen told them, "You were both very brave, and I hope it will not happen again to you," there was a torrent of letters and receptions to attend, and in November both Gledhill and McFall were nominated as 'Men of the Year' and attended a celebratory luncheon at the Savoy Hotel.

★   ★   ★

In October 1968 McFall was appointed detective constable and remained on 'P' Division, whilst Gledhill, still as a temporary detective constable, was making himself very busy, gaining a commendation in 1970 for valuable assistance in a case of murder, followed in 1971 with another, this time for valuable assistance in a difficult case of manslaughter and robbery. In October 1972 he was appointed detective constable and posted to 'C' Division's West End Central police station, but by this time McFall had voluntarily resigned from the Metropolitan Police in June 1969 and emigrated to Canada to join the Ontario Provincial Police.

McFall was not the only one with wanderlust; in October 1968 McVicar escaped from the high-security Durham Prison and remained on the run for over two years. He was arrested by the Flying Squad at a flat in Blackheath, SE3, in possession of two sawn-off shotguns, a pistol, an automatic, ammunition, some coshes, stocking masks and a postman's uniform. In September 1971 at the Old Bailey McVicar pleaded guilty to two cases of conspiracy to rob and associated firearms offices and was sentenced to a total of three years' imprisonment, to run consecutive to his existing sentence, making a total of twenty-six years. Released in 1978, McVicar has turned his talents to journalism.

Eighteen months later, McFall returned to England and rejoined the Metropolitan Police. He had thoroughly enjoyed working as a provincial constable patrolling the wide areas of Ontario, but his wife became homesick. Surprisingly, McFall had to undergo the basic thirteen weeks' training all over again and was posted as a uniform police constable to West End Central, where two years later he was reunited with his old comrade. McFall took the sergeant's examination and was posted as a uniform sergeant to Peckham.

In 1973 Gledhill was again commended, this time for arresting a burglar, and in February 1974 he was transferred to 'Z' Division. The following year, he was commended twice, firstly in a case of dishonest handling (where he was also praised by the Bench at Croydon Magistrates' Court) and then for the arrest of four youths for robbery. But McFall was not around to see it; he had resigned from the Metropolitan Police for the second and final time in May 1975 and had emigrated once more to Canada. He had never forgotten the beauty of the country but on this occasion he went to Victoria in British Columbia and was employed driving coaches and buses across western Canada and the north-west of the United States. He retired when he was sixty-three. He and his wife divorced, and she returned to England. McFall has since remarried and still lives in Canada.

Gledhill was promoted to detective sergeant in 1976 and eighteen months later was posted to the Yard's Stolen Vehicle Squad, where he was commended for skill in the arrest and conviction of a gang of car thieves. Mick Carter, a detective sergeant on that unit for many years, remembered Terry McFall at Bow Street from his early days as being, "Quiet ... a good copper," but especially remembers Tony Gledhill from the Stolen Vehicle Squad. "Although Tony worked on the South Squad and I worked on the East Squad," recalled Carter, "I regarded him as a good grafter, one who was conscientious and willing to get stuck in." Three and a half years later Gledhill was transferred back to West End Central and three years after that back to the Stolen Vehicle Squad, where he was commended twice more for arresting gangs of international car thieves.

Gledhill retired from the Force in March 1987, after exactly thirty years' service. He worked as an investigator for the Post Office, then for finance houses, until he finally retired for good in 1997. Since then, he has busied himself with the running of the ex-CID Officers' Association, becoming its president in 1999, and also with the Victoria and George Cross Association, becoming a committee member and later treasurer.

Neither Gledhill nor McFall have ever forgotten the events of 25 August 1966. Counselling in the police was unknown then, although Gledhill now honestly admits, "I could have done with some". McFall agrees. "At the time," he told me, "I did not feel that it had any adverse effect on my behaviour or affected me as a person. During later years, however, I have discovered that if I have had occasion to retell the incident, I would inevitably become emotional. My doctor has stated that I may be suffering from Post Traumatic Stress Disorder, even after all this time."

* * *

Apart from the excitement and stress of that day, the incident also held a series of uncanny coincidences; firstly, that the factory in Creekside which the gunmen had targeted for their raid was the same one where the crew of 'Papa One' intended to make the arrest of the former employee; secondly, the sixth sense which prompted Gledhill to stop, perceiving an ambush by the side of St Olave's hospital, the same hospital where Terry McFall had been born twenty-eight years earlier; there was the front offside tyre of 'Papa One' exploding which brought the Area Car to a halt (if it had happened during the chase, the consequences could have been catastrophic, yet there was no discernible reason for the tyre exploding – it had not been punctured by any of the shots fired at the car); then there was the fact that none of the officers were shot, despite the number of shots fired at them; and the misfire from Gentry's revolver which enabled the officers to overpower him; finally, and strangest of all, the fact that Gledhill's wristwatch stopped ticking at precisely 1.44 pm – the exact moment when the Area Car came to a halt. It was almost as though the watch felt it had done its bit, rather like 'Papa One' and two mightily courageous policemen.

CHAPTER 16

Shoot-out at Streatham

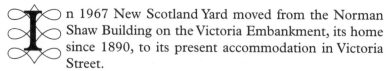n 1967 New Scotland Yard moved from the Norman Shaw Building on the Victoria Embankment, its home since 1890, to its present accommodation in Victoria Street.

With regard to criminal investigation, DNA testing was unknown at that time; if blood or hair samples were found at the scene of a crime, the best the scientists could say when comparing them with samples taken from a criminal (who, of course, was as guilty as sin) was that they 'appeared to be similar'. Similarly, there was no instant fingerprint recognition and no CCTV cameras to track the path taken by criminals or their vehicles. Criminals were unable to be placed at locations where they had made credit card transactions, neither could their whereabouts be pinpointed from calls made by their mobile phones, because such things did not exist.

Fortunately, when the files, records and administration were moved, lock, stock and barrel, that quarter-mile across London, they were accompanied by detectives – real detectives, who during their careers had amassed an enormous amount of knowledge of crime, criminals and criminal investigation. They relied upon speed, experience and intuition and by doing so they achieved impressive results.

In 1967, when you entered Victoria Block, the new premises in Victoria Street, and took the lift to the fourth floor, as you pushed through the double doors and turned left, you were in the long corridor housing two important crime-fighting departments on opposite sides of the corridor. On the left was the Flying Squad, which had been in existence since 1919. It was the Yard's top crime-busting unit, filled with detectives known for their intimate knowledge of the underworld, their informants, their physical toughness and their disinclination to accept the word 'no' from anybody. The Squad comprised a hundred officers, split into ten squads, each under the control of a detective inspector. The Flying Squad's chief was Detective Chief Superintendent Tommy Butler MBE, who had gained worldwide fame after the arrest and imprisonment of the Great Train Robbers. In 1968 he travelled to Canada to arrest one of the robbers, Charlie Wilson, who had escaped from prison four years previously; ten months later, Butler would arrest the mastermind of the coup, Bruce Reynolds.

On the opposite side of the corridor was C11 – the Criminal Intelligence Department, which had been formed in March 1960. They had a staff of fifty-six officers, four of whom had been posted in from constabularies in the Home Counties. C11 performed an excellent job of gathering information and providing surveillance, both human and electronic, in respect of what was known as 'docket criminals'. The docket system comprised an in-depth folder of intelligence maintained on the very top echelon of criminals. Next was the index of lesser (but nevertheless major) criminals, and finally a nominal index of known associates of the previous two categories, plus details of less significant criminals. The top layer of criminals were known as 'Main Index Men'.

Over the years, many officers would be posted to C11 from the Flying Squad (naturally taking their informants with them) and *vice versa*; in this fashion, there was a tremendous flow of top-notch intelligence between the two departments, who relied upon and admired each other. Quite often, C11 would accompany the Flying Squad on their operations, and a weapon in their armoury were the 'Four-twos'.

The 'Four-twos' were motorcyclists drawn from officers in Traffic Patrol units who had shown a propensity for crime-fighting. The call-sign emanated from the motorcyclists themselves; the 'four' referred to the fact that they had been seconded from each of the (then) four districts of the Metropolitan Police, the 'two' indicated that they were restricted to two wheels. On their powerful, anonymous motorcycles, they would lead surveillance teams comprised of officers in vans, taxis and fast cars on the trail of the top-level villains whom the Flying Squad specialised in arresting. In communication by radio with each other, the 'Four-twos' would unobtrusively follow the quarry, holding back then expertly weaving in and out of the traffic, and pinpointing their whereabouts so that at the most propitious moment the Squad could step in and make the arrests. The 'Four-twos' would not, of course, become personally involved in the arrests, being content to disappear unobtrusively. Usually, that is.

* * *

It became known to C11 that a number of active robbers were meeting, usually at lunchtime, at a public house in Battersea

High Street. It was simply a whisper of information, nothing more. Therefore, an experienced C11 operative and a woman companion arrived in the pub early and sat down at a table with their drinks. In this way, the C11 officer was able to positively identify no less than half a dozen known robbers. A number of vehicles used by the robbers were identified, and observations were carried out.

One man who was of particular interest was Peter Rose. Further information led C11 officers to follow Rose and another man over a period of weeks, and finally they were followed driving to Balham High Road, where a vehicle was stolen from the forecourt of a car showroom. Both vehicles were tailed, and the stolen car was left in a street close to Streatham High Road. The C11 officer in charge of the surveillance detail was Detective Sergeant Mike Purchase, and as a result of pertinent intelligence which he received he had every reason to believe that this vehicle would be used in connection with a bank robbery. However, the precise target was not known.

At lunchtime on 17 May 1968 a combined operation was under way involving C11 and officers from 4 squad of the Flying Squad (who had secreted themselves and their vehicles in the yard at Streatham police station), with Detective Inspector James William Marshall in charge. Marshall was then aged forty, and eleven years of his eventual thirty-year service would be spent with the Flying Squad and the Regional Crime Squad. He had been commended for the arrest of dangerous criminals involved in robbery with violence, officebreaking and possessing explosives and conspiracy to steal. Two months previously, the commissioner had commended him for detective ability and initiative in the arrest of a gang of active criminals for armed robbery, as had the judge at the Old Bailey and the Director of Public Prosecutions. It goes without saying that Marshall was quite used to leading from the front.

The four-man gang were on the move but they were not alone; one of the 'Four-twos', Detective Constable Reginald Alfred Walter George Jenkins, an officer with sixteen years service, was on their tail. He had previously seen them steal three cars and then place them at various points within a half-mile radius to facilitate their getaway. Mike Purchase was alone in an unmarked C11 car, behind Jenkins and listening to his radio commentary. Now he received the coded message he had been waiting for: "The parcel is being opened." It meant the gang had got into one of the stolen cars, and they were expertly followed. As they approached the District Bank on Streatham High Road, three of the men, wearing caps and carrying holdalls – obviously containing robbery impedimenta and known in Flying Squad parlance as 'Happy Bags' – got out of the car. Jenkins had experienced great difficulty in contacting the Squad by radio; finally he got through, and the Squad cars roared out of the yard at Streatham. The High Road was a dual carriageway and, ignoring the refinements of the Highway Code, the Squad cars thundered north along the south-bound carriageway, the oncoming traffic dutifully parting to make way for them, in much the same way that the Red Sea had divided for Moses, some time previously.

As the first Squad car, containing Detective Sergeant Pat O'Brien, screeched to a halt, Jenkins heard a shot fired; the second Squad car, containing Detective Sergeant Raymond Charles Adams and Detective Inspector Marshall, had mounted the central reservation in the High Road, and the shot had been fired at them. Purchase, too, had arrived at the scene. He heard the sound of the shot, and, as he told me, "A mêlée ensued immediately behind my car"; he got out of his car to assist. Jenkins saw the three men, two of them armed with sawn-off shotguns, the third with a pistol, dashing towards him. As O'Brien jumped from the Squad car, he saw that the men were armed and started chasing them. One of the men, Michael Engelfield, turned, pointed his shotgun at O'Brien and threatened to shoot, but nevertheless O'Brien continued pursuing him. Adams and Marshall leapt from their car and commenced chasing Michael Morris, who was holding a sawn-off shotgun. Meanwhile, Jenkins had been joined by Detective Constable Phillip John Dixon Williams, a fellow 'Four-two.' Williams, a former member of the RAF Regiment, had previously been commended for arresting a motorcyclist for dangerous driving by the chairman of Hendon Magistrates' Court, who described it as being "one of the most appalling and shocking cases I have ever had to deal with."

Now Williams revved his 500cc BSA motorcycle and drove straight at one of the men carrying a shotgun but missed him and, as he drove by, a shot was fired. Williams skidded to a halt, turned his machine around and drove at Peter Rose, who ran behind a parked car and aimed his revolver at Williams. "I zig-zagged as I approached him," Williams told me, over forty years after the event. "Being in the RAF Regiment had taught me never to approach the enemy in a straight line!" Williams' motorcycle crashed into Rose, lifting him momentarily on to the handlebars before both men fell to the ground with Williams on top, struggling to gain control of the gun. But Rose staggered to his feet and pointed the gun at Williams from a distance of two or three feet, threatening to shoot. Undeterred, Williams, a slim, six-foot athlete, leapt at Rose, a shot was fired and a tremendous struggle ensued. At that point Detective Sergeant O'Brien dashed up and used his truncheon on Rose, who during a violent tussle was also relieved of his revolver and eventually overpowered.

Meanwhile, Jenkins drove his 500cc Norton straight at Engelfield but missed, and as he turned his motorcycle round, so he was hit by a passing car and knocked to the ground. Engelfield now advanced on Jenkins, his sawn-off shotgun held at a threatening angle, but as Jenkins got up and faced him, Engelfield turned and ran. He was chased by Flying Squad officer Detective Sergeant John Stuart Northmore Wharton, a twenty-nine-year-old ex-police cadet with ten years' service. Wharton was used to dealing with dangerous criminals; just three weeks previously, he had been commended for the arrest and conviction of two violent criminals for armed robbery. Engelfield pointed his gun at Wharton, shouted at him and was chased into a nearby block of flats; losing sight of him, Wharton climbed to the top floor, where he saw Engelfield in a corridor, his back to him and the shotgun on the floor. Wharton called out his name; Engelfield turned and went for the sawn-off, but Wharton grabbed hold of him. There was a ferocious struggle, and Wharton succeeded in restraining him until assistance arrived.

In hot pursuit of the third member of the gang, Michael Morris, were Adams and Marshall. Morris had run off through the crowded thoroughfare, pushing his way through the pedestrians and pointing his shotgun at them. Purchase, having seen that Rose had been subdued, drove his car in the direction of flight which Morris had taken. Now Morris turned, shouting that he would shoot Marshall, but still the officers continued the chase. Morris darted into the front garden of a house and disappeared from view, but as the officers approached the garden, he emerged from cover pointing his weapon at them and again shouting that he would fire. But the officers approached him from different directions so as to widen the angle of fire, and at that moment Morris, suddenly nonplussed, lowered his gun. It was quite likely that he had seen Purchase driving towards him, and since the C11 vehicle was of the same colour and size as the stolen car, it was possible that he thought salvation was at hand. If so, it was a forlorn hope. His lapse in concentration was all the officers needed to spring at him, and as Marshall lashed out with his truncheon, so Adams grabbed the gun and pulled it away from Morris, who after a struggle was overpowered and arrested.

★   ★   ★

Calm had been finally restored at Streatham High Road, where during the space of the previous ten or fifteen minutes pandemonium had reigned. As the would-be robbers were bundled into police cars and vans, there was a smell in the air of burnt brake linings from the police vehicles and cordite from the discharged firearms. Frightened shoppers in that busy thoroughfare stood in groups, talking in whispers in the way that people do when they have just witnessed something momentous.

Many of the police officers stood breathing heavily, as though they had completed a rather gruelling race, as indeed, several of them had. Some had collected bruises; others cuts and abrasions. By a gracious dispensation of providence – and by exhibiting the most conspicuous bravery – none of them had been shot. Phill Williams was described by his colleagues as being 'the luckiest man alive'. Williams himself admitted, "It was the most hectic piece of action I have ever had in my life."

★   ★   ★

Five months later, the three men – all of whom had previous convictions – appeared at the Old Bailey. There had originally been four men in the car that drove up to the bank, but one man escaped, was later recaptured, stood trial and was acquitted.

On 25 October 1968 Peter Rose aged twenty-two, unemployed of Shillingdon Street, Battersea, was convicted of attempting to murder Williams, and for that offence, plus possessing a revolver – a Magnum – with intent to resist arrest, he was sentenced to a total of fourteen years' imprisonment. Michael Morris aged twenty-three, unemployed of Ferndale Road, Clapham and Michael Engelfield aged thirty-five, unemployed of Dorset Road, Lambeth pleaded guilty to conspiracy to rob, possessing offensive weapons and taking and driving away a car. Each was jailed for ten years.

The judge, Mr Justice Milmo, called the officers before him and, describing Phillip Williams' performance as 'outstanding', went on to say:

You arrested these gunmen when they were carrying arms, were prepared to use them and actually did so. Nevertheless, you pursued them and caught them whilst unarmed and ignoring the threats of Rose that he would fire at you, you chased him and brought him to justice. It was conduct in the highest police traditions.

The commissioner, Sir John Waldron KCVO, praised the officers, saying perhaps rather inaccurately, "This sort of thing, police do every day." He went on to say, "This was a very courageous thing to do against a determined band of armed robbers," adding, "They fired at us, but they did not stop us and we arrested them. What could be better?" Possibly a less ostentatious employment of his plurals, or his usage of the royal 'we'.

But once the commissioner had got his hyperbole under control, he highly commended the officers, who later received cheques from the Chief Metropolitan Magistrate for £20 from the Bow Street Reward Fund; all except Phill Williams, who received a cheque for £25.

On 8 August 1969 Her Majesty the Queen approved awards of the George Medal to Wharton and Williams (who, it was widely thought, would receive a George Cross), with British Empire Medals for Gallantry for Marshall, Adams, O'Brien and Jenkins.

The following day, the *Daily Mail* proclaimed, 'Honours ... for brave police who beat gun gang' and the *Sun* described the gallantry of the officers as a 'Portrait of courage'.

★   ★   ★

Williams and Wharton were two of the personalities voted 'Men of the Year', and this was celebrated by a luncheon at the Savoy Hotel on 13 November 1969. Marshall later took charge of the huge robbery investigation which resulted in 'Bertie' Smalls becoming the first supergrass, and he retired with the rank of detective chief superintendent of 'E' Division, thirty years to the day that he had joined. Adams became commander of C11 Department and O'Brien retired as detective chief superintendent of 'Y' Division.

Phill Williams returned for a short period to Traffic Patrol, long enough to be commended by the chairman at Barnet Magistrates' Court for tackling a drunken driver who drove off with Williams hanging on to the side of the car before he managed to climb into the vehicle and wrest the steering wheel from the driver. When civil unrest flared up in the Caribbean Britain was called upon for help, and Williams spent a three-month posting as part of 'The Anguilla Police Unit'; then in 1975 he rejoined C11, as a 'Four-two.' As part of an undercover team, he took part in attempting to recover a £4,000 stolen painting; a man who drove at Williams (he was charged with Williams' attempted murder but later cleared of that charge) was sentenced to eighteen months' imprisonment for other matters, and Williams was commended once again by the Judge.

In retirement, Williams is now waiting for the fourth generation of his family to join the police, where he enjoyed every moment of his service. Now in his seventies, and still an enthusiastic traveller and skier, he told me, "If I was nineteen again, I'd be first in the queue."

★   ★   ★

As for Mick Purchase, there were no commendations, no awards, although many of his contemporaries thought that he deserved recognition. He simply melted away into the shadows from whence he had emerged, to carry on the secretive work so necessary for so many successful operations.

Over forty years after that spectacular ambush he told me, "Some time later, other robbers identified from the Battersea public house were arrested, charged and convicted of conspiracy to rob, by again watching getaway vehicles being stolen and keeping observation on them until being put into use by the robbers. Albeit," he added, wryly, "in less dramatic circumstances!"

Shooting at Shepperton

Sunbury police station was situated right on the south-western boundary of the Metropolitan Police District (it is now part of Surrey Constabulary), and it was normally so quiet that when Anchor Square, Shepperton exploded into action on Thursday, 29 December 1970, with crashing cars and a gunman with blood pouring down his face being chased by police, the clientele of the Anchor Hotel believed that a crew from the nearby film studios were shooting a thriller. It was understandable, but they were wrong. This was real life.

★ ★ ★

It started earlier that month, when twenty-six-year-old Michael John Francis, a man with convictions for violence and a disqualified driver, together with Roger David Bethray aged twenty-three, stole a Ford Zephyr from London Airport. On 19 December the men broke into a butcher's shop in Hampton, Middlesex and stole £250 in cash, a knife and a meat cleaver. Three days later Bethray borrowed a shotgun from a friend, in order, he later stated, "to go shooting".

On Christmas Eve there was an attempted robbery at the White Lodge Garage in Staines Road, East Sunbury. The forecourt salesman, William Smith, was threatened by two men, one of them armed with a meat cleaver, who demanded money, but when he refused, the men drove off in a Ford Zephyr. In reporting this to the police, Mr Smith was unable to provide a registration number for the car. However, on Boxing Day Police Constables Gaitley and Fairweather spotted a Ford Zephyr, registration number BBJ 177H, in Shepperton High Street. The driver was talking to a pedestrian when PC Gaitley opened the door and asked him to get out. In response, the driver slammed the door shut, breaking Gaitley's thumb, and reversed sharply. Gaitley hung on to the car and Fairweather attempted to grab hold of the driver through the window, but as the car accelerated away the officers were obliged to let go. However, they were able to record the registration number of the rapidly disappearing vehicle.

Bethray would later say that on 28 December he met Francis and asked to borrow the Zephyr. When he returned the car to Francis later that night and Francis drove off in it, Bethray, to his horror, suddenly remembered the borrowed shotgun was still in the car.

The CID at Sunbury had already carried out a great deal of work, circulating the description of the car and its occupants as well as making more covert enquiries. These demonstrated the advantage of using underworld informants, because Francis had upset several of them by carrying a gun and threatening to use it 'if he was stopped by a cop'. Members of the underworld knew that if matters were to go badly awry in the police's search for a gunman, officers in the closing days of 1970 would *not* take action which nowadays would be considered 'proportionate, accountable or necessary' – in fact, they kicked in doors and turned *everybody* over. Therefore, one of those faceless, nameless informants picked up the telephone, and Sunbury's CID were informed that it might be worth their while to be in the vicinity of Anchor Square at 2.30 that afternoon.

Getting a team of men together at Sunbury was a problem at any time, particularly over the Christmas period, but six uniform officers plus Detective Constable Jack Hardwick were in and around the area of Anchor Square on 29 December 1970. Two marked police Panda cars were parked out of sight in Chertsey Road, when at 2.35 the officers received a call on the radio from Police Sergeant 89 'T' Brian Derek Parsons, that the suspect Ford Zephyr with one occupant – Francis – was travelling along the Chertsey Road. Parsons followed the car as it turned into the square, and as it stopped, some four feet behind a parked vehicle, so Parsons drove his Panda car behind the suspect vehicle and hemmed it in. Parsons, who had carried out his National Service with the Royal Artillery, was then forty years of age. Married, with two daughters, he was now in his twentieth year of service with the Metropolitan Police, had already been commended for arresting a persistent thief and for the past six years had been based at Sunbury. Now Parsons got out of the police car and went over to the driver's door of the Zephyr, only to find it was locked. Station Police Sergeant 2 'T' Arthur Howard Garner, wearing a civilian coat over his uniform, walked towards the car and tried the front passenger door, but it too was locked. Then Francis suddenly reversed, crashing the Zephyr into the Panda car; he then drove forwards, causing DC Hardwick and a uniform officer to jump clear, and drove on into Old Ferry Boatyard, a car park without any other form of exit – so he turned the Ford round and accelerated back towards Garner in the square.

A former cadet with Stockport Borough Police, Garner had joined the Metropolitan Police in 1961 and had been commended by the commissioner and a judge at the Old Bailey for ability and determination in catching a persistent criminal. Married, with two sons, Garner was a powerful adversary at just under six feet tall, and as an enthusiastic footballer, cricketer, squash and tennis player, he had acquired quick reactions, which would now be brought into play. As the Zephyr raced towards him, Garner drew his truncheon and smashed the driver's side of the windscreen. This caused Francis to crash the car into a parked vehicle; and at that moment, Police Constable 353 'T' Keith Victor Giles drove up in a police car, blocking any further advance by the Zephyr. Giles was then thirty-five, a former corporal in the RAF before joining the Metropolitan Police in 1955. Married, with two daughters, Giles was a keen rugby player.

Garner ran up to the car, saw that Francis was holding a shotgun and smashed the rest of the windscreen with his truncheon, shouting, "Don't be a fool, give yourself up, there's policemen all over the place." Francis shouted back, "You fucking bastards, I'll get you all," and Garner leant into the car and tried to pull him out through the broken windscreen, without success. Garner then attempted unsuccessfully to knock the shotgun away with his truncheon, telling Francis, "You don't stand a chance." Just then, as Parsons went to Garner's assistance, Francis shouted, "One of you bastards will pay for this," and with that, he levelled the gun at Garner. Immediately prior to Francis pulling the trigger Garner dropped to the ground, before hearing the ear-splitting roar of the shotgun's discharge. PC Giles later stated, "When Sergeant Garner ducked down, it was within a split-second of the gun going off." The shot blew a hole six inches in diameter through the roof of the Zephyr and hit a furniture van. Garner crawled to the rear of the Zephyr and through the back window he could see Francis brandishing the shotgun at officers around the car. Garner dashed back to the front nearside of the car and began hitting both Francis and the shotgun with his truncheon through the broken windscreen, while on the offside of the car Parsons was doing the same. Francis crawled out through the broken windscreen, stood on the bonnet and again pointed the gun at Garner, who dropped to the ground. Francis then pointed the shotgun at PC Giles, who threw his truncheon at Francis; Garner, believing (with some justification) that Francis was going to shoot Giles, also threw his truncheon at him.

Now Francis took to his heels and dashed off along Chertsey Road, followed by Garner in a police car. Stopping in a doorway, Francis pointed the shotgun at Garner from a distance of four feet. "Give yourself up," shouted Garner. "Put the shotgun down."

"Leave me alone," replied Francis, "or I'll do for one of you."

"You'll get life for murder," Garner told him reasonably, adding, "it's not worth it."

But Francis ran off again, stopping frequently and looking back. He was followed by Garner in the police car, which was then overtaken in another car by Parsons and Giles, who stopped ahead of Francis; both got out of the car and unsuccessfully tried to reason with Francis, who then ran into Range Way. Francis may not have known that this road was a cul-de-sac, but the officers certainly did, and as they chased after him they knew that when Francis reached the end of Range Way an already tense situation would become doubly fraught because there was nowhere else for him to go. As Francis pointed the gun at the officers Garner told him, for the last time, to put the gun down; but it was clear that Francis would not. Garner was now six feet away from Francis, and with enormous bravery he rushed him, pushing the barrel of the gun towards the ground and eventually wresting it from him. It was not the end of the affair; Francis continued to struggle violently in an effort to get away, but Parsons, Giles and other officers succeeded in overpowering him. When Garner examined the shotgun he found there was a spent cartridge in one of the shotgun's barrels, a live one in the other. The stolen Zephyr was searched; inside were the knife and the meat cleaver, part-proceeds of the burglary at the butcher's shop.

In the next few days Roger Bethray was picked up, and both men were committed for trial from Staines Magistrates' Court to Surrey Assizes. Both faced a whole range of charges, the most serious being that Francis was charged with the attempted murder of SPS Garner. To all of the charges both defendants pleaded not guilty.

A forensic scientist – a dour, Scottish former detective chief inspector – gave evidence that the shotgun was a lethal weapon and in good working order. He was asked by the prosecuting barrister, Ronald Bell QC, "What would have been the result if the blast from the shotgun had hit Sergeant Garner from a distance of two feet?"

"Dead," replied the scientist decisively, adding for good measure, "definitely dead."

During the course of the trial, Francis admitted some of the charges: the burglary at the butcher's shop, one charge of driving whilst disqualified, not possessing a driving licence, using a shotgun with intent to resist arrest and as an offensive weapon and having no certificate for it. Bethray still maintained his innocence of all the charges. Before sending out the jury to consider their verdicts, the trial judge, the Honourable Mr Justice Forbes, directed that not guilty verdicts should be brought in with respect to both defendants for the robbery at the petrol station and, with respect to Francis alone, for the assault on the police officer on Boxing Day .

After five hours of deliberations on 29 April 1971 the jury found Francis guilty of the attempted murder of SPS Garner, stealing the car and driving whilst disqualified. Bethray was also found guilty of stealing the car, the burglary at the butcher's shop and transferring the shotgun to Francis.

Telling Francis, "You have shown yourself as a thoroughly dangerous and desperate criminal," the judge sentenced him to a total of seven years' imprisonment and disqualified him from driving for ten years. "Be cautious of the people you mix with," the judge told Bethray, adding ominously, "Just see what happened to Francis." He then placed Bethray on probation for two years and fined him £10 for transferring the shotgun. Addressing Detective Sergeant Carr, the officer in the case, the judge stated, "Before I go, I ought – I think – to pass on the appreciation of the way the police behaved in that very difficult situation." Normally the sentence for the attempted murder of a police officer would have been two or even three times the seven years which was imposed, so many might have thought it was the least the judge could have said.

*   *   *

The three officers – Garner, Parsons and Giles – were all highly commended by the commissioner and all were awarded £20 from the Bow Street Reward Fund. Almost a year after the trial, Garner was informed that he would be awarded the George Medal and Parsons and Giles the British Empire Medal for Gallantry. The presentations took place at Buckingham Palace on 12 July 1972, and as Garner told me, almost forty years later, "Arriving for the investiture in my bright red Ford Corsair, I'm sure the crowds wondered how such an old banger could merit an invitation." As the medals were awarded, a small boy's voice was heard to shout, "That's my Daddy!" and though opinions now differ as to whose son identified his father, it was sufficient to bring a smile to the face of Her Majesty.

★ ★ ★

Parsons retired on an ill-health pension three years later, and Giles completed his thirty years service and lives in Spain.

One year into his sentence, Francis wrote to Garner, expressing both congratulations on his award and penitence for his own actions. But that was not the last Garner heard of his adversary. Four years after Francis' conviction, Garner (by then an inspector at Chelsea police station) was called to the Old Bailey to give evidence of the conviction at Surrey Assizes. Allegedly, Francis (released after serving half of his sentence) had tried to run down a police constable at the Oval. Francis was representing himself, and the prosecuting barrister required a little help because Francis had stated that the detective sergeant in charge of the case was having an affair with his girlfriend, and in consequence the officer had been excluded from the proceedings. It was bad strategy on Francis' behalf, because Garner did indeed assist the prosecution and Francis was later returned to prison. "When normal, he was lucid and intelligent," Garner told me, "but when roused ..."

Prior to the shooting in Shepperton, Garner had already passed a three-year course on 'The General Principals of Criminal Law' at Chiswick Polytechnic; then in 1974–75 he attended London University as an external student, studying 'Current Issues of Criminology' for which he was awarded a diploma. In 1982 he suggested to the Research and Planning Department a standard, national procedure for forwarding and recording details of persons reporting on bail, and one year later was awarded £100 for it. By now, he had been promoted to chief inspector, and the last two years of his service were spent on 'W' Division, before he retired after just over twenty-five years' service. Sadly, Garner and his wife divorced after thirty-five years of marriage, and he went to live on the south coast. Much of his time is now spent travelling all over the world.

When he is asked nowadays how he won his George Medal, Garner modestly replies, "Ducking at the right time." But we know different, don't we?

CHAPTER 18

One Gunman after Another

ohn Faulkner was not a criminal well known to London's police. True, he possessed a conviction for forgery in England, but he was better known to the authorities in France and especially Switzerland, where he had escaped from prison whilst serving a sentence for safe-blowing. However, he was about to move up a notch in the criminal hierarchy. During the early hours of 30 November 1970 Faulkner and an associate climbed on to the roof of a building close to the Trafalgar public house in the Kings Road, Chelsea; it appeared that they intended to break into the premises – until they were spotted, the police were called and both men fled.

Faulkner dashed up Chelsea Manor Street towards Britten Street, but at that moment Police Constable 516 'B' Rodney Andrew Phillips, who was attached to Chelsea police station and on patrol in a police car, heard the information regarding the suspects and drove towards the area. Phillips, a single man aged twenty-six, had almost four years' service as a Metropolitan Police officer. The former accountant was also an enthusiastic member of the Scout movement, having previously headed the 3rd Ilford West Troop; during a three month posting in 1969 as part of 'The Anguilla Police Unit' he had helped to run a Scout troop there. During his time with the Scouts he had impressed upon his young charges the need to 'Be Prepared' – and as a young copper, Phillips was prepared for anything. It was just as well.

★   ★   ★

Seeing Faulkner turn into Britten Street, Phillips immediately realized that this was one of the suspects, and as Faulkner ran towards him Phillips braked to a halt and flung open his driver's door in front of him and shouted at him to stop. But Faulkner ran round the open door, so Phillips jumped out of the car and chased him, again shouting at him to stop. As both men raced into Sydney Street, Phillips drew his truncheon and hit Faulkner, left-handed, on his left shoulder. Faulkner stopped, turned and Phillips saw he was holding a gun, which he pointed at the officer, shouting, "I'll shoot! I'll shoot!" Phillips lashed out with his truncheon at the pistol, but Faulkner avoided the blow and ran off. In the ensuing chase, Phillips again struck Faulkner on the shoulder, so hard this time that his truncheon snapped in two, causing Faulkner to slip and fall; but he rose immediately, adopted the classic shooter's position on one knee and, pointing the pistol directly at Phillips, again shouted, "I'll shoot!" Phillips rushed towards the gunman, who turned and ran, with the officer in pursuit. Faulkner again stopped, turned and levelled the pistol at Phillips, who leapt at him, seizing him in a bear hug. As Phillips tried to grab hold of the weapon, Faulkner hit him with the gun butt just above his ear. The blow caused Phillips to become dizzy and disorientated, but he kept hold of the gunman and both men crashed to the pavement. Faulkner was on top and he hit Phillips in the mouth with the gun butt and also punched him in the face with his other hand. "He still had hold of the gun and but for the fact that I'm left-handed and he was right-handed, I would have sustained more injuries," Phillips recalled, forty years later.

Phillips refused to relinquish his hold, and as the struggle continued he was suddenly aware that other police officers were approaching. "Look out, he's got a gun!" he shouted to his colleagues, and Faulkner, possibly thinking that these officers were armed, shrieked, "It's not loaded!" and immediately surrendered. Examination of the pre-war Polish-made P.64 Radom 9mm automatic pistol revealed that it was indeed unloaded; but even in its empty state, it still weighed over two and a quarter pounds and caused Phillips severe bruising to his face and head and a chipped tooth. He was detained for forty-eight hours at St Stephen's hospital, Chelsea, since for the first twenty-four hours following the attack he had suffered double vision; he was kept on the sick-list for the following two weeks.

* * *

On 11 May 1971 Faulkner appeared at the Old Bailey and stood alone in the dock – his accomplice had not been caught – before His Honour Judge Broderick QC, whose sentences were invariably evaluated by the Court of Appeal as being 'just right'.

Faulkner was indicted on seven counts, including possessing a firearm with intent to resist arrest, conspiracy to steal and assaulting PC Phillips, and after a week-long trial he was found guilty and sentenced to a total of six years' imprisonment.

The jury congratulated Phillips, as did the judge, who calling him before him, said:

I think you are a very brave and conscientious officer. I am sure the Force is proud of you, as well it ought to be. Indeed, the whole community should be grateful to you for the way in which, and the courage you displayed in tackling this man who may have been a very dangerous criminal. I propose to see to it that the Commissioner of Police is informed of the court's commendation and your conduct so that it may be placed on record.

On 29 June 1971 the commissioner highly commended Phillips for 'his outstanding courage and devotion to duty', and on 18 August he was handed a cheque for £25 from the Bow Street Reward Fund by the Chief Metropolitan Magistrate, Sir Frank Milton, who said, "This officer fully deserves this award because alone he persistently pursued this man and eventually overpowered him."

The press was full of the story; the *Chelsea News* commented, 'PC tackled gunman: court praise', but that was not all. Phillips' presence was 'requested' at Buckingham Palace on 28 March 1972, when for his outstanding courage Her Majesty the Queen invested him with the British Empire Medal for Gallantry.

★   ★   ★

The Diplomatic Protection Group (DPG) was formed to provide protection from terrorism to London's 160 embassies and high commissions (amongst a large number of other duties), and its personnel who operated in uniform and plain clothes, were armed with a variety of weapons and were highly mobile to respond to emergencies. But quite apart from protecting any of the 10,000 members of the diplomatic community in London, the ability of the DPG officers was often tested in situations beyond their remit. Police Constable Peter Slimon was shot by gunmen robbing a bank as he went to take up his protection post; although badly wounded, he drew his revolver, shot two of the robbers and was awarded the George Medal. Police Constable Stephen Peat similarly shot a man in the act of bank robbery, and Police Constable Gordon McKinnon opened fire on a kidnapper, freeing the person whom the man had taken hostage. And on 15 November 1978, Rodney Phillips, by now a sergeant with the Diplomatic Protection Group, was on mobile patrol in 'Ranger 500' (the DPG Central London Security Patrol) when he received a radio message which sent him and local officers from 'E' Division speeding to the Swinton Hotel, 18–24 Swinton Street, WC1, just off King's Cross Road.

At about 5.15 that afternoon, Paul David Booth, dressed bizarrely (and frighteningly) in a fireman's jacket, leather belt and armband, his face completely masked in a balaclava, had entered the hotel. At the reception desk he produced a pistol and, placing a parcel wrapped in Christmas paper on the counter, passed a note to the manageress, Mrs Peggy Hodgson, which read:

The Christmas present is a bomb. This gun is real and loaded. You have seven minutes to leave the hotel.

This was a threat not to be taken lightly; the IRA offensive on mainland Britain was still very active (and would continue to be for several more years), so with tremendous composure Mrs Hodgson sounded the fire alarm, thereby initiating the evacuation of the hotel; once the premises were clear, she herself left and telephoned the police.

Two unarmed local officers entered the hotel, but Booth, who was now on the upper landing, pointed the pistol at them and warned them off. They retreated outside the premises, but they could still see Booth, who now descended to the ground floor and handled the package, before retreating to the landing. The local duty officer, Inspector John Rowe, a police officer with twenty-three years' service who the previous year had been awarded a commissioner's high commendation for outstanding courage, arrived and took charge of the situation. A safety cordon was set up, with local residents and passers-by being warned to stay away from the area.

Inspector Rowe and Rodney Phillips advanced into the hotel in full view of Booth who, still on the landing, was crouched down pointing his gun at the officers. Phillips shouted, "We're armed police officers – throw the gun out and come down!"

There followed a long silence; then Booth threw the gun into the hallway of the hotel, and the officers 'talked him' down the stairs, whereupon he was arrested. A later examination of the parcel revealed that it was not a bomb at all, but a hoax; the gun with which Booth had threatened the officers turned out to be a starting pistol. Booth was not a terrorist or a blackmailer, just a very foolish and immature young man with (as would be said nowadays) 'issues'; and when he appeared at the Old Bailey on 9 February the following year, he pleaded guilty to making a hoax bomb and possessing an imitation firearm with intent to commit an indictable offence. His Honour Jack Abdela QC, normally known as a 'hard-line' judge when it came to sentencing, came to the eminently sensible conclusion that Booth was more to be pitied than punished, imposed a two-year probation order and ordered that he pay the whole of the legal aid costs of his defence or £200, whichever was the less of the two sums. But even though with hindsight, poor, sad Mr Booth had not represented a physical threat, nevertheless it had been a tense and fraught situation for everybody concerned, and the judge singled out Mrs Hodgson for special commendation, saying:

> I suggest Mrs Hodgson richly deserves suitable recognition for her exemplary coolness and courage when confronted with an armed man. Her prime concern was for the safety of the residents and her action in evacuating the hotel, with the minimum of fuss, made the job of the police much easier.

In addition, Judge Abdela commended several of the police officers. Inspector Rowe was later awarded a commissioner's commendation for 'courage, leadership and ability', and Phillips was one of four officers who were commended for 'courage and ability' by the Deputy Assistant Commissioner.

★   ★   ★

Three months later, Phillips, now Police Sergeant 95 'Q' attached to Wealdstone police station, received information that an armed robbery together with an indecent assault and the unlawful taking of a vehicle had occurred in Coventry and that the suspect – Peter Richard Mark Mardon, who had first come to the attention of the police two years previously – was likely to return to his home address in Edgware. Arming himself with a police issue .38 Smith & Wesson revolver, Phillips, together with Police Sergeant 46 'Q' Philippe de Chaumont Rambert, made his way to the vicinity of Mardon's home, where they made enquiries and kept observation. After three and a half hours a black London taxi appeared, and the passenger matched the description of Mardon. The taxi was followed at a distance until it stopped, then the two officers jumped from their vehicle and ran over to the cab, Rambert approaching the offside door and Phillips the nearside. As Rambert reached the door of the cab he saw through the window, which was slightly open, that Mardon was pointing a cocked crossbow at him and at the same time was fumbling with a black briefcase on the seat. "Put it down, put it down, don't be silly," shouted Rambert, but Mardon did not. The terrifying weapon, easily capable of causing mortal injury, was still pointed at Rambert. At that moment Phillips wrenched open the nearside door and, levelling his revolver at Mardon, he shouted, "I'm armed, put it down, do you hear me, put it down!"

With what appeared to be great reluctance, Mardon placed the crossbow on the floor of the cab, was taken out of the vehicle and arrested. The black briefcase which Mardon had been trying to open was searched; it revealed an open pack of crossbow bolts, plus a cocked Colt .45 automatic pistol, which turned out to be a replica. During an interview at the police station, where he was found to be in possession of £50, he admitted the money was the proceeds of the robbery in Coventry.

At his trial at Coventry Crown Court, two months later on 25 September, Mardon was convicted of robbery, taking a conveyance, indecent assault and possessing an offensive weapon, and was sentenced to a total of four years' imprisonment. The judge, His Honour Martin Wilson, said:

> Would you please ensure that it is passed on to the Metropolitan Police that this court thinks very highly of the behaviour of Sergeant Rambert and Sergeant Phillips, who went to arrest a man who, as far as they were concerned, was armed with a pistol.

Just over a year from the date of the incident, both officers were awarded a commissioner's commendation for courage and determination in effecting the arrest of a person wanted for robbery.

★   ★   ★

In January 1983 Phillips was promoted to the rank of inspector and posted to Cannon Row police station, where he attended the Harrods' bomb scene, as well as dealing with a viable Improvised Explosive Device (IED) and a number of suspect packages, including one at the Admiralty. Had it been necessary to evacuate the building, because a NATO exercise was in progress, it would have required the approval of the Prime Minister!

Now married, with two children, a boy and a girl, Phillips spent much of the rest of his service devising and implementing firearms training, public order practices and sports stadium evacuation procedures. He was teaching from the benefit of his considerable experience in keeping the police and the public safe. In addition, he was selected to travel to South Africa to be part of the Commonwealth Peacekeeping Advisor Group to help train the National Peacekeeping Force in policing the forthcoming multi-cultural elections in 1994.

Phillips retired, having completed thirty years' service, on 31 March 1997. Much of his service had been filled with excitement, carrying out deeds beyond the capabilities of many of his contemporaries, but in his later years, he assumed, as he put it, "a slightly lower profile."

It is debatable whether dealing with IEDs could be described as adopting 'a low profile', but in any event, Phillips arrested no more gunmen. As he told me, "I must have realized by that stage that the 'cat's lives' were running out!"

CHAPTER 19

The Scissors Punch

Forty years ago I attended the Initial (Junior) Course at the Metropolitan Police Detective Training School, one of the last to be held at Peel House, Regency Street, SW1. The course for fledgling detectives lasted ten weeks, and it was necessary to make the grade in a series of examinations, including the final one in which a pass-mark of 75 per cent was required. If one faltered, then it was the end of one's embryonic career in the Criminal Investigation Department. But even with a pass, it still required the skilful negotiation of two terrifying selection boards and the necessity of keeping up an impressive return of arrests for crime, before permanent entry into the CID was achieved. I – and many of my contemporaries – believe it was the finest course we ever attended. We were instructed in over seventy aspects of the criminal law and investigation, from 'Abduction – Procuration' to 'Wounds (other than firearm)' by a variety of instructors, the majority of whom really did not want to be there for their two-year posting; they were working detectives and had been press-ganged into the role of instructors. But they buckled down to the job, and we learnt from their tremendous experience. My instructors were two of the finest: Detective Inspector (later Detective Chief Superintendent) Lou van Dyke, who was already a legend, having been part of the Flying Squad's arrest team on the Great Train Robbery investigation; and Detective Inspector Jeff Southeard, a tall, slim northerner with a quiet voice and enormous charm. It was Southeard who instructed us in the art of taking a dying declaration: a statement to be taken only when a person was in imminent danger of death, in which the content contained the facts and circumstances of how they came by their injuries. The statement would commence with the ominous words:

I, (name) having the fear of death before me and being without hope of recovery make the following statement ...

And a whole (very complicated) rigmarole would have to be sedulously adhered to before that statement was admissible in court as evidence. All of us shuddered at the thought of having to write those dreadful words.

Years later, Lou van Dyke told me why Jeff Southeard gave such a competent lecture. "Jeff had to take a dying declaration from a nurse who had been badly attacked by her boyfriend," he told me. "It was a very emotional time, with Jeff quietly and very compassionately coaxing every bit of evidence from the poor woman, in order to convict the man responsible. Eventually, the declaration was completed, the woman signed it, as did Jeff and all the necessary witnesses, and the nurse died shortly afterwards. Jeff got up, blew his nose and wiped his eyes and went out and nicked the boyfriend." Lou smiled. "It appears he resisted arrest," he added, "because when he arrived at the nick, he'd sustained some facial injuries!"

I was thinking of that when I spoke on the telephone to Bill Griffiths. "I'm in my study, Bill, and I'm looking at a photograph of a very young you and me."

"I know the one you're talking about," replied Bill. "I've got one on my study wall as well. In fact, I'm looking at it, right now. Our hair was darker then."

"Our hearts were lighter then," was my rejoinder, pinching a line from Richard Brooks' 1966 film *The Professionals* which was too good to miss.

Bill and I laughed, but I – and I am sure, Bill too – recalled that within two years of that photograph being taken he would be experiencing the actuality of both 'Wounds (other than firearm)' and 'Dying Declarations', following a savage assault which almost cost him his life.

★   ★   ★

The story begins on 20 January 1973 when Police Constable 768 'E' Colin Smith, attached to Hampstead police station, stopped a car containing two occupants. The car had been stolen, although Smith was not aware of this at the time; it was the behaviour of the occupants which had prompted him to stop and question them, which he did as a matter of routine.

The pair were unprepossessing enough; the driver was Keith Richard Ravenhill, who was known to the passenger, Yolanda Maria Standen, as 'Joey'. Both were in their early twenties, white, thin, with dark hair. Ravenhill was approximately five feet nine, Standen shorter, but there were several matters with which PC Smith was unacquainted. Firstly, both were drug abusers. Secondly, both had serious criminal records; Ravenhill had made one appearance before a juvenile court and had eight other previous convictions, three of which were for possessing offensive weapons. He had been sent to a detention centre, received a period of Borstal Training and, fourteen months previously, been released from an eighteen-month prison sentence. Standen had appeared before the juvenile courts on three occasions and had seven previous convictions, one of which was for possession of an offensive weapon, a sheath knife.

Thirdly, both of them were circulated as being wanted: Ravenhill at Hackney, for inflicting grievous bodily harm – his mother was the victim – and also at Vine Street for attempted theft and possessing an offensive weapon. On that occasion, when a police officer had endeavoured to arrest him for attempted theft from a car, Ravenhill had threatened him with a pair of scissors and had made good his escape. He was also wanted at St Ann's Road, for unlawful taking of a motor vehicle. Standen was wanted on two counts: firstly, for shoplifting and failing to appear at Marylebone Magistrates' Court and secondly, again for shoplifting, and on this occasion for failing to appear at Tower Bridge Magistrates' Court.

Nowadays, Ravenhill and Standen would refer to each other as their 'partner'; then, they were known as common-law husband and wife. It was a common-law marriage made in heaven; apart from a liking for drugs and dishonesty, this charmless duo shared a passion for sudden, mindless violence, as PC Smith was about to find out.

★   ★   ★

Having provisionally questioned the two, Smith asked to look in the boot of the car. Ravenhill accompanied him to the rear of the vehicle and opened up, then Standen suddenly grabbed hold of the officer, pinioning him, and Ravenhill snatched an iron bar from the boot. As Standen held the officer, Ravenhill used the bar to hit him violently on the head, seriously injuring him. With great resolution, Smith struggled free from Standen, drew his truncheon and struck Ravenhill on the head with it before collapsing, whereupon the pair made good their escape on foot.

The car was taken to Hampstead police station and was forensically examined and searched. Two receipts were discovered relating to a transaction at Harvey & Thompson's Pawn Shop, 389 Walworth Road, London, SE17. The investigating officer at Hampstead contacted the pawnbroker, William John Burke, and asked him to contact the police if the holder of the receipt returned.

Meanwhile, although Ravenhill had sustained painful injuries as a result of coming into sharp contact with PC Smith's truncheon, he nevertheless had not sought treatment because he believed that police enquiries would be made at nearby hospitals, as indeed they were. However, three days after the incident he was in such discomfort that he attended King's College hospital, Camberwell, several miles away from Hampstead and south of the Thames, where he was admitted and kept under observation until 26 January, when he was discharged. He and Standen made straight for the pawnbroker in an endeavour to raise some money. It was whilst they were in conversation with an assistant, Albert Victor Ernest Keeble, that Mr Burke quietly telephoned the nearest police station – Carter Street.

★   ★   ★

Detective Sergeant Daniel Jackson was one of the officers who volunteered to attend the pawnshop; the other was Detective Constable William Ian Griffiths. Born in 1947, Griffiths had joined the Metropolitan Police in early 1967, and in June 1970 he had been appointed temporary detective constable (TDC) at Woolwich. A few months later, whilst on night-duty patrol, he and two other TDCs stopped some men who they thought were in the process of breaking into a shop. In fact, the men were urinating in the shop doorway but, drink having been taken by the urinators, matters suddenly escalated out of control. There was, as Griffiths told me, "an almighty fight and one of them hit me so hard from the side that my jaw broke away in two places and I lost some teeth, as well as consciousness."

But there was a positive side to this confrontation; during the period of sick leave which followed, Griffiths used his time productively, to study for – and pass – the sergeant's promotional examination.

Now, as he and Jackson made their way 100 yards along the Walworth Road to the pawnshop, Griffiths was a recently appointed (just four days previously) detective constable on 'M' Division. However, what neither officer knew was the true extent of their mission; they had been told purely that there was a suspect for theft or criminal deception in the pawnshop. They were completely unaware that they were about to confront two very dangerous criminals wanted for a variety of offences, including a serious attack on another police officer.

★   ★   ★

As the two officers entered the shop, Ravenhill and Standen were still talking to Mr Keeble. Jackson introduced himself, told them that they would be detained and went into a back room in order to telephone for police transport to convey all of them to Carter Street police station. "Had we known anything of the story, or that there were two suspects," Griffiths told me later, "I think we would have had uniform back-up, and there is no way that Danny would have left me to call the van."

Standen asked Griffiths if she might leave the shop in order to tell a friend outside that they would be delayed, and not unnaturally Griffiths refused, positioning himself in front of the door to prevent their escape.

Standen suddenly pushed Griffiths violently, at the same time shrieking, "Give it to him, Joey – we've got to get out!" and with that, Ravenhill punched Griffiths in the neck. What was not immediately apparent to Griffiths was that this was no ordinary punch; protruding between Ravenhill's fingers was a pair of sharp-pointed nail scissors which cut his jugular, the vein which carries a large volume of blood from the brain. As Griffiths staggered, Ravenhill hit him with two more blows from this 'scissor punch' – one on the left temple, the other over his left ear. Falling to the ground and bleeding heavily, Griffiths, with commendable presence of mind, kept his feet pushed against the front door of the shop to prevent the two escaping, but with only limited success. Both Ravenhill and Standen viciously kicked at his body and legs until the pain forced Griffiths to move, enabling Ravenhill to open the door wide enough to squeeze through. His departure caused Standen to scream, "For fuck's sake, do him, Joey – don't leave me!" By now, Jackson had heard the commotion and was trying to re-enter the pledge room, but as he did so, Griffiths, due to the pain in his legs, was forced to release his foothold on the door. Nevertheless, he managed to grab hold of Standen's ankle, but Ravenhill pulled her through the gap in the door and common-law husband and wife both dashed off along the Walworth Road.

Both officers chased after them, with Griffiths bleeding copiously from his neck wound; Jackson caught Standen, passed her to Griffiths and continued to chase Ravenhill for over half a mile, eventually losing sight of him in Trafalgar Street, SE17. Griffiths, now feeling extremely faint from loss of blood, pushed the furiously struggling woman against a shop window; this was witnessed by a number of passers-by, including Eric Richard Lawrence, a deputy supermarket manager, who saw Griffiths holding Standen with one hand whilst attempting to stem the flow of blood from his neck with the other. Fortunately, Police

Constable 330 'M' Michael Watson, who was in 'half-blues' (i.e. with a raincoat over his tunic), was on his way to the police station to report for late-turn duty. Although he was not immediately aware of Griffith's identity, he stepped in to take custody of the still fighting Standen.

At that moment, the local Area Car, call-sign 'Mike Three', drew up, driven by Police Constable 432 'M' Geoffrey Lowe, with Police Constable 623 'M' Reginald Dunn as the RT operator; on being appraised of the situation by PC Watson, as Bill Griffiths told me forty years later, "It was Geoff Lowe whose actions undoubtedly saved my life. He took one look at me, put the prisoner in the back with Reg the operator and sat me in the front." There was absolutely no time to wait for the ambulance which PC Dunn had quite properly summoned; 'Mike Three' took off like a rocket, blue light flashing and sirens wailing, and thundered down the Walworth Road, across the busy junction with Albany Road and into Camberwell Road. Lowe slowed momentarily, then drove into Camberwell Green, against the oncoming traffic, and turned into Denmark Hill and King's College hospital, which coincidentally Ravenhill had left an hour previously. "It was at this point," recalled Griffiths, "that the creeping numbness which had started in the extremities reached my chest and the lights went out."

With Griffiths fighting for his life in intensive care, Standen was taken to Carter Street police station. Now the investigation moved into top gear. Witnesses staring at the trail of blood in the Walworth Road were questioned about precisely what they had seen, and Michael Joseph Carlin, a GPO engineer, handed to police a pair of bloodstained and twisted nail scissors, mute testimony of the force which had been used during the attack on Griffiths. But finding the truly dangerous Ravenhill was now the absolute priority.

Meanwhile, Griffiths awoke to find an extremely concerned looking Detective Inspector Dave Little sitting by his bedside, notebook in hand. Griffiths had lost at least three litres of blood. Talking to me forty years later, Little – later a detective chief superintendent – said simply, "The hospital staff told me he was going to die. I was there to record his dying declaration." It was no thanks whatsoever to Ravenhill that Little did not have to.

It was soon established that Ravenhill was known to frequent a flat in King's Grove, Peckham, SE15, and a bare hour and a half after the incident he was seen to be approaching the front door of the premises. He had discarded his coat, but the watchers could see that he was in possession of a hammer and a screwdriver. Ravenhill shouted out to someone in the flat, and at that moment

Temporary Detective Constable Peter Atkins opened the front door and Detective Constable Malcolm Goldie ran up behind Ravenhill, who chose that moment to launch an attack on Atkins. Swinging the hammer at Atkins' head, he also attempted to stab him with the screwdriver, screaming, "I'll kill you, I'll kill you!" He was overpowered with the assistance of other officers and taken initially to Peckham police station, where he became so violent that over a period of almost half an hour he had to be forcibly restrained. Both Atkins and Goldie would later be commended by the commissioner for displaying courage and ability, as would Jackson.

Stitches were inserted in Bill Griffiths' wounds and after three days he was permitted to leave hospital, although for a month thereafter he still attended the outpatients department and was off sick for a total of seven weeks.

In July Ravenhill and Standen appeared at the Old Bailey. Ravenhill was sentenced to a total of twelve years' imprisonment – ten of those years were for the attack on Griffiths – and Standen to three years. It is slightly incredible that no reference was made to Griffiths' outstanding gallantry by the trial judge, an omission tactfully referred to as 'this possible oversight' by Detective Superintendent John Swain in his report to the commander of 'M' Division.

However, 'possible oversight' or not, it did not prevent a gallantry report being submitted, and on 16 October 1973 Griffiths was highly commended by the commissioner, the late Sir Robert Mark GBE, QPM, for 'courage and determination in detaining a violent woman suspected of theft, having received personal injury from a man armed with an offensive weapon'. Then, on the day before publication of this commendation in *Police Orders*, something almost unprecedented occurred.

* * *

Mark had been appointed commissioner in 1972. He loathed the CID, believing them to be a totally corrupt department, and he set about eradicating corruption with unprecedented zeal. Unsurprisingly, many of the CID detested Mark in return, because whilst they accepted that corruption existed, the vast majority of detectives were honest and hard-working. With Mark's policy of 'interchange' (the routine swapping of personnel between uniform and CID) and the devolving of the the power of the divisional CID to the uniform branch, many felt that he would be the ruination of the department; in the years which followed, many former members of the CID felt that their concerns were justified. In fact, after Mark retired he admitted that he might have been wrong in tarring all detectives with the same brush, but by then it was a case of too little, too late. Nevertheless, Mark was in many ways a good commissioner: outspoken, especially with regard to corrupt defence solicitors, forthright and a man of principle. Bill Griffiths was one of his many admirers, feeling that he had taken the only possible stance to resurrect public confidence in the police.

On Monday, 15 October Griffiths was at home in Bexley, Kent. Married, with three children aged six, three and ten months, he was ready to commence a two-week tour of night-duty CID that evening, when he received a telephone call from his Detective Chief Inspector, Bernie Warren, instructing him to attend the Yard that afternoon to see the commissioner. Griffiths was duly led into the commissioner's office by the Assistant Commissioner (Crime), Colin Woods, and Mark congratulated Griffiths on his high commendation. It was not the first time Griffiths had met Mark – he had also visited him during his hospital stay – but what Mark said next, as Griffiths told me, "almost knocked me off my chair".

Mark told Griffiths that he had displayed such exemplary leadership that he would be promoted to sergeant immediately, and he was; Griffiths had been a detective constable for less than nine months, and this was one of only twelve 'promotions in the field' which had been bestowed since the formation of the Metropolitan Police in 1829.

It was later revealed that the proposal had been strongly supported by the Deputy Assistant Commissioner (Crime) (Operations) Ernie Bond OBE, QPM. Bond, a pre-war regular in the British Army, had been Sir David Stirling's sergeant at the time when Stirling formed 'L' Detachment, the Special Air Service Brigade in the Western Desert in 1941. Stirling, the SAS and Bond all went on to greater things, with Bond working his way up through the Metropolitan Police, serving two tours with the Flying Squad and assisting in the formation of C11 Criminal Intelligence Department. Now, as head of operations of the CID, Bond was enormously popular and respected; he was also one of the few career detectives that Mark listened to.

With promotion, the proposed night-duty CID went out of the window; Griffiths was posted to C1 Department at the Yard, working with the central cheque squad, the murder squad and assisting with the bomb squad. Almost a year to the day of the pawnshop incident, Griffiths was awarded £20 from the Bow Street Reward Fund, and five months later, on 18 June 1974, the

London Gazette announced that he would be awarded the British Empire Medal for Gallantry, for 'displaying gallantry of a very high order'. This was one of the last of the BEMs for Gallantry ever awarded; two days after the announcement of the award, the Queen's Gallantry Medal was instituted in its place.

For the next seven years Griffiths remained a detective sergeant, gathering a wealth of experience, until his promotion to detective inspector in 1980. As he shot up through the ranks, postings included a three-and-a-half-year tour with the Flying Squad and, after a five-year spell in uniform, the position of operational head of the Flying Squad. Just twenty-seven years after his promotion in the field, Griffiths filled the chair vacated by his hero Ernie Bond as Deputy Assistant Commissioner, Director of the Serious Crime Group, a post he held for over five years. During his thirty-eight-year career with the Metropolitan Police Griffiths found time to attend firearms courses, the advanced CID course at Hendon and the junior, intermediate and senior command courses at Bramshill Police College. He attended the Hostage and Crisis Negotiator courses, at both Hendon and the FBI Headquarters in Quantico, USA, and also passed the Advanced Forensic Science course at Hendon, Advanced Public Order at Hounslow and eight other courses; this all led to the publication of four papers based on his experience – sound, common-sense policing.

Griffiths was showered with awards; his Long Service and Good Conduct Medal in 1989 were followed eight years later by the Queen's Police Medal for distinguished service, in 2003 the Queen's Jubilee Medal and in the following year, the Association of Chief Police Officers' Homicide Working Group lifetime achievement award.

Bill Griffiths retired as DAC on 31 October 2005; he took with him fourteen commissioner's commendations for courage, leadership and detective ability, but the following day he was back in a civilian role – as Director of Leadership Development, a post he held until 2010 when he and the Met finally parted company, but not before accepting one final award. In 2007 he was appointed Commander of the British Empire for his services to policing. He now runs a consultancy business and is also the proud grandfather of seven children.

Griffiths possesses strong opinions, as do I. We both served for over eight years with the Flying Squad and we are both immensely proud of that; similarly, both of us have profound, lip-curling contempt for lazy and corrupt police officers.

But on the emotive matter of Sir Robert Mark – Bill Griffiths and I agree to differ!

CHAPTER 20

Shots Fired in the Mall

ecently, the Princess Royal recalled the time when an attempt was made to abduct her in the Mall and gave her opinion as to why it failed. "The reason it didn't work is that there was only one of him," she stated. "If there had been more than one of him, it would probably have worked."

It could be she was right; but it must not be forgotten that on 20 March 1974 it was not through want of trying that her lone abductor failed in his attempt to kidnap Her Majesty the Queen's second eldest child in order to extort a ransom. It should also be remembered that during the attack a number of very gallant people, both police officers and civilians, went to her aid and that four of them were shot at the closest possible range, one of them three times. The incident resulted in the lunatic kidnapper being overpowered and seven gallantry awards being bestowed; it also revealed a shocking lack of security procedures in respect of the royal family.

★   ★   ★

The man who was eventually charged under the name of Ian Ball was born Peter Sydney Ball in 1947. Bullied at school, he acquired six 'O' levels before starting a series of undemanding jobs, interspersed with petty crime; he was convicted for offences of receiving stolen goods and obtaining property by deception, none of which led to custodial sentences. He was a loner and a dreamer; the desire for easy money and a grand lifestyle, plus a personality disorder which was becoming more severe, were inexorably leading to a plan which would culminate in worldwide headlines. In 1966 Ball had been diagnosed as schizophrenic and by 1972 he was suffering from depression; in the single furnished room in which he lived frugally in Bayswater, the social security benefits he received were meticulously set aside – as were the profits from a small mail-order fraud – for the grand coup he had started plotting the previous year.

The scheme, three years in the planning, was quite simply to kidnap Her Royal Highness, Princess Anne, and to demand a ransom from Her Majesty the Queen of £3 million. In fact, the preparation was meticulous; he obtained a false driver's licence in the name of John Williams and used this to hire a white Ford Escort, registration number SVL 282L. He used accommodation addresses, acquired two Astra handguns in Madrid with a sufficiency of ammunition, and had taken a house in Fleet, Hampshire on a six-month rental, using the name of Jason van der Sluis. There were sufficient provisions in the house for a week and in addition, there were four sets of handcuffs, two of them adapted to make leg shackles. All previous documentation relating to Peter Sydney Ball had been destroyed, as had the labels in his clothing.

A week before the attack, Ball hired a typewriter from a shop in Camberley, using his alias of John Williams – which would not in itself have attracted attention, although the fact that he was wearing white cotton gloves during the transaction did. Back at the house in Fleet, Ball typed his preposterous ransom note to the Queen, in which he demanded £3 million in used £5 notes, to be packed into suitcases with the amount in each suitcase shown on the outside. What he did not know is that a combination of grease and dirt adds to the weight of used notes, and the total weight of the money demanded would have amounted to approximately seventy-five kilos; Ball would have encountered grave difficulties in attempting to manage the cases himself. Perhaps he hoped Princess Anne would help load the suitcases on to the aeroplane which he also demanded, to fly them to Zürich. Incorporated in Ball's nonsensical demands was the stipulation that he would receive a free pardon for his crimes, including, chillingly, 'the murder of any police officers'.

Ball's initial plan was to ambush Princess Anne close to her home at Oak Grove House, Sandhurst Military Academy, Berkshire, where her (then) husband Captain Mark Phillips was a staff instructor. The academy was just a few miles away from Fleet, and twice in one week Ball was stopped and questioned by military personnel and police in that immediate area. In fact, a staff sergeant had spotted his distinctive white hire-car at eleven different locations during the space of four days, but although the car was searched, nothing incriminating was found and he was allowed to go. Now, on 20 March, Ball resolved that decisive action had to be taken. He knew from the Court Circular published in the *Daily Telegraph* that Princess Anne and her husband would be attending a charity film show at Sudbury House in the City of London that evening; he was also aware that five days hence she would be travelling to Germany. This latter information had been gleaned by telephoning the Press Office at Buckingham Palace.

So that afternoon Ball followed Princess Anne to London and parked up in Newgate Street, where he waited until 7.30, at which time Princess Anne and her husband left the film performance and got into the maroon Austin limousine, registration number NGN 1, which was used for royal duties. The elderly vehicle had no protection whatsoever; it was not armour-plated, did not have bullet-proof glass in the windows, nor was it accompanied by back-up vehicles of any kind. This in itself would not have presented so much of a problem had the vehicle possessed an R/T set to communicate with New Scotland Yard in the event of an emergency – but it did not. Only one person in that car possessed a weapon to use in the event of an attack; and as events would show, the firearm which had been issued was woefully inadequate.

The vehicle used by Ian Ball, on the other hand, was very well equipped. He had the two revolvers, fifty-eight extra rounds of ammunition, the handcuffs and three sets of cotton gloves, one pair of which he was now wearing. In his pocket was the absurd ransom demand addressed to the Queen.

During the next fifteen minutes the Austin headed west across London until it passed Admiralty Arch, and as it drove down the Mall towards Buckingham Palace, Ball decided it was time to act. How he thought he could abduct the Princess and then convey her to his hideout, over forty miles away, probably did not occur to him; a plan that he would kidnap Princess Anne, come what may, had become fixed in his fragmenting mind, and now that plan had to be carried out. "Ball was obsessive," Graham Melvin, one of the investigating officers told me, over thirty-five years later. "He believed it was a foolproof plan."

The Princess was sitting in the rear of the royal car on the offside, behind the driver, with Captain Phillips sitting next to her; opposite him sat Princess Anne's Lady in Waiting, Miss Rowena Brassey, on a fold-down 'dicky' seat. The vehicle was driven by a long-serving chauffeur to the royal household, Alexander Callender; next to him sat Inspector James Wallace Beaton, married, aged thirty-one, who had been a member of the Metropolitan Police for twelve years. He had served at Notting Hill, Harrow Road and Wembley before transferring as an inspector to the Royalty Protection Department in March 1973. One year later he had been appointed personal police officer to Princess Anne. Trained in the use of firearms, he was carrying a 9mm Walther PP semi-automatic pistol, serial number 17125A.

Named after their designer, Carl Walther, these pistols were first manufactured in Germany in 1929 and were considered both reliable and concealable. One was used with great success by Adolf Hitler, who blew his brains out with it in his bunker in 1945, and another by Ian Fleming's fictional secret agent, James Bond. Light, weighing just over one pound, Beaton's weapon was fitted with what should have been – according to the manufacturer's instructions – a standard clip containing eleven 9mm Parabellum rounds. But it was not. The 9mm ammunition which had been issued was the cheapest the Metropolitan Police could find. So that, plus the propensity for automatic weapons to jam, did not augur well for Beaton's personal protection weapon.*

★ ★ ★

Now, in the Mall, the Austin screeched to a halt as Ball's Escort cut in front of it. Ball got out of the car and walked towards Callender; Beaton, seeing this, initially thought that the man was going to remonstrate with Callender over some imagined traffic incident. Therefore he got out of the car and walked around the back of the Austin to approach the man and find out what was happening. What he did not know was that Ball was pointing his .38 revolver at Callender and telling him to turn off the ignition; as Beaton rounded the back of the car, Ball fired twice, one bullet tearing Beaton's jacket, the other hitting him in the right shoulder and puncturing a lung.

Initially, Beaton did not realize he had been shot; there was a feeling as though he had been kicked or punched in the shoulder, and as he later said, "It did not register I had been wounded." He immediately drew his pistol and fired in Ball's direction, but the strength had drained from his right arm, and as he lowered the weapon he realized that the bullet had hit the back of the royal car. Furthermore, he now noticed that he was bleeding from the shoulder and that this had distorted his aim. Stepping away from the car, Beaton adopted a two-handed stance to fire his weapon, but discovered that the pistol had jammed. He retreated to the rear nearside of the car and, crouching down, tried to clear the

---

* In fact, the author fired off thirteen rounds from a police-issue Browning Hi-Power automatic pistol which should, like the Walther PP (and according to the manufacturer) have been issued with 9mm Parabellum bullets; it jammed three times.

gun. The magazine slide was back; Beaton put his finger inside the mechanism but it was completely blocked. As he did so, on the other side of the car, Callender grabbed Ball's arm in an attempt to take the gun off him, but Ball said, "I'll shoot you," and did just that; the shot fired at point-blank range hit Callender in the chest, knocking him back into the driver's seat.

Suddenly Beaton saw the rear nearside door of the car open and Miss Brassey come out in a crouch, very low, leaving the door open as an avenue of escape for the Princess. He moved towards the door, seeing a man silhouetted in the open offside doorway opposite. As Beaton started to get in the car, Ball said, "Put your gun down, or I'll shoot her." Since the pistol had jammed and could not be freed, Beaton put the gun down in the roadway, then held his hands up to show Ball that he had done as he had been told and at the same time started to move into the car in an effort to get between Princess Anne and the gunman. Ball had hold of Princess Anne's wrist and was pulling her towards him, while Captain Phillips was holding her around her waist and attempting to shut the door.

With commendable presence of mind, Princess Anne tried to defuse the situation by asking, "Why are you doing this?" Ball replied, "I'll get a couple of million."

"I haven't got a couple of million!" replied the Princess indignantly, and when Ball told her, "Get out of the car," her response was predictable: "Not bloody likely!"

Beaton had managed to get closer and now, his elbow resting on the Princess's knees, he was still trying to get between her and the gunman. When, for some unaccountable reason, Ball took a step back, Captain Phillips took the opportunity to slam the door shut. Beaton was on his knees leaning against the Princess, and Ball, pointing the gun at the closed window, shouted, "Open the door or I'll shoot!" Ball pulled the trigger, and as Beaton later stated, "I immediately held my hand up in its path and everything seemed to explode at once." The window shattered and the bullet from Ball's gun hit the palm of Beaton's hand, lodging there. Captain Phillips was still holding the door shut and Beaton told him to release it, as he meant to kick the door open with the intention of knocking Ball back into what he imagined would be a crowd of people outside, in the hope that they would capture him. With a superhuman effort, Beaton kicked the door and the fragmented glass flew out of the window frame, but the door opened hardly at all. Ball wrenched the door open and shot Beaton for the third time, on this occasion in the stomach, the bullet ploughing through his intestines and lodging in his pelvis.

Now grievously wounded and in complete shock, Beaton would later say he felt 'drunk'; in fact, he was utterly disorientated. In common with many people who suffer great trauma, Beaton, who was wearing a new blue pinstripe suit, a red and white shirt and a dark tie, found he was concentrating on minutiae. He just wanted his new suit to suffer as little damage as possible – unlikely, since his blood was running from three separate bullet wounds – and he gently collapsed by a tree at the side of the Mall; there he would remain until the ambulance came for him.

Incredibly, only a few minutes had passed since the Escort had swerved in front of the royal car; but by now passers-by were stopping and traffic from the direction of Admiralty Arch was piling up. People were shouting, car horns were sounding and what appeared to be the sound of a car backfiring had attracted the attention of Police Constable 736 'A' Michael Hills, on duty outside St James' Palace. Running towards the scene, he immediately recognised the royal car and, believing that the vehicle must have been involved in a traffic incident, he radioed this information to Cannon Row police station. As he reached the car, he became aware that the rear offside window was shattered and that a man was leaning in through the open door. Someone shouted, "He's got a gun," but Hills grabbed hold of the man by the door, saying, "What's going on?" Ball turned and fired – by now, he had emptied his .38 revolver and was using the second of the Astra handguns, this one containing .22 ammunition. The bullet struck Hills in the stomach, coming to rest just by his liver; Hills managed to duck behind the limousine and sent a second, more accurate radio transmission to Cannon Row, with such precise information that police cars from all over Central London began racing towards the scene.

Attracted by the commotion, the chauffeur of a Jaguar, Glenmore Thomas Walter Martin, had pulled up in front of Ball's Escort. He looked back, saw the wounded Alex Callender in the driving seat of the Austin weakly beckoning for help and saw Ball discharge his revolver into the offside rear window, firing the bullet which hit Beaton's hand. He immediately reversed his Jaguar against the front of the Escort to prevent Ball's escape, then ran over to the royal car. Ball pushed the muzzle of the gun against his ribs and told him, "Clear off."

Martin turned to see PC Hills, who had picked up Beaton's discarded – and useless – Walther with the intention of shooting Ball, but the bullet wound had weakened him to such an extent that he staggered, and Glenmore Martin helped him to the pavement, where Hills collapsed.

John Brian McConnell, a forty-six-year-old journalist, had spent a convivial evening with lawyer friends at El Vino's in Fleet Street; now, they were en route to the Irish Club in Euston Square in a taxi, when he heard the sound of gunfire. Jumping from the cab, McConnell saw that Ball was holding a gun and, as he later told a reporter for the *Daily Mirror* who interviewed him at his hospital bedside, "I ran up to the gunman and stood in front of him. I said to him, 'Look old man, these people are friends of mine – don't be silly, just give me the gun.' He told me, 'Get out of the way, get out of the way!' I moved forward to take the gun from his hand and he pulled the trigger. There was a blinding flash and I remember thinking, 'Christ, the bastard's shot me!'" McConnell staggered to the rear of the royal car and collapsed; the bullet had passed between his fifth and sixth rib and lodged under his right armpit.

At that point, twenty-six-year-old Ronald George Russell, who was driving home on the opposite side of the Mall, saw what was happening. The six feet four former heavyweight boxer ('with no time for bullies or liberty takers') got out of his van and ran across the thoroughfare. By now, the car door was shut and Ball was smashing it with his gun butt. Russell punched him on the side of his head. This caused Ball to turn and fire – the bullet narrowly missed Russell and splintered the windscreen of a taxi. Russell then ran round to the nearside of the car; Glenmore Martin was still looking after PC Hills, and Russell said, "Give me his truncheon," but there was no time – two more shots sounded on the other side of the car. Ball had got the door open again; he grabbed Princess Anne by the wrist and was trying to pull her out, whilst Captain Phillips was holding her back inside the car. "Come on, Anne," said Ball. "You know you've got to come!"

"Why don't you go away?" replied the Princess, quietly. "What good is all this going to do?" – and at that moment she broke free from his grip. Now Russell leant in through the nearside door, saying, "Come this way, Anne, you'll be safe." She had almost reached the pavement when Ball came round the front of the car and Captain Phillips wisely pulled her back into the car. Russell stood in front of the Princess, prepared to 'take the bullet', but Ball tried to get past between Russell and the car; it was the last of many mistakes he had made. Russell punched him on the chin, so hard that he actually overbalanced. When he got to his feet, Ball had run off; but twenty-six-year-old Temporary Detective Constable Peter Roy Edmonds, crewing the local 'Q' Car and having heard the radio message that had flashed across one quarter of the capital, rushed to the scene. As he arrived, he took in the sight of four men on the ground who had been shot, before taking up the pursuit. Shouting at the gunman to stop, and seeing him turn and aim his revolver at him, Edmonds threw his coat over Ball's head and brought him crashing to the ground with a rugby tackle. Five more police officers piled on top, one of them knocking the revolver, still with five live rounds in its chambers, from Ball's hand.

Four men had been grievously wounded, but at least an act of violence against a member of the royal family – the most serious since the anarchist Jean-Baptiste Spirido had fired a shot at King Edward VII in protest against the Boer War, seventy-four years previously – had been averted. Unlike Spirido, the perpetrator of the carnage in the Mall had been caught. Now, as the injured were ferried to hospital, the investigation had to commence – to find out the who, the how and the why of the offence, and to discover who else (if anybody) was involved. This last was a perfectly reasonable supposition, since at that time mainland Britain was in the middle of a particularly vicious IRA offensive. Although kidnappings were not commonplace, shootings were.

Instead, an act of unparalleled stupidity was committed.

★   ★   ★

The commissioner of the Metropolitan Police was Sir Robert Mark GBE, QPM, and following a number of high-profile scandals, he had removed several of Scotland Yard's senior CID officers from office and replaced them with uniformed officers, the majority of whom, like their leader, had no expertise whatever in the world of criminal investigation.

Now, having initially heard the news of the attempted abduction of Princess Anne from Magnolia, one of the Yard's waitresses, Sir Robert received confirmation of the incident from the Assistant Commissioner (Crime), Colin Woods, who until recently had been in charge of supervising the flow of London's traffic. Having confirmed that Magnolia's information was essentially correct, Sir Robert set off to the Reform Club to deliver a speech. An hour later, Sir Robert spoke to the Home Secretary at the House of Commons, and Prime Minister Harold Wilson made a late statement in the House, confirming that an incident had occurred in the Mall involving Princess Anne, that shots had been fired, the Princess had not been injured and a man had been arrested who would appear in court in the morning. The statement was made with the same confidence that a custody officer might have in prophesying the simple appearance in court of someone who had been charged with being drunk and disorderly – whereas at that time no one knew anything about Ball, who he was, where he lived, whether he had plotted alone or been part of a wider terrorist conspiracy.

Fortunately, the calibre of the three-man investigating team was up to the job. At its head was Deputy Assistant Commissioner 'C' Department (Operations) Ernie Bond OBE, QPM, who was a dyed-in-the-wool career detective and a shrewd investigator. His second-in-command was Detective Chief Superintendent Roy Ransom, and newly-promoted Detective Inspector Graham Melvin completed the trio. They got to work immediately, Bond directing Flying Squad teams to work throughout the night establishing Ball's true identity, his antecedents and the possibility of anybody else being involved in the incident. Ball appeared at Bow Street Magistrates' Court the following day, and just two months later an extremely brief trial was held at the Old Bailey.

Ball pleaded guilty to two charges of attempted murder, two charges of wounding with intent to cause grievous bodily harm and attempting to steal and carry away Her Royal Highness, Princess Anne. There was little that could be said in mitigation; a Home Office psychiatrist certified that Ball was suffering from 'a severe personality disorder', and Lord Chief Justice Widgery ordered that Ball be detained under the Mental Health Act, without limit of time. He was sent to Rampton Mental Hospital and he remains incarcerated to this day.

★   ★   ★

Beaton and Hills were on the sick list for a considerable length of time; the bullet which lodged by Hills' liver had to be left where it was, because the surgeons believed it would be too dangerous to try to remove it. Beaton returned to duty after six months, and he, Hills and Edmonds were all highly commended by the commissioner. The following November, the heroes of the Mall were honoured at Buckingham Police. Jim Beaton's gallantry was recognised with the award of the George Cross – the highest award it was possible for him to receive. The George Medal was awarded to Michael Hills and Ron Russell, the latter saying that when he received the award the Queen told him, "The medal is from the Queen of England; the thank-you is from Anne's mother." Alexander Callender, Peter Edmonds and Brian McConnell were each awarded the Queen's Gallantry Medal, and Glenmore Martin, the Queen's Commendation for Brave

Conduct. And of course, Princess Anne had acted with cool courage throughout her ordeal; she was appointed a Dame of the Grand Cross of the Royal Victoria Order, although as her father the Duke of Edinburgh is said to have commented, "If the man had succeeded in abducting Anne, she would have given him a hell of a time in captivity!"

The American Secret Service, which amongst other duties is tasked with protecting the life of the President, awarded Jim Beaton the Director's Honor Award. He remained with Princess Anne until 1979, when he was promoted to chief inspector, and three years later he became the Queen's Police Officer. In 1983 he was promoted to the rank of superintendent and in 1985, chief superintendent. Two years later he was appointed a Lieutenant of the Royal Victorian Order and in 1992 he was promoted to Commander of the Order. Jim Beaton retired after thirty years' service and now lives quietly in the north of England.

Three years after the incident in the Mall, Peter Edmonds and a fellow officer were confronted by a gunman who had stolen a car in order to carry out a post office robbery. They chased the man, who fired at them during the pursuit, and overpowered him. Edmonds was twice highly commended by the commissioner for outstanding courage and received five other commissioner's commendations for bravery and detective ability. He served in the East End of London, as well as in postings with the Stolen Car Squad, and retired with the rank of detective sergeant in 1998, after twenty-seven years' service. He retired to Devon, but sadly died at the early age of fifty-six.

Michael Hills retired from the Metropolitan Police on medical grounds in 2000; he has always been reluctant to discuss the incident.

Brian McConnell died from cancer in July 2004, aged seventy-five; a reporter and author to his fingertips, he was still writing a column for the *South London Press* at the time of his death.

Ron Russell now lives in Cromer, Norfolk; he and his wife Eve ran a succession of pubs in villages in Norfolk, East Runton, North Creake and Worstead, before he started a roofing business. "I'm a 'get-involved' sort of person," he says, "and would do the same thing again, today."

Her Royal Highness Princess Anne – now the Princess Royal – and Captain Phillips divorced in 1992 and she re-married Commander (now Vice-Admiral) Timothy Lawrence. An accomplished horsewoman – she was a pupil at the Spanish Riding School in Vienna – the Princess competed in equestrian events in the 1976 Olympic Games and won a gold and two silver medals at the European Eventing Championships. With a host of British and foreign decorations, honorary degrees and military appointments, the Princess is the patron of over 200 organisations and on behalf of the Queen carries out over 700 royal engagements every year. In papers declassified and released after thirty years, in a written note for the then Prime Minister Harold Wilson, she stated, "It was all so infuriating; I kept saying I didn't want to get out of the car and I was <u>not</u> going to get out of the car."

★   ★   ★

As well as worldwide media coverage at the time, the incident inspired the 2006 Granada Television docu-drama *To Kidnap a Princess*, and was the basis for Tom Clancy's novel *Patriot Games* and Antonia Fraser's *Your Royal Hostage*. It also prompted a much-needed review of royal security.

Close protection skills were stepped up and the Walthers were hastily discarded; eventually Royalty Protection Officers were armed with the Austrian-made Glock automatic pistol, made of steel with a plastic covering. With a magazine holding seventeen rounds, it does not have a tendency to jam. The Royalty and Diplomatic Protection Department was formed in 1983; it embraced *inter alia* the Royalty Protection Department. Close and Personal Protection Officers liaise with each other as well as with intelligence agencies and are in radio contact with the Special Escort Group. Medical equipment is carried in their vehicles, and all personnel are trained to a high degree in advanced first-aid.

It all seems a long way from the elderly, defenceless Austin in the Mall in 1974; or rather it did until December 2010, when an equally defenceless Rolls-Royce Phantom VI, containing the heir to the throne, His Royal Highness The Prince of Wales, and his wife, Camilla, Duchess of Cornwall, was attacked in Regent Street by a howling mob of protesters. The car, which had been presented to the Queen three years after the incident in the Mall, was splattered with paint and kicked, and a window was broken. Denying that the Duchess had been struck with a stick, Home Secretary Theresa May nevertheless admitted that 'physical contact' had been made and, refusing to offer her resignation, smartly passed the buck to the commissioner of police, who did. His offer was not taken up, although after Prime Minister David Cameron promised that the protesters responsible should face 'the full weight of the law' it was of course stated that an investigation would reveal if 'any lessons needed to be learnt'.

Will they be? Time will tell.

★   ★   ★

Many long-term prisoners, sane or otherwise, with little hope of ever being released, turn to God. Instead, Ian Ball has turned to the internet and has kept his disintegrating mind busy composing a rambling blog in which he offers a £1 million reward to the person who can prove that the incident was a hoax; that it occurred one year later and therefore he cannot be responsible because he was in Rampton; that the whole matter was orchestrated by a police officer named 'Frank'; and that the woman in the car was not Princess Anne. She was a substitute, planted there by 'Frank' and so, claims Ball, since Princess Anne must know it was a hoax, she would have told her mother. Therefore, it is the Queen's fault that an innocent man has been kept incarcerated for over thirty years.

When the truth of this miscarriage of justice is finally made public, Ball believes his autobiography will be a best-seller – probably grossing in excess of £2 million.

CHAPTER 21

East End Mercenary

He was christened Brian Ernest Walter Pawley, but to his many friends and contemporaries he has never been known as anything other than 'Ernie', which is the way he will be referred to throughout this narrative. Now, at seventy years of age, Ernie still looks tough enough to punch holes through a brick wall; it was his physical fitness, strong constitution and resolve which saved his life, over thirty years ago – and the skill of the surgeons and the love and support of his family. All that, plus a generous indulgence of good luck.

It all happened because of an investigation which, if it had been allowed to run its course, would probably have culminated in a ticking-off for the perpetrator and the warning, 'Don't do that, again'. But the enquiry did not come to a satisfactory conclusion. It ended abruptly with one detective escaping death in a fusillade of bullets, another lying grievously wounded and close to death, and the man responsible, very definitely dead. And it all happened on Saturday, 11 March 1978, when Detective Constable Ernie Pawley wanted a day off.

★   ★   ★

Ernie had only been at Stoke Newington police station for two months; prior to that, he had been attached to the Yard's Serious Crime Squad for three and a half years, during which time he had been commended by the commissioner, the Director of Public Prosecutions, judges at the Old Bailey and the bench at Norwich Magistrates' Court in three cases, for his role in breaking up gangs of international criminals, as well as some home-grown ones. But when the Squad was not actively engaged in carrying out observations on criminals or arresting them, they had every weekend off. Not so at divisional police stations, which demanded a twenty-four-hour, seven-day-a-week cover by CID officers, especially a busy East End station like Stoke Newington. So when on the morning of 11 March Ernie phoned in to see if he could have a day off, it was curtly refused.

Grumpily getting dressed and putting on an old pair of shoes, thirty-seven-year-old Ernie kissed goodbye to his wife Val, and their three children, Neil, fourteen, Colin, ten and Sarah, eight. He then left their home in Romford and made his way to the insalubrious streets of Stoke Newington, where he was seen by Detective Chief Inspector Don Gibson, who informed him of a curious incident. That morning, a concerned father had arrived at the police station and told the officers that the previous day, his daughter aged nine and her friend, a girl aged eight, had gone to the local swimming pool where they had met a man named 'Alan', who had taken them to his flat 'somewhere near the children's hospital in Hackney'. The girls had travelled there in his car, which was red and had the part-registration number 'TUU'. It also had what the girls described as 'a loose boot'. In the flat he had shown the girls some guns he possessed and had given them some trinkets and, in the father's words, 'fifty bob [£2.50] each'. There had been absolutely no allegation of sexual impropriety, but 'Alan' had asked that the girls meet him at the swimming baths again the following day, Saturday.

The girl's father repeated this odd story to Ernie, who asked him to bring both girls to the police station to verify it, and this was done. "Take Russ Dunlop with you," said DCI Gibson, indicating a new detective constable. Booking out the CID car, Ernie, Dunlop, the father and the two girls drove out of the station in the direction of Hackney Road and the (now closed) children's hospital. As Ernie stopped at a set of traffic lights, across the junction amongst the oncoming traffic was a red car bearing the part-registration number 'TUU'. "Is that the man driving that red car over there?" asked Ernie, and both girls immediately replied, "Yes".

Ernie turned the CID car round, and as the red car moved off he followed it into a side street and stopped some distance behind it. Both officers got out of their car, walked over to the red car and introduced themselves to its occupant. Possibly thinking he had illegally parked, the man, whose name was Alan Murphy, replied, "Oh, I'm only going to the shops." In his early forties, Murphy was five feet six tall and very well built – he had enormously thick arms – and he was quite relaxed and unconcerned about being questioned by the two detectives. As Dunlop checked the boot of Murphy's car and discovered that it was indeed loose as the girls had described, so Ernie said casually, "I understand you've got some guns at home, Alan?"

"Yes," agreed Murphy, "but I have got a certificate for them."

"Well, let's go home and check it then," said Ernie, to which Murphy, with the calm he had exhibited all through this brief meeting, replied, "Certainly, let's go."

At no time had Ernie mentioned what the girls had said, nor had Murphy seen them, because the CID car had been parked some little distance away. So now, telling Dunlop to accompany Murphy in his car, Ernie went back to the CID car and followed the two men in the red car to 81 Goldsmith's Row, Bethnal Green, E2, a three-storey block of flats in a short street just off Hackney Road, between Queensbridge Road and Mare Street. Leaving the father and the two girls in the police car, Ernie walked over to Murphy and Dunlop and the three men walked up to Flat 4, situated on the first floor of the premises. The atmosphere between the three men was completely affable, but this was about to change dramatically. Murphy had told Ernie that he worked as a driver, which was true. What he had not told him was that he had also worked as a mercenary in Africa and six years previously had taken part in an abortive coup to overthrow Equatorial Guinea's dictator. Murphy was, in fact, a borderline psychotic, he was indeed in possession of firearms, he had killed a lot of people in Africa and now, here in England, he was about to try to add two more to the list.

★   ★   ★

The flat – or rather, bedsit – was unremarkable; there was a bed, a wardrobe, a chest of drawers, a table and chairs and at the back, a door leading to the kitchen. Murphy, a member of a gun club, handed Dunlop a firearms certificate and then from under the bed took a briefcase, from which he produced a large black handgun. Dunlop confirmed that that was one of the guns mentioned in the certificate, and Ernie commented, "Surely you shouldn't have this gun here, you should keep it at your club." Murphy agreed but said he had brought it home for cleaning. In a corner of the room by the chest of drawers Ernie noticed a long metal object, four feet in length, with a diameter of about two and a half inches at one end, tapering down to one inch at the other. He picked it up; it was very heavy, and when he asked Murphy what it was, he was told that it was an antique air rifle. Ernie kept hold of it for a little longer, examining it because he had never seen a weapon like it before, before putting it down on a chair by the wardrobe. It was the wardrobe which Dunlop was searching in Murphy's presence, so Ernie walked into the kitchen where he picked up one of several red plastic boxes containing empty shells. As he went to open it, Murphy called out, "Be careful how you open them or they'll all fall out," and that was just what happened. As Ernie bent down and picked up the shells, he noticed a lot of equipment in the kitchen; when he asked the purpose of it, Murphy replied, "Making bullets," and then asked Ernie what was going to happen to him. Ernie explained what the little girls had said, in detail, and Murphy replied, "Oh, you found out about the girls, then?" adding, "but I never touched them."

"In view of the allegations made by the girls and the fact that you have that gun in the briefcase that you shouldn't have here," said Ernie, "I want you to come to Stoke Newington police station with us to clear it all up." Murphy, as unconcerned as ever, replied, "OK, I'll come down with you."

Ernie looked down, saw a metal tool box underneath the table and said, "We're going to have another quick look round before we go." Bending down, he pulled the box out, opened it and saw a Mauser self-loading pistol lying on top. Then, before he could ask any questions about it, he heard Murphy say, very quietly, "That's enough."

Ernie looked up. The shocking sight that confronted him was his colleague Russ Dunlop, a thirty-one-year-old married man with two children, on his knees with Murphy behind him, staring fixedly at Ernie and holding a handgun with both hands, his knees slightly bent, forcing the barrel of the gun into the nape of Dunlop's neck. As calmly as he could in such a situation, Ernie said, "Don't be silly, let me sit down and we can talk about this." But as he went to sit on one of the chairs, Murphy replied, "Shut up and stay where you are."

Murphy now turned the gun one-handed from Dunlop to Ernie, pointing it at his chest from a distance of three feet. Although matters were now moving very quickly indeed, Ernie, who had been a police-authorised shot for the past eight years, and a marksman, spotted that the gun that Murphy was holding was a short-barrelled .38 revolver. Bullets were in the chamber, and there was no visible obstruction in the barrel to suggest that this was an imitation firearm. Moreover, although this did not become apparent until much later, it was not the weapon which Murphy had produced from the briefcase. It had been in his possession the entire time.

Murphy now pushed the gun barrel back into Dunlop's neck, forcing his head forwards, and Ernie, desperately trying to defuse the situation, again said, "Don't be silly – these are only small matters," but Murphy replied, "Shut up – I'm going to kill you both." His calm manner had now deserted him, and as Ernie looked at him he knew immediately that this was no hysterical outburst. As he told me, over thirty years later, "I knew negotiations were out!" He had faced dangerous men before, and

he realized at that moment that Murphy meant exactly what he
said and that unless immediate action was taken he was about to
witness his companion's execution.

Forced to his knees, Dunlop could do nothing to save himself,
so Ernie took the initiative, leaping at Murphy, seizing hold of his
wrist and pushing the gun away from Dunlop's neck. Although
this took Murphy by surprise, his reactions were extremely quick
and he turned the gun towards Ernie's chest. Even though Ernie
was exceptionally strong and fit, he was no match for Murphy, a
bodybuilder who could actually press porters' trolleys above his
head; so although Ernie was pushing with all his strength, slowly
but steadily the gun in Murphy's rock-solid grip moved across
Ernie's chest area until it reached the heart region – then Murphy
pulled the trigger.

"I felt as though I had been hit on the chest with a
sledgehammer," said Ernie. As he continued to hang on to
Murphy, he could actually feel the bullet burning its way through
his body, so he shouted to Dunlop, "Get out, and get some help!"
As Dunlop ran to the door, Murphy suddenly wrenched his arms
from Ernie's grasp and fired a shot at Dunlop, fortunately
missing him; as Murphy ran after him Ernie punched the
gunman to try to knock him off balance and give Dunlop a
chance of escaping, before he himself crashed to the floor. There
came the sound of another shot fired in Dunlop's direction. Ernie
was now on his hands and knees and experiencing great difficulty
breathing, so he rolled on to his right side in the hope that this
might assist him to breathe more easily. Initially, as he later told
me, "I was thinking of Val and the kids", and his second thought
was, "I don't want to finish in some shitty flat in the East End,"
because now he believed he was dying.

Murphy now came back into the room and fired a random shot
at Ernie, which missed; then, squatting down in front of Ernie,
Murphy ejected the empty bullet cases from the gun and began
reloading it, saying chillingly, "You're dead, anyway."

Believing that Russ Dunlop was either dead or wounded – in
fact, the bullet had narrowly missed Dunlop, who had fallen
down the stairs – Ernie suddenly noticed the antique airgun, and
to prevent any other police officer who might enter the flat being
killed or incapacitated, with a tremendous effort grabbed hold of
the airgun with both hands and jumped to his feet. Murphy was
taken by surprise, but he also got to his feet, still holding the gun.
Ernie smashed the airgun across Murphy's forearms and the
revolver went spinning across the room. But the struggle was by
no means over; Murphy with or without a weapon still posed an

enormous threat, and Ernie struck him across the arms and body to stop Murphy attacking him, before Murphy grabbed hold of the air rifle. Ernie managed to snatch the weapon back from Murphy's grasp before hitting him across the face with it and seeing blood start to run from his nose and mouth. Still hitting any available part of Murphy's body, Ernie finally knocked him face down on to a chair and continued to hit him across the head and neck as hard as he could; he only stopped when he was too weak to continue. Ernie believed – wrongly, as it turned out – that Murphy was dead; but he had one more task to accomplish. He had to drag Murphy out of the room and down the stairs, to prove to any police officers who arrived that it would be safe to enter the bedsit. He tried to lift Murphy but he was too heavy; he left the flat to look for Dunlop but was unable to find him, and as he did so he fell down the stairs. Staggering to the front door of the premises, he all but collided with Jim Campbell, a bank messenger who was passing by, and told him, "I've been shot – can you help me?" before collapsing in the street.

Uniformed officers were running towards him, having been summoned by Russ Dunlop, who recalled, "When I got back to the flat after raising the alarm, Ernie was sitting on the pavement, leaning against the wall with blood pouring out of him." In addition, people were spilling out of the pub opposite; one of the clientele brought a large glass of scotch over, saying, "Come on mate, drink this." It was obviously done with the best of intentions, but it was too much for Ernie, who groaned, "Oh, fuck off!"

With Ernie now being rushed by ambulance to St Leonard's hospital, Hackney, police ringed the flats and marksmen took up position. After an hour, Inspector Eric Lister from Bethnal Green police station heard a shot from within the premises, and Sergeant Alexander Moir from the Yard's D11 Firearms Unit led the way into the flat. There he found the lifeless body of Murphy. Moir later told the inquest, "His face was bloodstained and there was a hole in his chest and vest, apparently caused by a gunshot. There were four weapons around his body on the floor." The pathologist, Dr Peter Venezis, said that in his opinion the gunshot which had killed Murphy was self-inflicted.

Murphy's landlord, John Delaney, told reporters, "He was a nice person – respectable, shy and a bit of a loner," and added, "I just can't understand how this situation developed."

Neither could anybody else.

* * *

But now, in St Leonard's hospital, Ernie was fighting for his life. During its journey through his body, Murphy's bullet had bounced off his ribs, punched a 2cm hole his diaphragm, penetrated his gut and shaved off part of his pancreas, before lodging in his back by his spine. Professor Staunton had been summoned; he had treated soldiers for gunshot wounds in Northern Ireland and was an authority on this type of injury. Meanwhile, Ernie lay flat on his back as one nurse cut away his bloody clothing and another removed his shoes. One of the shoes – the old pair which Ernie had put on that morning – had a hole in the sole; the nurse held it up to show the doctor, and to Ernie's discomfort he rolled his eyes, as if to say, "Poor soul!"

But this was a small piece of humour in a fraught situation. Professor Staunton operated successfully, but because of the dirt, debris and fragments of clothing which the bullet had dragged with it, septicaemia set in. In addition, it was thought possible that some of Murphy's fellow mercenaries might wish to take revenge, and armed police officers were placed around Ernie's room. The guards were lifted when the Private Military Company which had recruited Murphy was contacted by Detective Chief Inspector Gibson, who was assured that no such action would even be contemplated.

The police rallied round as they always do in such an emergency. Detective Constable John Fowler, a friend of Ernie's from the Serious Crime Squad, volunteered to chauffeur Val Pawley to and from the hospital, and during those days of intensive care, newspaper photographs showed a frightened-looking Val by Ernie's bedside, together with a concerned-looking Russ Dunlop. 'The Suicide Siege', reported the *News of the World*, the day after the shooting, with the subheading, 'Gunman shoots hero detective'; and fellow police officers praised Ernie's courage, none more so than Russ Dunlop.

Six weeks had passed and the septicaemia was getting worse, with the poison having to be drained several times a day; then arbitrary action was taken by David Powis OBE, QPM, the Yard's highly controversial Deputy Assistant Commissioner, who ordered Ernie's removal to St Thomas' hospital. If Powis thought Ernie was not getting the best medical attention then he was wrong, because Ernie and his family were perfectly happy with the treatment he was receiving. No doubt Powis believed that he was doing this from the best of motives, but it caused resentment among Ernie's CID contemporaries (who for the most part loathed Powis) and probably ruffled a few feathers amongst the staff at St Leonard's, as well. Powis had a dislike of being addressed as 'Guv' (a usual form of address from a junior officer to those of and above the rank of inspector), since he thought it disrespectful, and this was matched by his dislike of seeing CID officers without jacket or tie, the sight of which was sufficient to have the offender sent back to uniform. Not that Ernie will have a bad word said about Powis who, he says, treated him with nothing but kindness. No respecter of persons (Ernie addressed his colleagues, male and female, as 'Babe') he recalled, much later on when he was posted to Romford, seeing Powis walk into the CID office. Ernie was without a tie and he nodded to Powis. "Morning, Guv," he said. The office collectively held its breath, until Powis smiled. "Ah, Ernie," he said. "Fancy some lunch?"

Back now to St Thomas' hospital, where Ernie received care just as good as he had at St Leonard's, and where the Chief Surgeon, Mr Lloyd-Davies, was keeping a careful eye on his recovery. Slowly, Ernie recovered. Ten months after the shooting he was allowed to resume duty – light duties – with a home posting at Romford police station. He gave evidence at the Coroners' Court of the events which led to the shooting, and the coroner, Dr Douglas Chambers, congratulated Ernie on his actions and returned the verdict that Murphy had taken his own life while the balance of his mind was disturbed. Nor was the coroner's the only congratulation forthcoming; the commissioner commended both Ernie and Dunlop for their courage (with Ernie receiving a high commendation) on 25 August 1978, and three months later Ernie was awarded £30 from the Bow Street Reward Fund.

And seventeen months after the shooting, the *London Gazette* announced that Ernie would be awarded the George Medal. "It was a day I will remember for the rest of my life," said Ernie, after receiving the medal from the Queen, adding, "it was a nice touch to be taken to the Palace by Rolls. It certainly beat travelling up on public transport!" Ernie received a scroll of honour after being voted one of 'The Men of the Year' and attending a luncheon at the Savoy Hotel – and then it was back to work.

Slowly Ernie's health improved, so much so that by March 1981, just three years after the near-fatal shooting, he was posted to the prestigious No. 9 Regional Crime Squad; for the next eight years he saw some of the toughest police work in Britain, going up against gangs of professional lorry thieves, armed robbers, warehousebreakers and receivers, as well as running informants and making arrests.

One such arrest, involving a seven-handed gang of lorry thieves, was recalled by former Detective Chief Inspector Peter

Connor. At the subsequent trial Ernie was in the witness box giving evidence of the arrest, and it was put to him in no uncertain terms in cross-examination that after he had confronted one of the lorry thieves he had turned and run away. Ernie simply denied the scurrilous allegation, but the defence barrister persisted in his accusation. Peter Connor, sitting behind the prosecuting counsel, scribbled a note and passed it to him, watched as the barrister read it and saw a smile creep across his face. When the defence barrister's vilification of Ernie ended, the prosecuting counsel got to his feet to re-examine Ernie.

"Tell me, Mr Pawley," asked the barrister, "has your courage ever been brought into question before?" Ernie stated that it had not.

"Have you ever been commended in the past?" enquired the barrister, and Ernie agreed that this had been indeed the case.

"Has your courage ever been the subject of any kind of award?" asked the barrister, almost casually, and Connor kept his eyes on the defence barrister who by now had realized that he had committed a gaffe of staggering proportions and appeared to be sliding further and further down into his seat, especially when Ernie agreed that it had.

Delivering his *coup de grâce*, the barrister asked mildly, "Was that award the George Medal for Gallantry?" and as Ernie nodded, the jury burst into laughter; this was probably a contributory factor to the conviction of the entire gang who, as Connor put it, "Went down like a stack of bricks," adding, "These moments come only too seldom in a detective's life!"

But by January 1989 the strain of his injuries was starting to tell, and Ernie was medically discharged with just over twenty-nine years' service. He was re-employed as a civilian, still working for the Regional Crime Squad but now as the office manager ensuring that the wheels of the organisation ran smoothly, until he retired altogether.

In retirement, Ernie, now with five grandchildren, is affectionately remembered by his contemporaries, many of whom – and I am one of them – were surprised that his actions did not merit the award of the George Cross. His biggest admirer is Russ Dunlop, who described Ernie to me as being quite simply, "The bravest of men and one to whom I owe my life."

CHAPTER 22

Justice Denied

Derek Hall is now in his eighties, but his handshake is firm and he is extremely alert. He has lost the sight of one eye but there is very little that he misses. When he left the Metropolitan Police, he not only took with him a lot of memories and commendations, he also took his courage; it would stand him in good stead.

★　★　★

Born in 1929, Derek Arnsby Hall left school at the age of fourteen and enlisted in the Royal Navy in 1947 for seven years. In 1954 he joined the Huntingdonshire Constabulary (to become known as the Mid-Anglia Constabulary in 1965, having amalgamated with Cambridge City Police, Peterborough Combined Police and the Isle of Ely and Cambridge County Constabularies); within a year of joining, he distinguished himself by being commended by the Chairman of the Bench at Huntingdon Divisional Magistrates' Court and also the Chief Constable for displaying courage and devotion to duty in dealing with four men who attacked him and who were later convicted and imprisoned for causing him grievous bodily harm. It would be the first commendation of many.

Hall joined the Criminal Investigation Department in 1962 where his successes continued; he was twice more commended, firstly for his ability in apprehending a mean thief who targeted offertory boxes and altar furniture in churches, and secondly for the detection of three men for a series of office- and storebreakings. Promotion to detective sergeant in 1964 also brought a posting to No. 5 Regional Crime Squad (RCS), specialising in major, cross-border crime; he was again commended for his work in bringing about the arrest of a man wanted for van theft offences and then received a surprising commendation from both the commissioner of the Metropolitan Police and the Chief Constable. He had been directed by the Assistant Chief Constable of Hertfordshire (and also No. 5 Regional Crime Squad Co-ordinator) Gerald McArthur MBE ("one of the finest police officers, ever," says Hall) to carry out surveillance work against the Richardson brothers' 'Torture Gang'. At five feet nine and looking nothing like the public's – or Torture Gang members' – perception of a police officer, Hall carried out his work so well that his position was not compromised, and the commendation praised his 'outstanding assistance'.

Hall had enjoyed his time working with the Metropolitan Police and at the instigation of Detective Superintendent Don Adams (a highly respected investigator with the Richardson enquiry) he decided to transfer to the Met. Within three weeks of his application being submitted in 1970, he was accepted, still retaining his rank of detective sergeant, and spent four and a half years as a divisional officer working in the East End of London. Promotion to detective inspector eluded him, since he failed the examination on four occasions, but his skills were put to better use – a posting in 1975 to No. 9 Regional Crime Squad, based at Horns Road, Barkingside.

In 1978 alone he was commended on three occasions for courage and ability in effecting arrests involving firearms, armed robbers and conspiracy to rob, and the following year he received another commendation for detective ability in a case involving 'numerous' armed robberies. But his time on the RCS was coming to a close, and he resigned from the Force in 1980.

★   ★   ★

Former CID Commander Ferguson Walker was in charge of security at Scaffolding Great Britain (SGB), and he provided Hall with a job in the company. Formed in 1922, SGB grew rapidly nationwide to become the country's biggest supplier of scaffolding and plant hire, and by 1984 had an annual turnover in excess of over £177 million. Hall's job as senior security officer was to cover part of London and the South East of England, visiting sites, maintaining staff discipline, recovering stolen property and liaising with police.

At eleven o'clock in the morning on 13 September 1984, Securicor had just delivered the wages for the depot at Gallions Close, Barking, East London, and Hall was in his office speaking on the telephone to a former Detective Chief Superintendent, the late Bob Chalk, who was employed at the company's head office at Mitcham. Suddenly he heard the sound of loud voices. "Hang on Bob, I'll quieten this lot down," said Hall. He turned to see a large black man wearing a ski-mask and boiler suit, carrying an axe and holding a bag containing stolen wage packets; looking through the office window, Hall saw a white man wearing similar apparel but carrying a sawn-off shotgun and threatening Kim Wallington, a typist, Don Ormiston from stock security, Lil Dayer a cleaner and Robyn Groom, a clerk. At fifty-five years of age, Hall's courage and fitness as a policeman had not deserted him; he charged the black suspect, and together with a colleague, Henry 'Lofty' Harrison, they made him drop the wage packets. Hall and the black robber crashed to the floor, where Hall was savagely hit in the face, head and arms with the axe. The axeman got to his feet and together with the man with the shotgun ran to the reception area. Although badly shaken up and injured – his face had already swollen up from the axe blows – Hall pursued the two robbers out of the reception area and into the yard, where he cornered the black man. "You're not going anywhere," Hall told him with difficulty through his swollen lips, but as he went to seize him the other man, who had pulled off his ski-mask and was about to crawl through a hole in the perimeter wire fence, stopped and turned. Hall saw the suspect full-face; the man then raised the shotgun and, from a distance of six yards, he fired. The blast hit Hall full on the left side of his face and he fell to the ground. Both men then escaped through the hole in the fence, jumped into a stolen blue Ford Cortina and roared off into Thames Road; the car was later found abandoned in Charlton Crescent. From there, it was thought that the men ran through a tunnel underneath the busy A13 trunk road. Although Detective Sergeant Jim O'Connell of the Flying Squad asked readers of the *Barking and Dagenham Independent* for sightings of two men running into Alfreds Gardens or Suttons Close, north of the A13, none was forthcoming.

Back at the depot, the staff had rushed out to render assistance, and an ambulance took Hall initially to Newham hospital, then to Whipps Cross, which had an ophthalmology unit; there he stayed for three weeks. Hall was immensely popular with his former police colleagues and also the workers at SGB, who all crowded around his bedside. Prior to the shooting, he had castigated two young employees at SGB for sloppy practices; to his surprise, they were amongst the first to visit him and wish him well. He received the best of care from the consultant, Mr Beveridge ("A wonderful man," says Hall, "who took time to come and visit me on Sunday mornings"), but Hall had experienced enormous damage and trauma to his left eye and the left side of his face. Two shotgun pellets had lodged in his eye, three more behind it, and another dozen pellets were embedded in his face and neck. Surgeons battled to save the sight of his left eye, without success; it would have to be removed. Hall's wife Joan told the press, "Derek has been in terrible pain and I've had to bathe the eye every day. We were worried that his right eye might begin to be affected." Hall said, "It's got to the stage now where losing the eye will mean good riddance to all the pain I've suffered."

In January 1985 the damaged eye was removed. But two months before that happened, there was another appointment which Hall had to keep. Although Detective Sergeant Jim O'Connell's newspaper appeal had not resulted in any assistance from the residents of Barking or Dagenham regarding the robbery, their reluctance was not shared by the investigating team's underworld informants. O'Connell picked Derek Hall up at home and drove him to Barking police station; he was going to attend an identification parade.

*   *   *

Although the Flying Squad had been in existence since 1919, in 1978 it had been mainly devolved from Scotland Yard, to four offices sited at different points in the capital, there to investigate and arrest those who participated in armed robberies, to the exclusion of any other type of offence. This left four squads at the Yard, but in 1983 two offences took place which stretched the Squad to its absolute limits. The first was the robbery at the Security Express vaults at Shoreditch where £5,961,097 was stolen; the other occurred seven months later, when gold bullion valued at £26,000,000 was stolen from Brink's-Mat warehouse in West London. The four squads at the Yard were mobilised to assist in these two massive investigations, which would continue for years. In order to investigate the other robberies reported at the area offices, the commander of the Flying Squad utilised the services of the RCS, who were also under his control. Therefore, the Flying Squad officers based at Walthamstow and the RCS officers based at Barkingside (where Hall had previously worked) formed an amalgamated team.

They had concentrated their efforts on identifying, then tracing, a gang who were running riot in the Barking and Dagenham areas. The gang had carried out an armed robbery at the Post Office in Becontree Avenue on 13 June 1984 and had got away with £17,256; on 21 August there had been an attempted armed robbery at a sub-Post Office in Goresbrook Road; and three days later Violet Atkins, the sub-Post Mistress at Green Lane, was robbed of £6,029 at gunpoint by six men.

Seven people were arrested and appeared at Barking Magistrates' Court; there was uproar in the public gallery when four men were remanded in custody, and the Chairman of the Bench, Leonard Wright, threatened to have the court cleared. Two days later, two more men appeared charged with similar offences, and the Chairman, Dorothy Revington JP, made it quite clear she would not tolerate any nonsense. She ordered the doors of the court to be locked, saying, "No one must come in or out of this room whilst this matter is being heard." It did not take long at all; she summarily dismissed applications from a defence solicitor that his client should be granted bail and that he should not be handcuffed to a police officer in the dock, and she had the prisoner remanded in custody.

The man who was the subject of the applications was accused of the three robberies whilst armed with a sawn-off shotgun and his name was Timothy Sullivan, aged twenty-two from Dagenham. Without the slightest hesitation, Derek Hall picked him out on the identification parade as being the man who had shot him in the face.

★   ★   ★

Although the identity of the masked, axe-wielding black man who had attacked Derek Hall was known as an absolute certainty to the investigating team who arrested him, there was insufficient evidence with which to charge him.

Hall returned to work and in October 1985 he went to Moorfields Eye Hospital in London, where further surgery was carried out, this time by a different surgeon, Mr Collin, to strengthen and support the structure of bone and flesh around the left eye; this operation was a success. After ten days the area around his right eye and the socket of his left were level. He was also invited, together with 'Lofty' Harrison, to the head office of SGB at Mitcham for a small 'thank-you' ceremony hosted by the Group Chairman, Neville Clifford-Jones.

At the Old Bailey in January 1986 Hall gave evidence at the trial of Sullivan. Mr Beveridge was also called to give evidence and was subjected to rather bad-tempered cross-examination from Sullivan's barrister, who suggested that Hall could not have given a reliable identification of his client because of his injuries. "Nonsense," replied Beveridge. "There was nothing wrong with his right eye, nor," he added, "his memory, either!"

The jury deliberated for three hours before returning a verdict of not guilty in respect of the robbery at SGB and the injury to

Derek Hall. In the public gallery Sullivan's family and supporters clapped and wept with gratitude as the verdicts were delivered, and why not? A totally innocent man had been vindicated and cleared.

Well, perhaps not entirely innocent. What the jury had not known was that another jury had already found Sullivan guilty of the other three armed robberies; and as His Honour Judge Neil Dennison QC jailed Sullivan for a total of twelve years, the joyful family's emotions changed to screaming abuse of everything to do with the British legal system, and the judge ordered the public gallery to be cleared. So Sullivan went off to join three of his associates who had been jailed for a total of twenty years, and the judge complimented Hall, saying, "It is a privilege to meet someone of such conspicuous bravery."

On 16 April 1986 Hall was awarded a cheque for £100 and a certificate to commemorate his bravery by Giles Shepherd, the High Sheriff of Greater London; also present was a commander representing the commissioner. Three months later came a rather belated letter of congratulations from an assistant commissioner at the Yard.

But in February 1987 Hall received the thrilling news that the Queen was going to honour his bravery by awarding him the Queen's Gallantry Medal. The medal had been struck in 1974, replacing the British Empire Medal for Gallantry, and like the other gallantry medals it is 36mm in diameter with the crowned effigy of the monarch on the obverse. On the reverse is the image of St Edward's Crown, and flanked with laurel sprigs are the words, 'The Queen's Gallantry Medal'. The ribbon is of three equal stripes of dark blue, pearl grey and dark blue, with a narrow rose pink stripe running down the centre. The recipient is permitted to use the letters QGM after his name, and at the time of writing fewer than 600 of the medals have been awarded. On the day of the investiture, 3 October 1987, Derek Hall, impressively decked out in a grey topper and a cutaway, was waiting for the transport to convey him to Buckingham Palace. He was so pleased with his apparel that he refused to sit down, in case the knife-edge in his striped trousers should become creased. There was a knock at the door; Hall answered it to discover a police constable standing there, who had just alighted from a very small police car. "Come to take yer to the Palace, ain't I?" he said. "Derek's face was a picture; you'd have gone miles to see it!" was the verdict of the chief prankster, former Detective Superintendent Alan Goodman, who then let Hall off the hook with the arrival of a beautiful, gleaming maroon Rolls-

Royce, the property of the relative of an RCS officer. And so, Derek Hall, his wife Joan and daughter Christine went to the Palace, where Her Majesty the Queen presented him with a very well deserved medal. The day was made complete by a well-attended party at the Bury Club in Ilford, that evening.

Hall returned to work, but the area which he covered was actually extended and the consequent driving caused such a strain on his right eye that further treatment was required by Mr Beveridge, who immediately wrote to the company insisting that SGB medically retire him, and so they did; they also paid him two-thirds of his salary until state retirement age.

But the list of Hall's awards had not quite come to an end; he had received a shoal of congratulatory letters, including one from the Recorder of London, Sir James Miskin, and several from his Member of Parliament, Vivian Bendall, and in October 1987 he was invited to attend the annual dinner given by the Association of the ex-CID Officers of the Metropolitan Police, as the guest of honour. Within days, he received a letter inviting him to attend the Goldsmiths' Hall, to receive a Binney award. On 10 December Hall, together with Henry Harrison, was awarded a certificate of merit by the Lord Mayor of London, Sir Greville Spratt GBE, DL, for the bravest act carried out by someone not a member of a Police Force.

Derek Hall's wife sadly died in 2002, but despite her death and his disability, Hall's spirit, as ever, is indomitable. His courage had accompanied him into his retirement, illustrating – if any demonstration was necessary – that Derek Hall is among the bravest of the brave and an inspiration to young coppers everywhere.

Bibliography

BROWNE, Peter, *Seven Minutes in the Mall* (The Reader's Digest, Vol. 106, June 1975)

CATER, Frank & TULLETT, Tom, *The Sharp End – The Fight Against Organised Crime* (The Bodley Head, 1988)

CORNISH, G.W., *Cornish of the Yard* (John Lane, The Bodley Head, 1935)

DARBYSHIRE, Neil & HILLIARD, Brian, *The Flying Squad* (Headline, 1993)

DIVALL, Tom, *Scoundrels and Scallywags* (Ernest Benn, 1929)

FIDO, Martin & SKINNER, Keith, *The Official Encyclopedia of Scotland Yard* (Virgin Books, 1999)

FIRMIN, Stanley, *Scotland Yard – the Inside Story* (Hutchinson, 1948)

FORBES, Ian, *Squad Man* (W.H. Allen, 1973)

GLEDHILL, Tony, *A Gun at my Head* (Historic Military Press, 2006)

HART, Edward T., *Britain's Godfather* (True Crime Library, 1993)

HIGGINS, Robert, *In the Name of the Law* (John Long Ltd, 1958)

HONEYCOMBE, Gordon, *The Complete Murders of the Black Museum* (Leopard Books, 1995)

HUNTLEY, Bob & EDGINGTON, Harry, *Bomb Squad* (W.H. Allen, 1977)

JACKETT, Sam, *Heroes of Scotland Yard* (Robert Hale Ltd, 1965)

JACKSON, Sir Richard, *Occupied with Crime* (Harrap, 1967)

KENNISON, P. & SWINTON, D., *Behind the Blue Lamp* (Coppermill Press, 2003)

KIRBY, Dick, *You're Nicked!* (Constable & Robinson, 2007)

KIRBY, Dick, *The Guv'nors: Ten of Scotland Yard's Greatest Detectives* (Wharncliffe Books, 2010)

KIRBY, Dick, *The Sweeney: the First Sixty Years of Scotland Yard's Top Crimebusting Department – the Flying Squad* (Wharncliffe Books, 2011)

KRAY, Reg, *Villains We Have Known* (Arrow Books, 1996)

LAWRENCE, Jane R., *From the Beat to the Palace – 175 years of Gallantry* (Brewin Books, 2005)

LUCAS, Norman & SCARLETT, Bernard, *The Flying Squad* (Arthur Barker, 1968)

LUCAS, Norman, *Britain's Gangland* (W.H. Allen, 1969)

MARK, Sir Robert, *In the Office of Constable* (William Collins, Sons & Co, 1978)

McCALL, Karen (ed), *London Branch NARPO Millennium Magazine* (Orphans Press, Leominster, 1999)

McFALL, Terence, *The Miracle of 'Papa One'* (Privately published, 1999)

McVICAR, John, *McVicar by Himself* (Artnik Publishing, 2004)

MORTON, James, *Supergrasses & Informers* (Little, Brown & Co, 1995)

MORTON, James, *East End Gangland* (Little, Brown & Co, 2000)

MORTON, James & PALMER, Gerry, *Gangland Bosses* (Time Warner Books, 2004)

NARBOROUGH, Fred, *Murder on my Mind* (Allan Wingate, 1959)

RUMBELOW, Donald, *The Houndsditch Murders and the Siege of Sidney Street* (Macmillan, 1973)

SAVAGE, Percy, *Savage of Scotland Yard* (Hutchinson & Co, 1934)

SCOTT, Sir Harold, *Scotland Yard* (Andre Deutsch Ltd, 1954)

SELLWOOD, A.V., *Police Strike – 1919* (W.H. Allen, 1978)

SIMPSON, Keith, *Forty Years of Murder* (George G. Harrap & Co Ltd, 1978)

SWAIN, John, *Being Informed* (Janus Publishing Co, 1995)

THOMAS, Donald, *Honour Among Thieves* (Weidenfeld & Nicholson, 1991)

THOMAS, Donald, *Villains' Paradise* (John Murray, 2005)

WALDREN, Michael J., *Armed Police* (Sutton Publishing Ltd, 2007)

WENSLEY, Frederick Porter, *Detective Days* (Cassell & Co Ltd, 1931)

WHIBLEY, Charles (ed), *Poems of Byron* (Caxton Publishing Co, 1907)

WILLETS, Paul, *North Soho 999* (Dewi Lewis Publishing, 2007)

YOUNG, Hugh, *My Forty Years at the Yard* (W.H. Allen, 1955)

Index